DANGEROUS TRADE

DANGEROUS TRADE

Histories of Industrial Hazard across a Globalizing World

Edited by

CHRISTOPHER SELLERS and
JOSEPH MELLING

TEMPLE UNIVERSITY PRESS
PHILADELPHIA

TEMPLE UNIVERSITY PRESS
Philadelphia, Pennsylvania 19122
www.temple.edu/tempress

Library of Congress Cataloging-in-Publication Data

Dangerous trade : histories of industrial hazard across a globalizing world / edited by
Christopher Sellers and Joseph Melling.
    p. cm.
    Includes bibliographical references and index.
    ISBN 978-1-4399-0468-8 (hardback)
    ISBN 978-1-4399-0469-5 (paperback)
    ISBN 978-1-4399-0470-1 (e-book)
1. Industrial hygiene.   2. Hazardous substances.   3. Industrial toxicology.
4. Industrial safety.   5. Environmental health.   I. Sellers, Christopher C.
II. Melling, Joseph.
    RC967.D36 2011
    363.1109—dc22

                                                                2011015413

∞ The paper used in this publication meets the requirements of the American National
Standard for Information Sciences—Permanence of Paper for Printed Library Materials,
ANSI Z39.48-1992

Printed in the United States of America

2 4 6 8 9 7 5 3 1

Contents

PART II THE MIDDLE TO THE LATE TWENTIETH CENTURY

New Transfers of Production

New Knowledge and Coalitions

New Arenas of Contest

Tables and Figures

Tables

Figures

Acknowledgments

We thank the National Science Foundation for funding the Stony Brook University conference in December 2007 at which contributors to this volume first presented their papers to one another. At Stony Brook, we also appreciated the support provided by the Fine Arts, Humanities, and Social Sciences Initiative (FAHSS); the Center for Global Studies; the Humanities Institute; the Center for Interdisciplinary Environmental Research; the dean of the College of Arts and Sciences; the dean of the School of Medicine; the Office of the Provost; and the Departments of History, Chemistry, Preventive Medicine, and Technology and Society. The Wellcome Trust in the United Kingdom also supported many of those attending the conference, including Joseph Melling. A few individuals also deserve thanks for their contributions to the organizing of the conference: Susan Grumet, the history department's vital administrator; Jeff Hall, who handled much of the logistics with dispatch; and Ann Brody, who was invaluable in making the local arrangements.

We also are appreciative of the many around the world who sought involvement in our efforts to build a transnational "invisible college" around the conference themes. We attracted many fine papers that we were unable to include in this collection for reasons of space and time; we look forward to the further work of these scholars. They, as well as nonauthor participants at the conference, made important comments and criticisms along the way. In the current volume, we have tried to absorb and include as many of these as possible but have inevitably given short shrift to some. We hope that this book, itself a culmination of much dialogue, will provide a means by which these discussions, and the network of those participating in them, will continue to grow.

In preparing the volume itself, we benefited from the assessments provided by the readers of Temple University Press. We have been fortunate to have such a supportive editor at the press, Mick Gusinde-Duffy, as well as others at TUP who so painlessly shepherded the volume along. More generally, we are grateful to the history department at Stony Brook University for being so friendly to this kind of initiative, at once transnational and interdisciplinary. Both editors gained much from Chris Sellers's time as a visiting professor at the University of Exeter's Centre for Medical History. We particularly thank Nancy Tomes for her backing of this project in so many ways. Joseph Melling offers special thanks to his son, Ross Leslie Sproule, for his wisdom and support as well as critical insights into research questions.

Introduction

From Dangerous Trades to Trade
in Dangers: Toward an Industrial
Hazard History of the Present

CHRISTOPHER SELLERS AND JOSEPH MELLING

At the beginning of the twenty-first century, industrial diseases elicit only mild curiosity among most readers in affluent corners of the world. They seem part of a vanishing past, slipping out of modern memory, long since vanquished by previous battles against antiquated processes and brutal working conditions. This impression is misleading at best and, by the light of this book, utterly mistaken. Depending on where you stand at present, industrial dangers can be at once new or old, mostly occupational or mostly environmental, unknown or widely recognized, unregulated or tightly controlled—and all the while, on a global scale, ever more deadly. Health and other ecological hazards long found in factories and mines have reappeared in lethal forms and on epidemic scales, especially in developing nations. Add to this the dangers we keep discovering from toxins beyond the workplace, be they lead poisons passed along via toys or beach-blackening oil spills or discards from the latest digital or pharmaceutical innovation, and another conclusion beckons. Industrial hazards remain a major, arguably still growing, threat to the global community.

Asbestos offers a primary, sinister example of how industrial hazards may continue to afflict a citizenry worldwide, although in ways that differ dramatically between countries with contrasting histories of development. Exposure to what used to be known as a "magic mineral" has long produced lethal yields: asbestosis, lung cancers, and mesothelioma (a cancer of the lung lining). As these began to be recorded over the middle of the twentieth century in developed nations such as

Britain and the United States, heavy regulation ensued. Use of asbestos then tumbled, first in these nations and then worldwide, halving from a peak in the 1990s. At the same time, human contacts with asbestos continued to rise in developing countries such as India. Indian output of and exposure to asbestos had developed on a significant scale only during the latter half of the twentieth century, as industries like ship breaking drew in asbestos-laden walls and wastes of vessels constructed decades earlier in developed nations. The Indian government did draft protective regulations, almost as rigorous as those in Europe and North America. But enforcement remained severely hindered. Nine-tenths of India's occupational contacts with asbestos now occur in "unorganized" sectors, beyond the reach of government regulators. Within an informal economy, the low cost of this toxic fiber has fueled a continuing thirst for products laced with asbestos among Indian consumers, as a building material, a fire retardant, and an insulator. In today's India, far more people are inhaling more asbestos fibers than in 1990, making current Indian campaigns to ban it not just fresh but urgent.[1] One conclusion seems unmistakable: knowledge of the hazard in Indian public health and medical circles has not provided a sufficient spur to controlling the risks.

Meanwhile, though current exposures to asbestos are now much less in both Britain and the United States, past use in these countries still asserts its deadly legacy. The half-century of reliance on asbestos in American and British construction of all sorts has bestowed a fearful inheritance of lethal threads, in clouds that continue to seethe. Intensive and worrisome exposures still arise when schools or tenements are renovated, or when terrorists or hurricanes decimate downtown blocks. Asbestos fibers from earlier exposures, still lurking in the lungs of hundreds of thousands, touch off deadly tumors, and so mortality from asbestos-related disease quietly continues to rise.[2]

In the starkly dissimilar threats it poses to different parts of the world, and in its widening arc of damage, asbestos is not alone. Today across the globe, annual deaths from work-related disease and injury amount to two million, roughly twice those from malaria and equaling tuberculosis as a killer. These figures do not include the additional millions who sicken and die from toxic pollution beyond the workplace. Projections suggest that over the next half-century, these tolls will continue to mount.[3]

Practitioners, activists, policy makers, and citizens who tackle such dangers today must confront the long-standing dynamics that have propelled their spread and resurgence and, also, the limitations of earlier efforts to combat them. How well we understand this present, in other words, hinges on how well we have fathomed the past that made it. This volume, the outcome of an international conference of scholars and practitioners in 2007 at Stony Brook University, seeks to establish the historical groundwork that is necessary for a better understanding of how and why industrial hazards like asbestos have continued to trouble today's world. Our historical vision, contributors agreed, had to take a long view, across decades and centuries rather than just the past few years. We concurred as well on the need to better comprehend the transnational dimensions of this history, those cross-border circulations so integral to the geographic variations in industrial hazards across the world, not just today but yesterday. From the movement of firms, industries, and goods bearing dangers, to those passages of politics, knowledge, and regulatory strategy that seek to tame them, the history of these perils is one that keeps escaping the confines of nation-states.

In completing these studies, our contributors have built on that oldest way of writing about the history of "dangerous trades": as a succession of individual, pioneering practitioners. Still prevalent in the literature of occupational and environmental medicine today, this vein of history writing has origins among early-twentieth-century pioneers in industrial health such as Thomas Oliver, the British medical factory inspector and editor of a landmark volume, *Dangerous Trades* in 1902. Oliver and his compatriots made historical sense of their own work by noting its continuities with that of the Italian physician Bernardino Ramazzini some two centuries before.[4] Ever since, practitioner-historians have continued to situate their own work-a-day present within this lengthy clinical tradition, often wedded to broad if vague narratives of industrialization. In these accounts, industrial "progress," conceived as fundamentally Western and modern in nature, gives rise not only to new workplace hazards but also to the technocratic instruments of their alleviation: heroic experts and the controls they espouse.[5] This style of history still has its uses—among others in the inspiration it furnishes contemporary practitioners.[6] Nonetheless, a starting point for the present volume is that the key suppositions of this historiography have not held up well. The continuing plague of asbestos is just one example of how expert knowledge, professionalism, and workplace-centered laws, long celebrated by this tradition as solutions, have resulted, at best, in only partial victories over the industrial hazards of today's world.

While including contemporary experts and practitioners among its contributors, this volume also marshals the skills and insights of an array of specialists in history and the social sciences. In particular, works written by social historians mainly in the United States, Britain, and Europe during the past two or three decades have brought out groups, themes, and conflicts often ignored in an heroic history of industrial health practitioners.[7] They have stressed the importance of workers' and other laypeople's agency and advocacy, which is also affirmed by many of the essays in this volume. Additionally, both in our conference and in the follow-up discussions leading to this book, the economic historians among us have highlighted the importance of corporate forms and labor migration; the environmental historians, the material history and ecology of those settings where industries emerge, thrive, and pollute.[8] Together, often in alliance with our geographers, the conference participants nudged us toward a greater appreciation of the influential, often pivotal, roles played by extra-workplace participants in industrial hazard history, from ecologists or geologists to farmers and to those living in the vicinity of factories or waste dumps.[9] Our conferees drew on other intellectual lineages as well, from feminist critiques of the scientific enterprise to the study of public understanding and uses of science and technology.[10] Especially influential were two veins of sociological scholarship: environmental justice and contested diseases and a new political sociology of science, which plumbs the political, institutional, and power dynamics that have shaped policy-relevant knowledge.[11] We were joined, as well, by a political scientist studying how certain issues become framed as "public" problems, and an anthropologist looking at "cultures of control" in high-hazard organizations.[12]

Such convergences have made the history of industrial hazards a topical "contact zone"—the anthropologists' term for a shared ground between cultures—where historians of health, medicine, and environment have met up with other social scientists and contemporary practitioners. For all the intellectual divides among us, some powerful common threads aided our interweaving of perspectives and emphases. All participants agreed about the serious, burning relevance of that past we were studying to today, to a tenacious problem faced by the modern global economy. A major inspiration for many at the conference had been the movement for "environmental justice." First forged among minority and working-class mobilizations against hazardous wastes in the United States, this label has since been applied to parallel struggles against industrial hazards across the developing world.[13] Several participants had been motivated by witnessing the modern ravages of industrial hazards close up, whether on a Malayan plantation, in a French metallurgical factory, or at a North Carolina quarry. In the meeting's aftermath, the activist interests and commitments of many of us led to a collective endorsement and publication of a corporate "Code of Sustainable Practice in Occupational and Environmental Health and Safety."[14] From our discussions of each others' work, we also arrived at a modest but valuable beachhead of agreement about a more comprehensive and interdisciplinary framework for understanding the history of industrial hazards.

Industrial Hazard Regimes

In situating such different perspectives on industrial hazards alongside one another, and in scrutinizing cases from such a wide array of places and times, conference participants had, by the end of our meeting, settled on a shared definition of our subject: the *industrial hazard regime*. Industrial hazard regimes are those arrangements, formal as well as informal, by which public bodies, private interests, and civic mobilizations handle the danger and damage associated with an industry.[15] Especially in its breadth, this notion draws more or less directly on what we know about industrial hazards today: that they may extend from afflictions of workers caused by factory emissions to those imposed via consumer uses and ecological chains of consequence. Yet it also opens the door to reflection on a narrower versus a wider conception of hazards. Indeed, the concept of an industrial hazard regime demands that we take seriously the conceptions of industry-related hazards active in the time and place under study. We mean this notion of "regime" to encompass the sociocultural side of hazards: the variety of perceptions, institutions, groups, and dynamics through which these hazards may be produced, recognized, and controlled. In the making of these regimes, as depicted in chapter after chapter, private actors—companies, workers, professionals, other local residents—figure notably, as do grassroots movements and other communal initiatives. So, too, do state laws and agencies, from the local to the national. In particular, our contributors attend to larger transnational scales of action, those arenas outstretching any single national experience, which help to explain and elucidate important trends.

One key challenge for our authors has been to articulate the interaction between this overarching scale and other, "lower" scales of analysis. The people and processes in these pages, the knowledge and strategies, the products and institutions, circulate between locales, regions, and nations. At the same time, portable and reputedly universal technologies, areas of expertise, or legal prescriptions must be effectively attuned to local interests and contingencies in order to work. Many of our chapters therefore offer variations on what anthropologists studying the modern international economy have styled "global assemblage." They frame events and outcomes as evolving, integrative mixtures of the global with the national or local.[16]

For these reasons, the studies herein unpack the importance, to a given country's industrial hazard history, of markets, people, events, and other influences beyond that nation's boundaries. Not just in our own era of globalizing but also in the early twentieth century, foremost among these influences were the demands of finance and capital, projecting out from metropolitan centers to remote corners of the globe. On this front, Wallerstein's celebrated, if somewhat dated, arguments about the mutual growth of core and peripheral regions in the world economy may still yield explanatory insights into the resulting distribution of industrial hazards.[17] Both labor and hazardous processes continued to migrate, the one in search of higher wages; the other, lower costs. The result was often intense exploitation of vulnerable populations, either because hazards arrived anew or because people themselves were moved. What David Harvey has called the "spatial fix" abounds in these essays: from Kaur's paper on the engineered migration of Indians to Malayan plantations, to Santiago's on the shift of multinational oil companies into Veracruz, Mexico, and to Zalik's on the shift of liquefied natural gas processing, a hazardous new technology, to the Mexican Gulf Coast.[18]

Another way these essays show how the industrial hazard regime in one corner of the world could become engaged with places elsewhere is through danger-bearing trade in commodities. Carter and Melling show how, from the late nineteenth century, anthrax came to be recognized as a hazard in Britain thanks to contaminated wools that circulated into English weaving centers from the Near East. So, too, Bohme explores how, in the late twentieth century, toxic pesticides banned in the United States found their way to Central American banana plantations, to cause sterility in workers. In such instances, when hazardous processes commence in a given place, local ignorance of or indifference to the risks has long bolstered the balance sheets of employers as a consistent, if untallied, asset.

One point seems clear in regard to industrial hazard regimes over the period of these essays: that even if the scientific, political, and regulatory focus of our historical actors often falls on hazards inside the workplace, historians as well as activists must also consider attendant environmental damage outside. As with asbestos, the hazards of industrial activity can threaten not only workers but surrounding residents, and even the consumers of toxic products. Moreover, the threats are often not confined to human bodies. They may also extend to untrammeled despoliation of a surrounding nature and its resources. Those clouds that spilled across continents from the disasters of Bhopal and Chernobyl offer only the most massive and most remembered instances of the suffering that mismanaged technologies have inflicted on regional food chains of flora and fauna as well as on human livelihoods. These essays point to many other such episodes, all the more tragic for having remained so unknown. From the jungles of Malaysia and Mexico to the industrial cities and towns of France, to the fields of rural England, that more far-flung damage may go little noticed beyond the circle of its victims. Yet, in the right time and place, it can also provoke more outrage and mobilize greater political energies than any workplace struggle can, as Henry's research on the French asbestos scandal suggests.

Perpetually useful in clarifying questions about the costs of industrial hazard—just how they are incurred as well as just who bears them—is economists' theories of "externalities."[19] The earliest operators of hazardous processes often found it easy to externalize the full bodily and ecological costs of their activities: to make others pay while reaping greater profits for themselves. The overall history suggested by our essays is one in which these externalized costs came to be, if not fully absorbed into producer costs through regulation, at least more widely recognized and contested. Over the last century and a half, our contributors suggest, the global patterns by which hazardous producers have externalized these costs have also evolved.

A Globalizing World: Two Periods of Industrial Growth

Lax talk about "globalization" often obscures more than it explains about the growth of international trade and its associated divisions of labor by country, yet more rigorous definitions are now available. Economic historians have usefully suggested that two waves of widely shared growth since the nineteenth century both have roots in new step-ups in global economic integration.[20] Industrial hazards have nevertheless received little attention from these historians, or from those historians of business and labor who have also turned to illuminating this extended history of globalizing.[21] Similarly, medical and public health historians recently taking up transnational and global dynamics have been more concerned with infectious and epidemic rather than industrial diseases, even when they consider illnesses like tuberculosis that may have workplace or environmental causes.[22] To this day, the book-length studies we have of the links between global economic integration and industrial hazards center on the past couple of decades, by journalists like William Greider as well as activist scholars like David Pellow.[23] Our essays, read alongside the emergent scholarship on globalization's longer history, suggest the value of distinguishing between this more recent period in the history of industrial hazard regimes and an earlier one, starting in the nineteenth century.

In the mid- to late-nineteenth century, new regimes of hazard enabled the making of what would become known as the "developed" parts of the world via the huge expansion of markets via railroads and steamships and the growth of intensive manufacturing and extractive industries. European and North American economies exploited these innovations most effectively. Catalyzing new demands for labor, powering the great migrations of the period, they also spawned organized movements of workers across the industrializing world. Over the later nineteenth century, those who sought to bolster oversight of factory and workshop "nuisances" in Europe and America confronted legal systems that heavily favored industrial development. As for the large corporations that suddenly took over great shares of the economic activity in these same nations, their innovations could intensify long-standing risks, as they did in the Almaden mercury mines described by Menéndez-Navarro. Or they could introduce technologies and processes that brought new dangers altogether, as happened in the making of artificial silk described by Blanc. As suggested by Carter and Melling's chapter on anthrax, and confirmed by the chapters by Menendez-Navarro and Blanc, those campaigns that arose in response, starting in Britain and other forerunning European nations during this period, were often spearheaded by workers' groups. They centered largely on compensation laws for "occupational" disease and injury. By comparison, the dangers imposed on surrounding residents and land could be slighted.

This same period was also one of imperial dominance and colonial expansion in Africa and Asia and one of economic neocolonialism across less developed regions of the Americas. The essay by Kaur on Malayan plantations explores the hazard-bearing ways that colonization opened up new extractive frontiers. Uprooting local peoples and land uses, it forced an importation of labor from elsewhere. Here, with other remote plantations or mines, not just the work involved but attendant imperatives, such as those for housing, affected workers as well as surrounding residents, with implications not just for health but for livelihoods. Santiago's piece tells of another, more exclusively private effort in Mexico: as American firms set up oil fields across the border, their workers confronted a similar array of problems. There, however, as in our British and European examples, it was a workers' movement that sought to address the perils of this industry more thoroughly, via a succession of new labor laws that culminated in nationalization.

A second wave of globalization gained momentum from the booming conditions of the international economy during the middle and later decades of the twentieth century. Throughout much of the developing world, the confrontations of the Cold War set the climate, as did fresh economies of speed, scale, and scope. As innovations in transport and communications enabled production to be dispersed to unfamiliar regions, competitive pressures on older economies resulted in large-scale dismantling of heavy industries such as coal, steel, shipbuilding, textiles, and potteries. In Europe and North America, these older sectors came to be replaced by newer ones involving lighter chemicals, synthetic materials, assembly work, and soft skills linked to knowledge creation and transfer (including financial transactions, customer call centers, and so on). Though meeting with abrupt downturns in the early 1970s, 1980s, and 1990s, these transformations have steadily reconfigured the economies of the developed world, at least up until the great financial crisis of 2008–2010. Over this same period, the older and heavier industries shed by these nations, ever more associated with health and environmental problems, have set up shop in former colonies and other countries where, prior to 1950, modern versions of manufacturing had been rare.

In those very nations from which these dangerous trades were departing, our papers for this period point to a new environmental and ecological oversight of industrial hazards, adding to the workplace-centered concerns of earlier times. One avenue of scholarship has characterized the associated institutional and legal achievements of these nations as "ecological modernization."[24] Our contributors raise questions about just how ecologically modern many developed nations became, and about what modernization in one nation might mean in those other places where ecologically damaging industries gravitate. As factory and extractive (and, more recently, office) work has fled developed-world sites, a so-called "race to the bottom" has not just sought out the lowest labor costs. What Thomas Friedman has termed the "flat world" of global competition is also a world in which industrial risks have been ever more effectively redistributed, with developing-world nations acquiring an ever greater share.[25]

Across period as well as place, our essays suggest a fundamental distinction between two types of industrial hazard regime. There are those regimes that prevail as a risk-laden industry is born in, or relocated to, a particular place. Then there are those that arise in response to controversies over established production, via a dawning or widening recognition of its impacts. A pivotal question threading through this history then becomes just how and why industrial hazard regimes have shifted from tolerating imposed risks to protecting against them.

Exposed Bodies, Voice, and Resistance

The question just posed, more than any other, is what makes industrial hazard history of such compelling interest, not just to historians but to social scientists, practitioners, and activists. This book, in keeping with much scholarship over the last few decades, locates the roots of change not so much in a smooth progression directed by rational investigation as in social conflict. If such a conflict has proven transformative, our essays suggest the importance of starting with those physical and material changes that grounded it—particularly what has or might have happened in the bodies of those exposed to a given hazard. It is their experience of damage, after all, that is at stake in all the other questions raised by this history, whether the interests be local or transnational, whether the actors be workers or WHO officials. In highlighting this bodily engagement of the exposed, many of our essays respond to recent calls by labor historians to "follow the bodies," to attend more closely to historical variations in the bodily experiences of a working class. As similar-minded environmental historians might add, fleshing out these experiences often requires similar attention to the physical environments in which they unfold.[26] Although historians do well to come to their conclusions about the damage involved, one other step is indispensable: To understand how an industry's physical impacts have translated into resistance against an existing industrial hazard regime, we also need to study how existing bodily as well as environmental damage was given a contemporary voice. Only with this voice could the dangers become a basis for mobilization and for the wielding of political force.

A key starting point here, as labor historians have long insisted, is with the voices of the victims. An industry's employees as well as those living near the industry bore the early brunt of so many of the hazards explored in these pages: workers shipped from India to Malaya, those living in the vicinity of Nigerian oil fields or along the lead-smoked streets of Montevideo. Communities of the exposed, though often without access to the tools and know-how of modern science, encountered industrial risks in ways that were often local, direct, and immediate. They could develop their own acute awareness as well as a working knowledge of the hazards involved. The purest example in this volume is Santiago's study of a 1930s rebellion in the Mexican oil fields. But other chapters confirm the import of a similarly local and lay knowledge in mobilizations, from Barca's of 1970s labor environmentalism in Italian industrial towns, to Allen's of a popular epidemiology challenging the Louisiana Delta oil industry, to Renfrew's of the anti-lead movement in Uruguay, and to Castleman and Tweedale's of the late-twentieth-century asbestos wars.

At the same time, these and other essays suggest the limitations of attributing resistance movements solely to the voices and agency of workers or other lay victims. Lay knowledge about production hazards did not inevitably yield a more collective resistance against threats to health, land, or livelihood. It could just as well propel local residents to change jobs or living quarters, or to push for higher wages. Moreover, in Allen's and Barca's stories, workers and communities activists themselves acquired voice and agency, not just by organizing among themselves but by recruiting—or being recruited by—medical or scientific allies. Evidently, not just appropriations of "elite" knowledge but elite knowers can aid lay mobilizing. Just as the knowledge around which lay groups mustered could be produced or facilitated by scientists or doctors, so scientific and medical innovation could come as experts lent more of an ear to aggrieved laypeople. In Melling and Sellers' essay, for instance, a group of experts coalesced not just around a new methodology but around a new industrial health association. By including union representatives, this group opened doors to more worker input into their field.

A related question runs through many of these papers: Just whose interests and ends are being voiced in expert accounts of an industry's impact on bodies and environments, beyond the experts' own? Expertise may indeed work to ameliorate the impacts of industry on workers' and others' bodies, even in the absence of much lay input; the essays of Carter, Melling, Sellers, and Blanc serve as cases in point. At least in some times and places, expert-endorsed, objective claims about the environmental and health impacts of an industry undoubtedly bolstered lay resistance to a reigning industrial hazard regime. Yet other essays make clear how easily experts' objectifications of workers or other victims' bodies and terrains may downplay important dangers or damages. From the laboratory science of 1920s Spain to the dismissals of cancer clusters in Louisiana's "Cancer Alley," claims to greater scientific accuracy and objectivity have often served either as prelude or postlude to a far-ranging imposition of industrial risks. Consequences claimed, at a given time, to be all-too uncertain may then turn provable, but too late, because the arc of damage has already widened. Through much of the twentieth century, whenever lay as well as scientific dissents have challenged an existing industrial hazard regime, they have come face to face with the voices of established experts, whose insistence on objectivity or certainty serves existing arrangements of power.

Many other aspects of industrial hazard regimes emerge in the essays that follow: dilemmas of the state and its officials, of supranational organizations, of firms and their managers, as well as of a host of other private actors. One further point consistently stands out. Throughout the history of industrial hazard regimes, voices for change, be they lay or expert, have proven vulnerable. In our modern world, hazardous industries and commodities have often traveled and taken root with greater ease than has knowledge about their dangers, much less about any corrective action. Those of us relieved of the worst threats nevertheless remain connected to those who still face them. We share a common humanity, and those who are protected most—the likely readers of this volume—continue to consume the production of those whose bodies and communities are protected the least. The editors of this volume dedicate it to the hope that, through a dawning sense of obligation, through innovative actions over the coming decades, the history recounted here may cease to repeat itself.

NOTES

1. Barry Castleman and Tushar Kant Joshi, "Global Asbestos Struggle Today," *European Journal of Oncology* 12 (2007): 149–154; Tushar Kant Joshi, Uttpal B. Bhuva, and Priyanka Katoch, "Asbestos Ban in India: Challenges Ahead," *Annals of the New York Academy of Sciences* 1076 (September 2006): 292–308; V. Subramanian and N. Madhavan, "Asbestos Problem in India," *Lung Cancer (Amsterdam, Netherlands)* 49, suppl. 1 (July 2005): S9–S12; Furquan Ahmad Ansari, Iqbal Ahmad, Mohd Ashquin, Mohammad Yunus, and Qamar Rahman, "Monitoring and Identification of Airborne Asbestos in Unorganized Sectors, India," *Chemosphere* 68, no. 4 (June 2007): 716–723.

2. V. C. dos Santos Antao, G. A. Pinheiro, and J. T. Wassell, "Asbestosis Mortality in the USA: Facts and Predictions," *Occupational and Environmental Medicine* 66, no. 5 (May 2009): 335–338; "Asbestos-Related Disease—A Preventable Burden," *The Lancet* 372, no. 9654 (December 6, 2008): 1927; Geoffrey Tweedale, *Magic Mineral to Killer Dust: Turner & Newall and the Asbestos Hazard* (New York: Oxford University Press, 2001); P. E. Enterline, "Changing Attitudes and Opinions Regarding Asbestos and Cancer 1934–1965," *American Journal of Industrial Medicine* 20, no. 5 (1991): 685–700; Jock McCulloch and Geoffrey Tweedale, *Defending the Indefensible: The Global Asbestos Industry and Its Fight for Survival* (New York: Oxford University Press, 2008); Ronald Johnston and Arthur McIvor, *Lethal Work: A History of the Asbestos Tragedy in Scotland* (East London, UK: Tuckwell Press, 2000); Peter Bartrip, *Beyond the Factory Gates: Asbestos and Health in Twentieth Century America* (London: Continuum, 2006).

3. T. Driscoll, J. Takala, K. Steenland, C. Corvalan, and M. Fingerhut, "Review of Estimates of the Global Burden of Injury and Illness Due to Occupational Exposures," *American Journal of Industrial Medicine* 48 (2005): 491–505; Annette Prüss-Üstun and Carlos Corvalán, "How Much Disease Burden Can Be Prevented by Environmental Interventions?" *Epidemiology* 18 (2007): 167–178.

4. Thomas Oliver, *Dangerous Trades: The Historical, Social, and Legal Aspects of Industrial Occupations as Affecting Health, by a Number of Experts* (London: J. Murray, 1902); Bernardino Ramazzini, *A Treatise of the Diseases of Tradesmen Shewing the Various Influence of Particular Trades upon the State of Health, with the Best Methods to Avoid or Correct It, and Useful Hints Proper to Be Minded in Regulating the Cure of All Diseases Incident to Tradesmen* (London: Printed for Andrew Bell and eight others, 1705).

5. Thomas Morison Legge, *Shaw Lectures on Thirty Years Experience of Industrial Maladies: Delivered before the Royal Society of Arts, February and March, 1929.* (London: Royal Society, 1929); R.S.F. (Richard Selwyn Francis) Schilling, *Modern Trends in Occupational Health* (London: Butterworths, 1960); George Rosen, *The History of Miners' Diseases: A Medical and Social Interpretation* (New York: Schuman's, 1943); Alice Hamilton, *Exploring the Dangerous Trades: The Autobiography of Alice Hamilton, M.D.* (Boston: Little, Brown, 1943); Ludwig Teleky, *History of Factory and Mine Hygiene* (New York: Columbia University Press, 1948); Franz Koelsch, *Beiträge zur Geschichte der Arbeitsmedizin* (Munich: Bayerische Landesärztekammer, 1968).

6. Among the more recent examples are Antonio Grieco, Sergio Iavicoli, and Giovanni Berlinguer, *Contributions to the History of Occupational and Environmental Prevention* (Amsterdam: Elsevier Science, 1999); and Antonio Grieco, *Origins of Occupational Health Associations in the World* (Amsterdam: Elsevier, 2003).

7. Among the early landmarks of this literature are Paul Weindling and the Society for the Social History of Medicine, eds., *The Social History of Occupational Health* (London: Croom Helm, 1985); and David Rosner and Gerald Markowitz, eds., *Dying for Work: Workers' Safety and Health in Twentieth-Century America* (Bloomington: Indiana University Press, 1987).

8. Ronald Johnston and Arthur McIvor, *Lethal Work* (Aldershot, UK: Ashgate, 2007); Arthur McIvor and Ronald Johnston, *Miners' Lung: A History of Dust Disease in British Coal Mining* (Aldershot, UK: Ashgate, 2007); David Rosner and Gerald E. Markowitz, *Deadly Dust: Silicosis and the Politics of Occupational Disease in Twentieth-Century America* (Princeton, NJ: Princeton University Press, 1991); Gerald E. Markowitz and David Rosner, *Deceit and Denial: The Deadly Politics of Industrial Pollution* (Berkeley: University of California Press, 2002); Christopher C. Sellers, *Hazards of the Job: From Industrial Disease to Environmental Health Science* (Chapel Hill: University of North Carolina Press, 1997); Paul Kirkbride and Karen Ward, *Globalization: The Internal Dynamic* (New York: Wiley, 2001); Amarjit Kaur, *Wage Labour in Southeast Asia since 1840: Globalisation, the International Division of Labour and Labour Transformations* (Basingstoke, UK: Palgrave Macmillan, 2004); Andrew Hurley, *Environmental Inequalities: Class, Race, and Industrial Pollution in Gary, Indiana, 1945–1980* (Chapel Hill: University of North Carolina Press, 1995); Christian Warren, *Brush with Death: A Social History of Lead Poisoning* (Baltimore: Johns Hopkins University Press, 2000); Allison L. Hepler, *Women in Labor: Mothers, Medicine, and Occupational Health in the United States, 1890–1980* (Columbus: Ohio State University Press, 2000); Linda Lorraine Nash,

Inescapable Ecologies: A History of Environment, Disease, and Knowledge (Berkeley: University of California Press, 2006).

9. Gavin Bridge, "Contested Terrain: Mining and the Environment," *Annual Review of Environment and Resources* 29, no. 1 (2004): 205–259; Gavin Bridge, "Environmental Economic Geography: A Sympathetic Critique," *Geoforum* 39, no. 1 (January 2008): 76–81; Barbara L. Allen, *Uneasy Alchemy: Citizens and Experts in Louisiana's Chemical Corridor Disputes* (Cambridge, MA: MIT Press, 2003).

10. Alan Irwin and Brian Wynne, *Misunderstanding Science? The Public Reconstruction of Science and Technology* (Cambridge: Cambridge University Press, 1996); Lorraine Daston and Peter Galison, *Objectivity* (Brooklyn, NY: Zone Books, 2007); Sandra G. Harding, *Is Science Multicultural? Postcolonialisms, Feminisms, and Epistemologies* (Bloomington: Indiana University Press, 1998).

11. Robert D. Bullard, *Unequal Protection: Environmental Justice and Communities of Color* (San Francisco: Sierra Club Books, 1994); Laura Pulido, *Environmentalism and Economic Justice: Two Chicano Struggles in the Southwest: Society, Environment, and Place* (Tucson: University of Arizona Press, 1996); Phil Brown and Edwin J. Mikkelsen, *No Safe Place: Toxic Waste, Leukemia, and Community Action* (Berkeley: University of California Press, 1990); Phil Brown and Stephen Zavestoski, *Social Movements in Health* (New York: Wiley-Blackwell, 2005); Scott Frickel and Kelly Moore, *The New Political Sociology of Science: Institutions, Networks, and Power* (Madison: University of Wisconsin Press, 2006).

12. Jacques Lagroye, François Bastien, and Frédéric Sawicki, *Sociologie politique* (Paris: Presses de Sciences Po et Dalloz, 2002); Claude Gilbert and Emmanuel Henry, "Divergences or Complementarity within the Research into Crises in France?" *International Journal of Emergency Management* 3, no. 1 (2006): 5–10; Constance Perin, *Shouldering Risks: The Culture of Control in the Nuclear Power Industry* (Princeton, NJ: Princeton University Press, 2006); Charles Perrow, *Normal Accidents: Living with High-Risk Technologies* (New York: Basic Books, 1984).

13. For an overview, see note 11; also see Mei Mei Evans and Joni Adamson, *The Environmental Justice Reader: Politics, Poetics, and Pedagogy* (Tucson: University of Arizona Press, 2002).

14. Barry Castleman et al., "Code of Sustainable Practice in Occupational and Environmental Health and Safety for Corporations," *International Journal of Occupational and Environmental Health* 14, no. 3 (September 2008): 234–235.

15. Our definition loosely parallels that of the "urban regime" that has helped enable comparative study of cities, and Michelle Murphy's "regimes of imperceptibility." Karen Mossberger and Gerry Stoker, "The Evolution of Urban Regime Theory: The Challenge of Conceptualization," *Urban Affairs Review* 36 (2001): 810–835; Michelle Murphy, *Sick Building Syndrome and the Problem of Uncertainty: Environmental Politics, Technoscience, and Women Workers* (Durham, NC: Duke University Press, 2006).

16. Aihwa Ong and Stephen Collier, *Global Assemblages: Technology, Politics, and Ethics as Anthropological Problems* (Malden, MA: Blackwell, 2005); Saskia Sassen, *Territory, Authority, Rights: From Medieval to Global Assemblages* (Princeton, NJ: Princeton University Press, 2006).

17. Immanuel Maurice Wallerstein, *World-Systems Analysis: An Introduction* (Durham, NC: Duke University Press, 2004).

18. David Harvey, "The Spatial Fix: Hegel, Von Thunen, and Marx," *Antipode* 13, no. 3 (1981): 1–12.

19. For more discussion, see Christine Meisner Rosen and Christopher C. Sellers, "The Nature of the Firm: Towards an Ecocultural History of Business," *Business History Review* 73, no. 4 (Winter 1999): 577.

20. Michael D. Bordo, Alan M. Taylor, and Jeffrey G. Williamson, *Globalization in Historical Perspective* (Chicago: University of Chicago Press, 2005); Jeffrey G. Williamson, *Globalization and the Poor Periphery before 1950*, illus. ed. (Cambridge, MA: MIT Press, 2006); Kevin H. O'Rourke and Jeffrey G. Williamson, *Globalization and History: The Evolution of a Nineteenth-Century Atlantic Economy* (Cambridge, MA: MIT Press, 2001).

21. Alfred D. Chandler, Jr., *Scale and Scope: The Dynamics of Industrial Capitalism* (Cambridge, MA: Belknap Press, 1994); Beverly J. Silver, *Forces of Labor: Workers' Movements and Globalization since 1870* (Cambridge: Cambridge University Press, 2003);

Jefferson R Cowie, *Capital Moves: RCA's Seventy-Year Quest for Cheap Labor* (Ithaca, NY: Cornell University Press, 1999).

22. Ichiro Kawachi and Sarah Wamala, *Globalization and Health* (Oxford: Oxford University Press, 2007); Kelley Lee, Kent Buse, and Suzanne Fustukian, eds., *Health Policy in a Globalising World* (New York: Cambridge University Press, 2001); Roy Smith and Christine McMurray, *Diseases of Globalization: Socioeconomic Transitions and Health* (Sterling, VA: Earthscan, 2001).

23. William Greider, *One World Ready or Not: The Manic Logic of Global Capitalism* (New York: Simon and Schuster, 1998); David Pellow, *Resisting Global Toxics: Transnational Movements for Environmental Justice* (Cambridge, MA: MIT Press, 2007); Nancy Lee Peluso and Michael Watts, *Violent Environments* (Ithaca, NY: Cornell University Press, 2001). Other exceptions, including recent efforts at world environmental history, concentrate more exclusively on the global scale and on resource extraction. See John Robert McNeill, *Something New under the Sun: An Environmental History of the Twentieth-Century World* (New York: W. W. Norton, 2000).

24. Maarten A. Hajer, *The Politics of Environmental Discourse: Ecological Modernization and the Policy Process* (New York: Oxford University Press, 1997); Arthur P. J. Mol, *Globalization and Environmental Reform: The Ecological Modernization of the Global Economy* (Cambridge, MA: MIT Press, 2003).

25. Thomas L. Friedman, *The World Is Flat: A Brief History of the Twenty-First Century* (New York: Farrar, Straus and Giroux, 2005).

26. Ava Baron and Eileen Boris, "'The Body' as a Useful Category for Working-Class History," *Labor* 4, no. 2 (June 1, 2007): 23–43; John Kasson, "Follow the Bodies: Commentary on 'The Body' as a Useful Category for Working-Class History," *Labor* 4, no. 2 (June 1, 2007): 45–48; Jody A. Roberts and Nancy Langston, "Toxic Bodies/Toxic Environments: An Interdisciplinary Forum," *Environmental History* 13, no. 4 (October 2008), available at http://www.environmentalhistory.net/articles/134_roberts-langston_toxicforum.pdf.

PART I

THE LATE NINETEENTH CENTURY TO THE EARLY TWENTIETH CENTURY

Creating Industrial Hazards
in the Developing World

1

Rubber Plantation Workers, Work Hazards, and Health in Colonial Malaya, 1900–1940

Amarjit Kaur

By the early twentieth century, Britain had created an externally oriented colonial economy in Malaya (the Malay Peninsula and Singapore before 1948) based on rubber and tin. Rubber cultivation centred on the plantation mode of production, incorporated new agricultural techniques and scientific methods, and exemplified capitalist ecological interventions in agriculture. For the most part, companies with European management ran the plantations, where work was extremely labour-intensive. Labourers were imported from South India and settled on large interior estates, where they formed isolated migrant communities. The environmental and health consequences of this new mode of agricultural production were far-reaching and primarily affected the labouring population. Exploitative working conditions and constant exposure to work hazards amplified the workers' vulnerability to nutritional and infectious diseases, resulting in high morbidity and mortality rates. Consequently, intergovernmental and imperial regulation led to greater intervention and supervision of workers' health and the promotion of plantation medicine. Health care provision was expanded to embrace preventive measures, including maternal and child health codes. The specific political and administrative relationships between the Colonial Office in London, the India Office, and the Malayan administration were crucial to these transformations.

This chapter focuses on key aspects of Indian workers' economic, social, and health engagement with plantation owners, subimperial India, and the global trade in commodities. The study first examines the

development of the rubber plantation industry against the backdrop of colonial developing-world agriculture and the recruitment of Indian labour. Then
it analyzes the consequences of this encounter through the prism of workers'
plantation life, the epidemiology of migration, and plantation work hazards.
Finally, the investigation turns to the unique labour and health experiences
of Indian plantation workers by examining labour codes and other administrative legislation that registered and contended with the resulting health
consequences for the workers.

Colonial Economies, Commodities of Empire, and Malaya

The expansion of trade and conquest by European powers in Southeast Asia
after the 1870s involved the restructuring of the economic landscapes of col-
onized states. Southeast Asian economies and societies were integrated more
completely into the global colonial economy and mobilized for expanded
commodity production. Since the imperial drive was fueled by an agenda
of competitive state building overseas, these states were transformed into
colonies, protectorates, or informal empire and assigned roles in subimperial
and global commodity chains. In the Malayan region this process climaxed
between 1870 and 1914. By 1914, too, Britain had extended its influence over
all of "British" Malaya, which included three administrative units: the original Straits Settlements ports (SS), the Federated Malay States (FMS), and the
Unfederated Malay States (UMS). The unified trading networks in Asia, the
open-borders policy, and the imperial web of connections established spaces
that produced new networks, creating officially authorized opportunities for
Indian (and Chinese) labour migration to Malaya.

Prior to the dominance of rubber, Malaya's chief commodity exports
were tin, coffee, and sugar. Chinese producers dominated the tin industry
using Chinese labour, while European planters chiefly controlled coffee and
sugar, employing indentured Indian workers. The early uses of rubber were
limited, and low production levels in Brazil (the principal rubber producer)
and high prices characterized the industry. This situation changed following
Charles Goodyear's improvement of the vulcanization process and thus the
suitability of natural rubber for hoses, tires, and shoes. The popularization
of the bicycle and the development of the automobile and tire industries in
the twentieth century subsequently resulted in a rubber boom. High prices
provided an incentive to British and other entrepreneurs to invest in rubber,
particularly since sugar and coffee were facing stiff competition from other
producers. Malaya's competitive advantage in climate, low population density, and vast tracts of suitable land for the plantation mode of production, as
well as Britain's access to cheap Indian labour, guaranteed the rapid development of the Malayan rubber industry after 1910.

The British helped transform the cost structure and capacity of the
industry by privileging plantation production, and Western (mainly British)
investors obtained large land grants on very long leases at charges of 3 to 4
percent per annum. European trading agencies or agency houses dominated

the rubber industry. The agency houses floated limited-liability companies, principally in London, to mobilize substantial funds for the industry. In Britain alone, they floated 260 rubber companies between 1903 and 1912 to acquire plantations in Malaya. Typically, the agency houses were appointed as managing agents and/or secretaries to the boards of directors of the new plantation enterprises. In addition to receiving management fees, the agencies earned commissions on the sale of rubber and tin and also became involved in labour recruitment.[1]

The colonial administration established modern bureaucratic structures, introduced new administrative and legal frameworks, and built a unified transportation system in the country. The new road and rail networks guaranteed planters access to ports and markets, while railway sidings connected inland plantations with the trunk railway line.[2] By 1910, rubber covered approximately 225,000 hectares, rising to 891,000 hectares in 1921. This accounted for 53 percent of the total land under rubber cultivation in South Asia and Southeast Asia, and Malayan rubber exports rose from 6,500 to 204,000 tonnes between 1910 and 1919.[3] Robert Heussler asserts that since rubber occupied a key position in Malaya's economy, the organized rubber interests "occupied positions not unlike those of similar [groups] in Britain and America, powerful combines that dealt with the government on equal terms or better."[4]

Rubber cultivation necessitated recruitment of a large, cheap, and "disciplined" workforce that had to be settled and organized to work under pioneering conditions in Malaya. British India, with its poverty-stricken millions and caste-ridden society, was the preferred source. Low-caste docility fit well into the dependent relationship between management and employee. Indians were also cheaper and less aggressive than the Chinese. The historical trade and cultural networks between India and Malaya thus expanded to create an integrated labour market extending from southern India to Southeast Asia. Indians were transported into alien surroundings where their language, religion, and cultural norms kept them apart from indigenous populations. Kernail Singh Sandhu notes that the South Indian peasant was seen as "malleable, worked well under supervision, and . . . was the most amenable to the comparatively lowly paid and rather regimented life of estates . . . and cost less in feeding and maintenance."[5]

Indian labour migration was consistent with the international division of labour and laid the framework for a migrant labour diaspora in Malaya. It involved mass migration and the organization of travel arrangements and employment in British colonies by intermediaries and state officials. Labour regimes that depended on the use of sanctions to enforce wage labour agreements, or coercion through intermediaries, were also developed. The Malayan administration and planters used regulations, immigration controls, and recruitment mechanisms to manage migrant labour.

The recruitment of Indian workers was consistent with a rather elastic use of labour in Malaya. These workers were young, predominantly illiterate, unskilled adult males who emigrated as individuals and thus had low dependency ratios. After periods of employment, they usually, but not always, returned to India. Colonial authorities viewed them as sojourners, to be repatriated when the demand for their services no longer existed.

Two migration methods were used—the indenture system and the *kangani* system. The indenture system allowed employers to use enforceable, usually written labour contracts, according to which workers were contracted or, rather, bonded to individual employers for between one and three years; planters used these contracts to handle their labour cost and supply. Breaches of written contracts were regarded as criminal rather than civil offences. Since most workers were impoverished, they were reindentured for further periods.[6] Penal clauses for assisted Indian workers were progressively abolished in the Malayan Labour Codes of 1921 and 1923.[7]

Some planters relied on an intermediary, or *kangani*, to recruit Indian workers. The *kangani* method was a personal recruitment system, and it became more popular when indentured labour was abolished in 1910 (the final contracts ended in 1913). Several conditions were introduced as the system developed, including the licensing of the *kangani* to minimize potential abuse of migrants and the stipulation that migrants be employed on a monthly basis only. Since the *kangani* recruited primarily from within his own village, the probability of workers absconding decreased as kith and kin networks were established on plantations.[8]

Eventually the government's own labour needs for state projects, together with growing competition for labour and an upsurge in "crimping" (poaching) activity, foreshadowed centralization of recruitment. Thus in 1907 a central quasi-official body, the Indian Immigration Committee (IIC), was formed to facilitate and administer South Indian labour immigration to Malaya. The Tamil (later Indian) Immigration Fund (TIF), associated with the IIC, was also established to provide free passage for Indian emigrants. A quarterly levy or tax to cover the travel and related costs of free Indian labour immigrants was imposed on all employers of Indians. The IIC and the TIF resulted in increased voluntary immigration to Malaya.

The IIC was placed under the authority of the Controller of Labour, representing all official (government) and private-sector interests in Malaya (except Terengganu state). In addition to transporting immigrants, the TIF had funds to repatriate unemployed Indians during depressed economic conditions. Its responsibilities subsequently included upkeep of a home for "decrepit" Indians, an orphanage for Indian children whose parents had died in Malaya, and, in the 1930s, an asylum for those suffering from melancholia brought about by the Great Depression.[9]

Until 1923, first the Indian government and then the SS and the FMS administrations regulated Indian labour immigration. In 1923, following passage of the Indian Emigration Act of 1922, the Indian government reestablished control over the management of Indian labour emigration to Malaya. New regulations were framed that defined work hours, working conditions, and welfare provisions for Indian labourers. Significantly, an agent of the government of India was appointed in Malaya to supervise

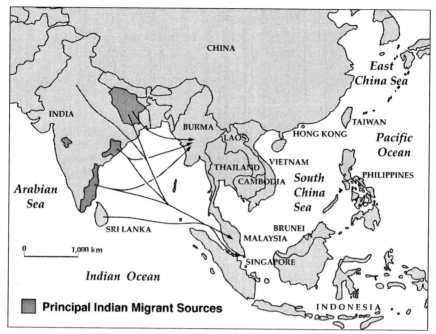

Figure 1.1 Indian migration flows to Southeast Asia. (Amarjit Kaur, *Wage Labour in Southeast Asia: Globalisation. The International Division of Labour and Labour Transformations* [Basingstoke, UK: Palgrave Macmillan, 2004], 67).

compliance with regulations. The origins and direction of South Indian labour flows to Malaya and Southeast Asia during this period are shown in Figure 1.1.

Broad estimates of the magnitude of Indian migrant flows provide some interesting insights. Labour recruitment peaked in the second decade of the twentieth century, when about 50,000 to 80,000 Indian workers arrived per annum. Moreover, whereas in 1920 only 12 percent of Indian workers were voluntary emigrants, this proportion had increased to over 91 percent by the 1930s.[10] In the first four decades of the twentieth century, Indians formed between 70 and 80 percent of the FMS plantation labour force (see Table 1.1).

It is significant that for about every 100 acres (1 acre is equal to 0.40468 hectare) under Western rubber cultivation, there were approximately fifteen to twenty workers, of whom between twelve and seventeen were Indians.

As stated previously, Indian labour migration was a male proletarian system. As plantation work became differentiated and specialized, with different pay scales for tapping, weeding, and performing factory tasks, women's migration was encouraged and assisted through the *kangani* system. Female immigration was also intended to improve the sex ratio and

TABLE 1.1   RACIAL COMPOSITION OF THE FMS ESTATE LABOUR FORCE,
            MALAYA, 1907–1938

YEAR	INDIAN	CHINESE	JAVANESE	OTHER	TOTAL	INDIANS AS PERCENT OF LABOUR FORCE	NUMBER OF ESTATES
1907	43,824	5,348	6,029	2,872	58,073	75.5	287
1911	109,633	31,460	12,795	12,127	166,015	66.0	711
1915	126,347	27,446	8,356	8,592	170,741	74.0	719
1920	160,966	40,866	8,918	5,808	216,588	74.3	1105
1925	137,761	37,879	4,165	4,549	184,354	74.7	1206
1930	132,745	30,860	3,665	2,411	169,681	78.2	1757
1935	118,591	29,950	1,941	2,658	153,140	77.4	2345
1938	137,353	28,925	1,762	2,892	170,932	80.4	2388

Source: J. N. Parmer, Colonial Labour Policy and Administration: A History of Labour in the Rubber Plantation Industry in Malaya (Locust Valley, New York: J. J. Augustin for the Association for Asian Studies, 1960), 273. Reprinted with permission of the Association for Asian Studies, Inc.

the reproduction of workers and to facilitate the settlement of Indians on plantations. The *kangani* earned a higher commission for women workers and married couples. Moreover, the Indian Emigration Act (Act VII of 1922), Rule 23, stipulated that unaccompanied males were not to exceed one in five emigrants: two out of every three male emigrants thus had to be accompanied by their spouses. The growth in female migration led to more children traveling to Malaya, and by the 1920s women accounted for 30 percent of all Indian arrivals. More children were also born in Malaya and raised locally, contributing to the transition toward permanent settlement and the availability of a pool of workers. Subsequent amendments to the Malayan Labour Code further stipulated the provision of rooms for married couples as well as child care and educational facilities on plantations.[11]

The Environment, Marginalisation, and Disease on the Plantation

Malayan plantations were developed in forested areas in the foothills or on plains in the interior, far from urban centres and coastal Malay settlements. They formed a belt about thirty miles wide in the western half of the peninsula. This belt extended from Perlis in the Northwest to Singapore in the South, a distance of about five hundred miles. Plantations were fully integrated enterprises, and both cultivation and processing were done in situ. The distribution of Malayan rubber plantations is shown in Figure 1.2.

Why did the physical environment cause health problems for Indian plantation workers in particular? Answering this question requires an examination of the factors that impinged on Indian workers' social determinants of health—that is, working and living conditions, wages, the physical/geographical environment and disease prevalence, and access to health care.

Prior to their arrival in Malaya, Indian migrants had to undergo a health screening designed to "weed out" medically unfit workers. On arrival at the

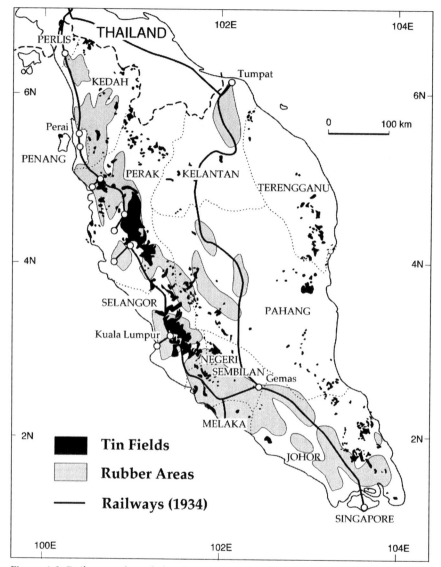

Figure 1.2 Rail network and the distribution of rubber, Malaya, 1935. (Amarjit Kaur, "Economy and Society" in *The Shaping of Malaysia*, ed. Amarjit Kaur and Ian Metcalfe [Basingstoke, UK: Macmillan, 1999], 147.)

Malayan ports, they were quarantined for about five days, their clothing was disinfected, they were vaccinated against smallpox, and then they were "readied" for employment.[12] With these procedures carried out to ensure that the workers had neither cholera nor the plague, it is reasonable to assume that they were in a fairly healthy state before starting their employment.

However, the workers entered a brave new world on the Malayan plantation in which the remoteness of plantations, the inability to speak English or
Malay, and vagrancy laws prevented workers from absconding. Moreover,
production relations on plantations differed from those in other enterprises.
Labour production costs were split into two processes: maintenance and
renewal. The workers were paid a daily minimum wage that was calculated
on the basis of their dietary and subsistence requirements and tied to the
prevailing price of rubber. The employer provided certain amenities, including simple housing, subsidised foodstuffs, and occasional medical attention.
Labour force renewal was provided by new recruitment to fill vacancies
created by death or departure or to expand the workforce. Workers became
trapped in an unending cycle of dependency and poverty, and the plantation
became their "boundary of existence." Charles Gamba explains that the
provision of housing and other amenities had a built-in mechanism for social
control. Labourers living in estate housing were not charged rent (which
was included in the wage calculation). Consequently, if they were dismissed,
they faced eviction. They were thus effectively bonded to the estates and tied
to the low-wage structure inherent in the plantation system.[13] The planter-
labourer arrangement has been described as a "community sub-system"
within the plantation organization as a "total" institution.[14]

The consequences of the plantation's location and its isolation were intensified by the presence of native wildlife that presented a constant danger.
Predators included tigers, elephants, wild boar, and snakes, which occasion-
ally attacked and sometimes killed workers. But less-visible threats were far
more dangerous.

Housing and the Spread of Disease

The three-tier stratification system on the plantation—European management at the apex, an intermediary Asian clerical class, and the *coolie* (or
labourer) class at the bottom—was pervasive in all facets of social life and
reinforced the coolies' low position in the hierarchy. The workers' accommodations basically consisted of rows of temporary *attap* (thatched-roof),
open-barrack structures, called labour lines, with mud walls and verandas.
The buildings were supported on posts with space underneath for storage
and cooking. The abolition of indenture and the introduction of the first
systematic labour "welfare" code in the FMS in 1912 (revised in 1923)
resulted in improvements to barrack construction. The new back-to-back
labour lines were raised from the ground, were supported on brick pillars,
and had corrugated tin or iron roofs. They were also divided into separate
sections. Beds were essentially pieces of wood or planks, sometimes raised.
Overcrowding and lack of privacy were the norm, and living conditions were
grim. Subsequently, the 1916 Labour Code made it obligatory for a separate
room to be provided for a married couple and stipulated that no more than
three adults were to be housed in a room with "less than 100 square feet of
floor."[15]

In the early years, workers were not provided with "modern" sanitation facilities or even bucket latrines. The river was their toilet, bathtub, and water supply, which meant that their drinking water was bacteria-infested and their method of storing it in large containers near their living quarters created ideal conditions for mosquitoes to breed in the vicinity. Impure water supplies and poor sanitation were also responsible for the spread of cholera and dysentery among workers. The Labour Code of 1923 stipulated that estates had to provide a sufficient supply of "wholesome" water and improve sanitary conditions. The latter provision depended on the size and locality of the estates. On larger estates, there were communal toilet and shower facilities and a common cooking area.[16] On smaller estates, the poorer working and living conditions had a far greater impact on workers' health, with cramped and unhygienic living conditions enabling diseases to spread rapidly and resulting in workers' susceptibility to disease. High morbidity rates were consistent with poverty and poor diet.

Malaria was the greatest scourge on estates because of its widespread distribution (especially in the lower hill country) and because the recurrent attacks of fever steadily reduced and weakened a patient's capacity to resist other, more deadly diseases. The clearing of jungle for new planting created the most serious hazard, since it left large pools of stagnant water that "invaded" the plantation with a new malaria vector. In 1829 a third of all deaths in Penang were attributed to malaria.[17] Almost eighty years later, in 1908, the death rate from malaria on twenty-one estates in the FMS was over two hundred per thousand people.[18]

Compared to rates in southern India, malaria was "hyper endemic in nearly all of Malaya and in particular on estates that had been established by clearing jungle. On one estate . . . the mortality rate was 23.3 percent in 1910, 10 percent in 1911, and 10 percent in 1912. . . . [In] three years nearly half the average population died."[19] Mortality rates for plantation workers for the period 1911–1923 are listed in Table 1.2. Comparative deaths and death rates for the FMS population as a whole for 1914 to 1923 are shown in Table 1.3.

In the UMS, conditions on plantations were much worse, and planters had to offer higher wages to attract workers. British Malaya was also less safe than other colonies. Comparative mortality rates for Indian indentured labourers in Malaya (Province Wellesley and Perak) and in three other British colonial states (Assam, Fiji, and Surinam) are provided in Table 1.4. As shown in the table, Indian mortality rates were highest in Malaya, indicative of the abysmal conditions there. In Surinam, moreover, unlike in Malaya, Indian workers were allowed to make the transition to a land-owning peasantry.

Fearing that the India Office would ban emigration to Malaya in the midst of a rubber boom, the FMS administration introduced several new measures after 1910. It established a Labour Department to tackle the high mortality rates and formed a Malaria Advisory Board to direct an antimalaria campaign.[20] Subsequently the administration incorporated an Estate

26 / CHAPTER 1

TABLE 1.2   ESTATE MORTALITY RATES, FMS, 1911–1923

YEAR	TOTAL NUMBER OF ESTATE LABOURERS	DEATHS	DEATH RATE PER THOUSAND
1911	143,614	9,040	62.90
1912	171,968	7,054	41.02
1913	182,937	5,592	29.60
1914	176,226	4,635	26.30
1915	169,100	2,839	16.78
1916	187,030	3,299	17.61
1917	214,972	3,906	18.71
1918*	213 425	9,081	42.55
1919	216,573	3,384	15.16
1920	235,156	4,367	18.57
1921	175,649	3,195	18.19
1922	159,279	2,556	16.05
1923	147,276	1,924	13.06

* Influenza pandemic.
Source: Estates Health Commission, *Report 1924* (Kuala Lumpur: Estates Health Commission, 1924), appendix 3, A56.

TABLE 1.3   DEATHS AND DEATH RATES, FMS, 1914–1923

YEAR	TOTAL POPULATION	DEATHS	DEATH RATE PER THOUSAND
1914	1,136,500	39,000	34.31
1915	1,172,336	33,899	28.92
1916	1,208,177	36,985	30.60
1917	1,244,018	42,514	34.17
1918*	1,279,859	67,639	52.85
1919	1,315,700	38,645	29.37
1920	1,351,541	43,705	32.34
1921	1,304,825	38,077	29.18
1922	1,360,876	35,028	25.74
1923	1,389,667	33,914	24.40

For a similar distribution of age and gender, the death rate on estates equals the general death rate if all deaths from illness contracted on estates are attributed to residence on them, but this is difficult, especially in the case of small estates and contractors' labourers.
* Influenza pandemic.
Source: Estates Health Commission, *Report 1924* (Kuala Lumpur: Estates Health Commission, 1924), appendix 3, A56.

Labour (Protection of Health) Enactment in the Labour Code of 1912 and required planters to report all deaths from malaria on their estates. By 1920 Malaria Destruction Boards had been established throughout Malaya to contain the spread of the disease.

Ancylostomiasis, or hookworm infection, followed malaria as the second most serious disease that afflicted plantation workers. Hookworm infection was consistent with unhygienic conditions, the absence of latrines with washing facilities, "uncontrolled" defecation on estate grounds, and walking barefoot. According to Norman Parmer, Indian workers were often infected

TABLE 1.4   COMPARATIVE MORTALITY RATES FOR INDENTURED INDIAN
LABOUR IN ASSAM, FIJI, SURINAM, AND MALAYA, 1871–1910

	1871–1880	1881–1890	1891–1900	1901–1910	1871–1910
Death rate per 1,000					
Assam	79.8	59.4	50.3	40.9	52.6
Fiji	n.a.	31.3	20.9	15.4	19.8
Surinam	53.6	20.9	16.8	14.1	22.3
Province Wellesley	57.3	39.7	49.6	56.9	48.0
Perak	n.a.	57.0	73.7	85.7	79.6
Average population					
Assam	45,770	73,899	127,472	71,269	84,436
Fiji	n.a.	3,836	4,508	8,975	5,911
Surinam	2,435	3,966	4,854	3,448	3,741
Province Wellesley	2,078	3,588	3,749	2,283	3,136
Perak	n.a.	986	1,493	3,499	2,148

n.a. indicates data are not available.

Source: R. Shlomowitz and L. Brennan, "Mortality and Indian Labour in Malaya, 1877–1933," *Indian Economic and Social History Review* 29, no. 1 (1992): 72.

on arrival in Malaya, and the incidence increased greatly after a period of residence on the estates. Parmer notes that in 1919 "an estimated 70 percent of persons dying from malaria in Perak also had hookworm."[21]

Tuberculosis was rife among plantation workers[22] and even in 1930 was reported to be the fourth most frequent cause of death in the FMS.[23] This was principally because of overcrowding in the "cubicle" accommodations, unsanitary conditions, and poverty among the workers, who lived in a state of semistarvation. Deaths from dysentery and diarrhoea also contributed to high mortality rates, as did deaths from beriberi. Planters and officials often laid the blame for malarial infection and ancylostomiasis (as well as other diseases) on the workers, disregarding the poverty, unsanitary living conditions, lack of potable water, and absence of proper medical facilities on plantations.[24] Data on deaths and death rates from the principal diseases in the FMS for the period 1911–1923 are provided in Table 1.5.

Labour legislation and the changing attitude of the Malayan government, rather than employers' actions, played an important role in improving the working and living conditions of Indian plantation workers.

Wages and Working Conditions

Institutionalized Indian labour recruitment meant that plantation workers possessed very little bargaining power. Demand for labour varied with the widely fluctuating price of rubber, and planters endeavoured to keep wages depressed. In the late nineteenth century, the daily work hours of indentured labourers were variable, with some estates stipulating nine hours and others requiring ten. The norm was eight hours.[25] Conditions improved marginally in the twentieth century, when the workday was limited to six consecutive

TABLE 1.5   PRINCIPAL DISEASES, DEATHS, AND DEATH RATES, FMS, 1911–1923

YEAR	MALARIA		DYSENTERY AND DIARRHŒA		PULMONARY TUBERCULOSIS		BERIBERI	
	DEATHS	RATE	DEATHS	RATE	DEATHS	RATE	DEATHS	RATE
1911	17,440	17.47	7,659	7.31	2,300	2.20	1,469	1.40
1912	17,870	16.52	5,885	5.44	1,353	1.25	1,212	1.12
1913	16,414	14.69	5,317	4.75	1,623	1.45	1,190	1.06
1914	13,634	11.99	5,235	4.60	1,655	1.45	1,223	1.07
1915	15,208	12.97	3,148	2.68	1,995	1.70	871	0.74
1916	17,627	14.58	3,197	2.64	2,193	1.81	757	0.62
1917	18,750	15.07	4,942	3.97	2,446	1.96	1,207	0.97
1918	31,515	24.62	4,280	3.34	3,184	2.48	1,277	0.98
1919	16,975	12.90	3,712	2.82	2,445	1.86	939	0.71
1920	20,595	15.24	3,804	2.81	2,634	1.95	431	0.32
1921	17,168	13.16	2,999	2.30	2,255	1.73	422	0.32
1922	15,570	11.44	2,419	1.78	2,393	1.76	443	0.33
1923	15,516	11.17	2,142	1.55	1,934	1.39	378	0.27

These figures are for the general population, not for estates only.
Source: Estates Health Commission, Report 1924 (Kuala Lumpur: Estates Health Commission, 1924), appendix 3, A57.

hours and could not exceed nine. Labourers had to work six full days a week, and if they complied, they were eligible for a paid day off on the seventh. Overtime was paid at double the hourly rate. These regulations governing hours of work were retained in all subsequent statutes, including the Labour Code of 1923.[26]

With respect to wage levels, the Straits Settlements Ordinance of 1884 had stipulated the following rates for Indian labourers on three-year contracts: 12 cents a day for the first year and 14 cents a day for subsequent years for adult males, and 8 cents a day for the first year and 10 cents a day for subsequent years for females and males under 21 years of age. The higher rate, however, was not to be offered until workers had paid off their debt (transport and other costs incurred on the journey to Malaya). Following the abolition of indenture, wages were freed of Indian government control. The practice of calculating pay on the basis of individual subsistence continued. The average monthly wage approximated (in Straits dollars) $6.00 in 1910, $13.90 in 1918, and $12.40 in 1920. Labour benefits such as housing added a further $2.00 to $2.50 per month.[27] After the introduction of the Indian Emigration Act of 1922, factors such as estate locality and health conditions on estates became part of the wage determination equation. Malaya was divided into two geographical regions: key and nonkey. Key areas (mainly the SS and FMS) included "healthy," better-located districts on the western half of the peninsula. Nonkey areas were located in more-expensive and inaccessible areas (eastern Malaya). It has been estimated that wages in 1930 were about 40 cents per day. They dropped to between 25 and 30 cents at the end of 1931 and were lowered to 20 to 25 cents in mid-1932. At the end of 1932, they stood at between 25 and 28 cents.[28]

Workers were categorised on the basis of their job/skills classification—factory work, rubber tapping, and fieldwork. Tapping was classified as skilled, fieldwork as unskilled. There was also a gender-based differentiation, with women workers earning lower wages than men (normally between 70 and 80 percent of the male wage). Indian child labourers, for their part, earned between 30 and 40 percent of the adult male wage.[29] Under depressed conditions, wages were reduced and workdays were shortened. Consequently, in 1927 the Labour Code made it mandatory for employers to provide one-sixteenth of an acre of land for cultivation or grazing to workers who had dependents on plantations. Planters resisted this regulation, as they did most others. It was only during the Great Depression, when unemployment was rife and many destitute Indians had nowhere to go that the first small steps were taken to implement these land provisions.

A key indicator of poverty among Indian workers in this period was the high infant mortality rate. On one estate, there were fifty women on average between 1892 and 1898, but, although women became pregnant, no living child was born.[30] Infant mortality rates averaged 195.62 per 1,000 annually in the second decade of the twentieth century and remained at nearly 1 in 5 in the 1920s.[31] The colonial government's policy of dealing with these issues through legislation only aggravated the situation.

Welfare and Access to Health Care

The colonial government first legislated the provision of estate hospitals in the SS and FMS under the 1884 Indian Immigrants Protection Enactment. The 1904 Immigrants Protection Enactment made it obligatory for planters to provide medical attention and hospital accommodations for their workers. Compliance with this legislation varied, and even in 1907 planters still looked to the government to establish and maintain workers' hospitals. Following the establishment of a health branch in the FMS in 1910, the hospital ruling was enforced; however, the hospitals were essentially "garden" dispensaries.

In 1924 the FMS government appointed a commission to investigate the state of health, sanitation, and medical amenities on plantations as a basis for the provision of improved health care. The commission confirmed the deplorable living and health conditions of plantation workers. Its most important recommendation was the establishment of a comprehensive health and medical scheme and health boards with oversight for all estates of more than twenty-five acres (ten hectares). In 1926 the government passed the Health Boards Enactment, but because of the costs involved and the exemption of smaller producers, planters' associations opposed it. As a result, only a few local boards were established; following the onset of the Great Depression and reduced demand for Malaya's primary commodities, the health boards scheme was terminated.[32]

On the subject of the "survival" of Indian migrant workers, the colonial government was essentially a "night watchman." Public health services focused on the application of medical research findings to direct campaigns against diseases, especially malaria; the enactment of appropriate legislation to provide oversight on plantations; and the organisation of estate hospitals.

The Pathological Institute (later the Institute for Medical Research [IMR]) was established at the turn of the century. Its main mission was to research the treatment and control of the "twin scourges of the country, malaria and beri-beri."[33] Apart from drainage measures to remove the mosquito-borne malarial threat, early antimalarial sanitation measures were constrained by financial considerations.[34] In the interwar period, a number of alternative/experimental sanitation measures were introduced on a trial basis, including sluicing, alternative methods of subsoil drainage, the contamination of *A. maculatus* breeding areas, and the introduction of larvae-eating fish.[35] Labour lines were also relocated to mosquito-free "sanitary circles."

Quinine was provided and "forcibly" administered—often somewhat indiscriminately by "dressers" (male nursing staff)—on most estates affected by malaria. Mass dosages administered by unqualified medical staff invariably led to various forms of cinchonism that not only tended to reduce the labour capacity of already ravaged plantation workforces but also reinforced Indian misgivings about the use and efficacy of quinine.[36] In the late 1940s, it was widely believed that the introduction of the insecticide DDT would eliminate the disease and that new drug treatments, such as Paludrine, would achieve more effective malarial control in Malaya.[37] However, expanded planting in the early 1950s showed that there was a strong and ongoing correlation between increasing rates of malarial infection and the opening of new plantations. This pattern is illustrated in Figure 1.3.

As shown in the figure, the peaks in malarial infection rates corresponded to new rubber planting. Nevertheless, it was "sensible" to "keep and maintain" the workforce and its expatriate managerial staff in good health so that the enterprise could thrive, rather than to halt new production. Thus,

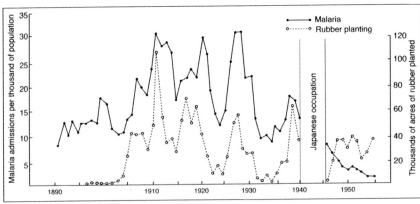

Figure 1.3 Admissions to government hospitals in the FMS for Malaria, and the planting and replanting of rubber, Malaya. (R. E. Anderson, *Federation of Malaya, Annual Report of the Malaria Advisory Board, 1955* [Kuala Lumpur: Government Printer, 1956], 2.)

public health provisions had to be equally disbursed and yet be customised to each plantation to be effective. Untrained hospital assistants or dressers managed the estate hospitals under the direction of visiting medical practitioners. Group hospitals were larger and better equipped and served several estates. In 1927 there were 169 plantation hospitals in the FMS (estate and group), but the number declined to 126 by 1939.[38]

Continuity and Change

The end of empire in Malaya witnessed a switch by the independent government to manufacturing industries for national development and economic growth. Oil palm gradually replaced rubber as the main agricultural commodity, and the race downward to reduce operating costs resumed. Indians are currently regarded as high-priced workers, and "cheaper" Indonesian and Bangladeshi contract plantation workers have replaced them in the new migration flows.[39] The future for Indian rubber plantation workers in current-day Malaysia is bleak.

NOTES

Acknowledgments: I am grateful to the Wellcome Trust Centre for the History of Medicine, University College London, and the Wellcome Trust (United Kingdom) for providing financial support for this study.

1. Amarjit Kaur, *Wage Labour in Southeast Asia: Globalisation. The International Division of Labour and Labour Transformations* (Basingstoke, UK: Palgrave Macmillan, 2004), 64.

2. Amarjit Kaur, *Bridge and Barrier: Transport and Communications in Colonial Malaya, 1870–1957* (Singapore: Oxford University Press, 1985).

3. John Drabble, *An Economic History of Malaysia, c. 1800–1990* (Basingstoke, UK: Palgrave Macmillan, 2000), 3–4.

4. Robert Huessler, *British Rule in Malaya: The Malayan Civil Service and Its Predecessors, 1867–1942* (Westport, CT: Greenwood Press, 1981), 176.

5. Kernail Singh Sandhu, *Indians in Malaya: Some Aspects of Their Immigration and Settlement* (Cambridge: Cambridge University Press, 1969), 56.

6. Ibid.

7. Granville St. John Orde Browne, *Labour Conditions in Ceylon, Mauritius and Malaya* (London: HMSO, 1943).

8. Sinnapah Arasaratnam, *Indians in Malaysia and Singapore* (London: Oxford University Press, 1970), 63.

9. P. P. Pillai, *Labour in South East Asia* (New Delhi: Indian Council of World Affairs, 1947), 146.

10. Virginia Thompson, *Post-mortem on Malaya* (New York: Macmillan, 1943), 123.

11. R. N. Jackson, *Immigrant Labour and the Development of Malaya* (Kuala Lumpur: Government Printer, 1961), 62–69.

12. *Annual Report of the Agent of the Government of India in British Malaya* (Kuala Lumpur: Government Printer, 1926), 8, para 11.

13. Charles Gamba, *Labour Law in Malaya* (Singapore: Donald Moore, 1955), 24.

14. Ravindra K. Jain, *South Indians on the Plantation Frontier in Malaya* (New Haven, CT: Yale University Press, 1970).

15. Jackson, *Immigrant Labour and the Development of Malaya*, 163.

16. Amarjit Kaur, "Indian Labour, Labour Standards, and Workers' Health in Burma and Malaya, 1900–1940," *Modern Asian Studies* 40, part 2 (May 2006): 393–444.

17. B. W. Hodder, *Man in Malaya* (London: University of London Press, 1959), 117.

18. Lennox A. Mills, *British Rule in Eastern Asia* (London: Oxford University Press, 1842), 300.

19. Highlands and Lowlands Para Rubber Company Limited, *History of the Company 1906–1956* (Kuala Lumpur: Highlands and Lowlands Para Rubber, 1956), 5. (Copy provided by Henry Barlow.)

20. Malcolm Watson, *The Prevention of Malaria in the Federated Malay States* (1921; repr., Kuala Lumpur: Malaysian Branch of the Royal Asiatic Society, 2000).

21. Norman Parmer, "Estate Workers' Health in the Federated Malay States in the 1920s," in *The Underside of Malaysian History: Pullers, Prostitutes, Plantation Workers*, ed. P. J. Rimmer and Lisa M. Allen (Singapore: Singapore University Press, 1990), 179–192.

22. *Report of the Commission Appointed to Enquire into Certain Matters Affecting the Health of Estates in the Federated Malaya States 1924* (Singapore: Government Printer, 1924), B11.

23. Parmer, "Estate Workers' Health in the Federated Malay States," 183.

24. *Report of the Commission*, B15.

25. Jackson, *Immigrant Labour and the Development of Malaya*, 104–105.

26. Browne, *Labour Conditions in Ceylon, Mauritius and Malaya*.

27. John Thoburn, *Primary Commodity Exports and Economic Development: A Study of Malaysia* (London: J. Wiley, 1977), 285.

28. P. T. Bauer, *The Rubber Industry: A Study in Competition and Monopoly* (London: Longmans Green, 1948), 58.

29. Kaur, *Wage Labour in Southeast Asia*, chap. 4.

30. Watson, *The Prevention of Malaria in the Federated Malay States*, 96.

31. Parmer, "Estate Workers' Health in the Federated Malay States," 183.

32. Ibid., 190.

33. *Institute for Medical Research Jubilee Volume No. 25* (Kuala Lumpur: Government Printer, 1951), 40.

34. Watson, *The Prevention of Malaria in the Federated Malay States*.

35. *Institute for Medical Research Jubilee Volume No. 25*, 167.

36. Kaur, "Indian Labour."

37. *Institute for Medical Research Jubilee Volume No. 25*, 167.

38. Kaur, "Indian Labour."

39. Compiled from *The Annual Report of the Agent of the Government of India in British Malaya 1927–39* (Kuala Lumpur: Government Printer, 1927–1939).

2

Work, Home, and Natural Environments

Health and Safety in the Mexican
Oil Industry, 1900–1938

Myrna Santiago

José G. Ramírez had worked for the East Coast Oil Company since adolescence. Between 1908 and 1916, he worked twelve-hour shifts. For the next seven years, he also worked Sundays. By 1927 Ramírez had suffered serious illness and two major accidents. In 1924 he nearly lost one eye, stabbed by splinters at a construction site. The next year a pipeline crushed his right foot. In 1923 and 1926 he caught malaria and missed work for weeks. The company lowered his salary once, and when he objected to a reduction in 1927, East Coast Oil fired him—after nineteen years of employment. Half-blind and limping, Ramírez sued the company for failing to pay overtime and compensation for injuries. He was bitter but hopeful that Mexican law would protect him. After all, Mexico had experienced a social revolution (1910–1920) to end oppressive labor conditions. Ramírez felt entitled to the rights and protections won as a result of the upheaval.[1]

However, until 1938 Mexican oil workers in northern Veracruz worked for an industry that was private and foreign-owned. Like workers elsewhere, from Malayan plantations to Spanish and Nigerian mines, men toiled under severe physical stress. The job was risky, the workday was long, and the evening whistle brought little relief. For oil workers, "home" did not mean comfort, rest, or reprieve from danger. Quite the contrary. Mexican workers' quarters were extensions of the workplace. The men lived on refinery grounds, meters away from wells, storage tanks, and other installations. The geographical location of extraction areas, moreover, increased workers' bodily stress. The industry operated in the tropical rain forest of northern Veracruz, fertile ground for disease since the nineteenth century.

Where the history of Ramirez differs most from others in this volume is in the recognition that work, home, and natural environment were integral parts of the labor process that shaped workers' activism. Mexican oil workers have been described as "precociously" political because their militancy contributed not only to the ascendancy of a new national government but to the expropriation of foreign oil companies. After 1938, workers received their paychecks from an industry that belonged to the Mexican state.[2]

The historiography of Mexican oil documents the clashes among workers, their employers, and the state.[3] What the literature overlooks is that the oil workers were active on behalf of their safety and health as well.[4] In broaching the topic, this article is mindful of scholars urging labor and environmental historians to think of "the body" as a category of analysis for examining how workers understood the effects of their work and how those ideas evolved.[5] The scholars' suggestions are intriguing. Arthur McEvoy, for example, proposes looking at industrial health and safety "in terms of the interactions between a number of systems: the worker's body and its maintenance, the productive processes that draw on the worker's energy, and the law and ideology that guide them," the purpose being to think of the workplace "as an ecological system, of which the worker's body is the biological core."[6]

Other environmental historians point to the body as a kind of middle ground, where biology and culture meet and mix in complex, historically significant ways. Emphasis on working-class bodies as at once material, cultural, and ecological fits the historical experience of oil workers. It makes clear how the "ecological system" encompassed space beyond the workplace. That is, to understand health and safety, it is fruitful to locate workers in their lived spaces on and off the job, "follow[ing] the bodies," as John F. Kasson suggests and as Christopher Sellers does in the case of lead poisoning.[7]

Mapping the geography of Mexican oil workers' bodies through their spatial habitats—workplace, home, and ecosystem in their built and natural environments—yields a rich picture. Workers become biological organisms in motion, interacting with chemical, biological, and other natural elements within and across the shop floor, the neighborhood, and the tropical ecology, integrated as so many biological objects. Such a view emerges because in the early twentieth century the physical distance between work and living quarters in the Mexican oil industry was minimal: "home" did not mean leaving the workplace behind. No boundaries separated the two spheres. The work environment diffused into the home environment, and both existed within a tropical rain forest. That spatial-ecological arrangement had implications for workers' safety and health, as their bodies were exposed to toxic petrochemical compounds and biological agents of epidemic and endemic disease, all in a day.

In addition, attention to the cultural lenses through which workers viewed their bodies offers glimpses of how they analyzed conditions as historical subjects and political actors. Rarely did they speak of disease or toxins, the biological language then evolving among "industrial hygiene" or "public health" experts. The workers' views about safety and health, forged in the context of revolutionary politics, connected instead the threats they faced across spaces in a more holistic and aggressive manner. Oil workers saw the health effects of exposures on the job, at home, and in the natural environment as a coherent whole, concluding that "Capital" was responsible for them all.[8] The companies disagreed, creating political strife across the industry. This chapter teases out how workers developed their views, acted on them, and affected the course of Mexican history.

Industry

American and English entrepreneurs founded Mexico's petroleum industry in 1900 in northern Veracruz and Tampico, Tamaulipas. They expertly navigated the Mexican Revolution (1910–1920), reaching third place in global production in 1921 and selling out to Standard Oil and Royal Dutch Shell afterward. As the Great Depression gripped the world in the early 1930s, the behemoths shrank production and labor, but the rise in Mexican consumption allowed for modest expansion until union activism led to nationalization in 1938.[9] Throughout, the industry followed a model of extraction developed in the United States in the nineteenth century and applied thereafter in oil regions as far away as the Caspian Sea,[10] a standard seen in other industries addressed in this volume, from Nigerian mining to Malayan colonial production. Outsiders brought capital, technology, and expertise, while local elites facilitated access to isolated geographical locations and cheap migrant labor. Products and profits were repatriated to Europe or the United States, leaving nationals with low wages, little tax revenue, and plenty of environmental effects. Anna Zalik's chapter on the Nigerian oil industry demonstrates the resiliency of this model into the late twentieth century. What surfaces as particular in Mexico is the workers' forceful response to labor conditions, including the struggle over their bodies, their health, and their safety.[11]

Work

To say that oil work is dangerous is to state the obvious. Perhaps better than any other, the petroleum industry defines "flammable" from start to finish. The risk of bodily harm extends from the point of origin—the oil well—to the finished product. Until the 1920s, men used handheld tools that required little energy beyond human muscle; they worked without sophisticated technology, a factor that McEvoy identifies as a key to health and safety.[12] Technologies introduced in the 1920s (tractors and steam- or oil-powered machines), moreover, saved time but did not make work safer. Machinery allowed companies to increase the pace of work.[13] Thus the period of foreign oil in northern Veracruz can be divided into two phases: between 1900 and 1921, when work focused on felling the rain forest for infrastructure, and from 1921 to 1938, when refining was more important. Bodily risks changed, but persisted throughout.

The task of demolishing the rain forest for industrial installations was exhausting and dangerous. Chopping down towering trees entailed swinging machetes for twelve hours a day into the mid-1920s.[14] Bodies falling from great heights or trampled by falling trees were not unusual; broken ribs or limbs, contusions, and "minor injuries," as one hospital reported, were routine. Heavy lifting led to hernias, as men's bodies literally ripped apart from physical effort.[15] The tractors and machinery of the 1920s brought new injuries: the crushing of limbs as man and machine interacted with no protective barriers at the point of contact between skin and metal.[16]

Risks increased as wells flowed. Northern Veracruz crude was extremely hazardous: boiling hot and saturated with hydrogen sulfide (H_2S), a chemical that displaces oxygen in the lungs and can provoke death within minutes.[17] When the driller perforated the rock that kept the lid on the pressure cooker, oil at temperatures of 140°F to 150°F burst with immense power.[18] Such "gushers" became iconic in Mexico.[19] The immediate danger of a gusher was fire, a frequent occurrence. Lacking evacuation procedures, workers ran for their lives.[20] Deaths were not rare when wells exploded, but no one tallied the bodies.[21]

Firefighting was no better. Until nationalization, fire control was unsuccessful. The main suppression method entailed dumping gravel and sand on the fire with hand shovels. Until 1923, the only protective equipment the companies provided to firefighters was a thin metal shield or a "wet sac" for heads and hands. Thereafter, experimental gas masks came into use, although their effectiveness was questionable.[22] By 1927, chemical foams replaced water in some cases, but equipment remained primitive. Firefighting exposed men to extraordinarily high temperatures, deafening noise, and at times "an almost blinding deluge" of boiling oil splashing on their bodies. The hydrogen sulfide around fire sites produced "agonizing pain" and swelling of the eyes, temporary blindness, and in extreme cases unconsciousness or death. How many workers died extinguishing fires between 1900 and 1938 is unknown. No one kept track.[23]

If infrastructure and gushers in the great outdoors exposed workers to acute danger, enclosed refinery work was no safer. Burns were routine. Slips and falls on oily floors happened daily. Heat stress was constant.[24] Tank and still cleaners were twice in jeopardy, as they had to introduce their whole bodies into containers steaming with poisonous vapors at temperatures of 122°F to 140°F.[25] Mexican refinery workers thus exhibited the poisoning symptoms that American oil workers reported to Alice Hamilton in the early 1920s: nausea, heartburn, headaches, eye irritation, sore throats, tremors, and difficulty breathing.[26]

By the mid 1930s workers were feeling the effects of long-term biological interaction with toxic petrochemicals. As their bodies absorbed more hazardous substances through nose, mouth, and skin than their lungs, livers, and kidneys could excrete, the chemical load their bodies carried gnawed at cellular structures and internal organs. Doctors began diagnosing oil workers with severe anemia, heart anomalies, digestive tract irritation, and impaired respiratory systems.[27] Only mining was more dangerous than the oil industry, a reality worldwide.[28]

Home and the Natural Environment

The miner William D. "Big Bill" Haywood, one of the most prominent leaders of the American labor movement in the 1920s, once noted, "I've never read Marx's *Capital*, but I have the marks of Capital all over me."[29] The same applied to Mexican oil workers. They were exhausted and sometimes maimed and disabled. Theirs was the body scarred, but they found no relief at the end of the workday. The physical proximity of dwellings to oil installations meant that the hazards of work followed them home.[30] The tropical rain forest where the industry operated, moreover, subjected workers' bodies to the stresses of the local ecology.

When oil workers went home, their muscles relaxed but their bodies continued interacting intimately with the hydrocarbons that emanated from the worksite through air and water. Refinery stacks belched "dense" clouds of compounds onto the neighborhood, meaning that workers inhaled toxins in their sleep.[31] The water supply was likewise contaminated by petroleum.[32] Workers bore more than the scars of Capital. They represented the polluted body, marked externally and internally, consumed by oil as their bodies literally consumed oil on and off the job.[33]

Infectious disease compounded the risks. Company housing was segregated by nationality, with Mexicans assigned to unhygienic, crowded, and substandard quarters. Biological agents of small pox, typhoid fever, influenza, and bubonic plague found easy targets in bodies living under such conditions.[34] By 1931, medical professionals reported that "proportionally" Tampico had the highest rate of tuberculosis in the country.[35] Thus the difference between work and home lay in the type or dose of noxious substances and organisms the men absorbed, not in their presence or absence. Workers never had sufficient time to recover from the physical and chemical abuses of the workday. Their bodies were under perpetual strain, placing them further at risk in the ecosystem that surrounded the industry.

Since the nineteenth century, Veracruz had been infamously "unhealthy." Temperatures and humidity were high, the rainy season was long, and hurricanes were as destructive as they were predictable. Abundant rainfall fed dense forests, rivers, lakes and lagoons, marshes and bogs, and coastal mangroves. Yellow fever was endemic and afflicted oil workers: California magnate Edward L. Doheny, for instance, reported losing forty-five oil workers to yellow fever in a single outbreak.[36] Still, the deadliest biological organisms that workers confronted were the pair responsible for malaria: the single-celled parasite *plasmodium* and its carrier, the mosquito. Thousands of bodies working outdoors meant a never-ending food supply for both.[37] The workforce was thus wracked by "the fever": by 1921 malaria was the primary cause of death in Tampico.[38]

The oil companies were not blind to the health challenges the rain forest represented, even as they ignored worksite hazards. Their response was to open clinics and, by 1937, six hospitals.[39] The problem was that the companies offered effective prevention measures—potable water, toilets, garbage collection, mosquito netting—only to foreign employees. Health care for Mexicans, plagued by racial segregation, was sporadic and inferior.[40] The natural environment where the industry operated, then, exacerbated health problems for workers. What could they do? As historians of medicine note, responses to health issues often depended on what the afflicted knew, and what they knew depended on what they were told or what they learned experientially.[41] In the oil workers' case, what they men knew was revolutionary politics.

Fighting for Body and Health

Mexican oil workers fought hard to improve working conditions, including health and safety. Three periods punctuate their efforts until 1938. The first, running from 1914 to 1924, in the realms of what McEvoy termed law and ideology, encompassed the immediate gains of revolution. The second phase revolved around the mid-1920s union drives, which sought to turn legal guarantees into contracts. The final period was from 1936 to 1938, when failed contract negotiations led to nationalization. Over those times, the oil workers developed sophisticated views of their bodies at work in a tropical environment.

Workers' health and safety emerged as an important topic in Veracruz, where labor activism was strong throughout the revolution. The oil workers staged twenty-nine strikes between 1911 and 1921, for example, but longshoremen and railroad and textile workers did their share.[42] As a consequence, Veracruz passed one of Mexico's first labor laws in 1914. Three of the eighteen articles focused on health and safety, making employers responsible for providing "medical services and medicines," paying "for subsistence and treatment in case of accidents," and setting up "hospitals or infirmaries."[43]

Three years later, labor gained more through Article 123 of the new 1917 Constitution. Article 123 guaranteed labor rights, including health and safety. It made employers liable for "labor accidents and occupational diseases arising from work" and responsible for compensation for accidents, disability, and death. Section XV specifically made employers responsible for

all the provisions of law regarding hygiene and sanitation and to adopt adequate measures to prevent accidents due to the use of machinery, tools and working materials, as well as to organize work in such a manner as to assure the greatest guarantees possible for the health and lives of workmen.[44]

The Constitution thus established a framework for health and safety that made prevention the governing principle in workplace organization.

However, the Constitution only laid out principles. Laws were needed to make them applicable. Once again, Veracruz took the lead, updating its labor law in 1918. Health and safety were addressed in detail, charging "the big industries" with responsibility for prevention and provision of medical and hospital services and for compensating workers for accidents. The law also adopted the concept of occupational illness and provided a broad definition: "that which is contracted and develops during the habitual exercise of work and as a consequence thereof, causing in the worker death or temporary or permanent inability to work."[45] In 1924, Veracruz went further, passing the "Law on Occupational Risks." It addressed oil work directly, listing over thirty occupational hazards, including benzene—although no one knew its carcinogenic properties—asphyxia, ulcers, vision problems, skin lesions, and malaria.[46] Thus worker activism elicited a positive legal and ideological response from the post-revolutionary state. Effective application of the law, however, required more.

Oil workers acted on their own behalf individually and collectively, offering a window into their worldview in the process. At the individual level, they sued for compensation for injuries, revealing a profound alienation from their bodies.[47] Men referred to severed or injured limbs as "defects" or "useless," yet they rhetorically embraced the law as a tool for individual empowerment and as a claim of employer social responsibility.[48] José Ramírez thus asked defiantly, "Well, doesn't the businessman or owner pay from his own pocket the repairs that have to be done to the machines when these wear out in the production process?"[49] Men's bodies deserved just as much from their employers. Other men deployed language indicative of hurt feelings in addition to hurt bodies also to invoke notions of employer obligation toward workers. They spoke of *desgaste orgánico*—that is, their bodies being biologically spent after years of arduous work—arguing that the companies "should understand that the human body isn't run by electric or steam machinery" without requiring rest. They accused the companies of "robbing" them of their youth and giving them "inhumane" treatment.[50]

In this way, injured men claimed the moral high ground over bosses who cared less about live bodies than about machinery. The hurt tone expressed resentment at how the companies, literally adding insult to injury, forced the men to sue for compensation, although the law dictated that workers were entitled to indemnity. In an industry that jeopardized men's bodies by its very nature, in which technology and men were instruments of profit, injured men emphasized their humanity—the biological and cultural qualities that separated man from machine and made them flesh and feeling rather than inert inputs of production. Discursively at least, disabled men claimed that the core of work was indeed the human body.

At the collective level, the activism was intense and the worldview was critical. Between 1924 and 1926 oil workers held twenty-five strikes across northern Veracruz and Tampico to gain union recognition and contracts.[51]

The proposed contracts adopted the compensation tables inscribed in the law, something one worker criticized as "the monetarization of risk" and what scholar Keith Wailoo calls "the commodification" of working-class bodies.[52] Yet prevention of illness and injury and protection of bodies were just as important, as men demanded, for the first time, safety equipment, the end of forced entry into hot containers, a maintenance schedule "to keep installations in good conditions and avoid workplace accidents," and "clear and precise signs in dangerous places."[53] Furthermore, workers made evident that they collapsed, or integrated, work, home, and rain forest into one. Mexican Gulf workers, for instance, sought full salary for illnesses "caused by the unhealthy conditions of the region" and "poor climate," while the men from the Pierce refinery demanded double pay for work in "dangerous and unhealthy locations."[54] What workers were saying, in effect, was that there was no distinction between work site, neighborhood, and natural environment, something confirmed by demands for houses "properly conditioned" for the tropics like those foreign employees enjoyed, with fans, ice, showers, and indoor toilets.[55] The men were following their own bodies and holding the employer accountable for what befell them throughout.

The companies, however, were formidable opponents. They skirted legal obligations and rejected health and safety demands, arguing that the men were sick or injured because they lacked "moral character" and engaged in "disorderly living."[56] The companies thus made workers individually responsible for the premature deterioration of their bodies, turning poor health into a morality tale: bodies decaying due to reprobate personal conduct rather than deplorable environments. The knowledge of assumed risk coupled with the theory of free will wrapped up the employers' argument: workers knew the risks yet chose the work, so why complain?[57] Malaria, yellow fever, and tuberculosis were not even an issue. They were "natural," not work-related.[58]

The question and its resolution were ultimately political. Labor, capital, and the state, at odds since the start of the revolution, clashed one last time over the 1936 contract. Union demands were unprecedented in their comprehensiveness. The proposal was 175 legal-size pages, with 250 clauses.[59] And while it focused on making the companies pay for subjecting workers to danger, following the model of the commodification of workers' bodies,[60] there is no doubt that the men integrated work, home, and natural environments holistically. Clauses that revealed that viewpoint included demands for double wages for working in the rain (nine out of twelve months) or in the mud, in "swampy locations," underwater, and along coastal waters—that is, all of northern Veracruz and Tampico. Also applicable were demands seeking company "cooperation" with campaigns against tuberculosis and "tropical diseases"; recognition of malaria and tuberculosis as occupational diseases; providing "comfortable and hygienic" housing free of charge; making available seven kilos of ice daily per worker; and medical service for "themselves and their families in view of the unhealthy nature of the region."[61]

The companies cried communism—not a comprehensive viewpoint of worksite ecology. The state was caught in the middle, trying to uphold the law. But since the legislation was indeed on labor's side, enforcing it meant a union victory. The companies' defiance of legality ultimately left the state with few options. Under threat of a national strike by all unions, President Lázaro Cárdenas chose nationalization on March 19, 1938.

The Aftermath of Nationalization

Did the now truly Mexican oil industry mean healthier and safer workers? The record is mixed. Workers made substantial gains under Petróleos Mexicanos (PEMEX). Their victories included recognition of malaria as an occupational disease, with fourteen more diseases so recognized by 1986. PEMEX also provided safety equipment, prevention training, and improvements in medical care, including a hospital for tuberculosis.[62] Nevertheless, accidents continued apace, at an average of eighteen per one hundred workers through 1942. Prevention was slow: the first occupational safety and industrial hygiene program was not drafted until 1945 and its implementation was secondary to production.[63] The expansion of PEMEX, moreover, amplified risks. Its legacy includes grisly accidents affecting not only workers but entire communities.[64] The fight to protect health and life on the shop floor, in the neighborhood, and in the natural environment therefore continues.

Mexican oil workers escaped the ravages of revolution but not those of oil. Safe from the violence that consumed Mexico, oil workers nevertheless suffered severe casualties. They did not die on battlefields, but their bodies littered oil camps—anonymous dead summarily buried alongside pipelines. They were spared the wounds of battle, but not the torture of industry. And while American oil workers' bodies became iconic as men drenched in oil from head to toe, Mexican workers did not even earn that dubious glory: the companies reserved drilling work for foreigners. The Mexican male was not masculine enough to be represented; his body was used more as a beast of burden in the daily war for energy production. His was a body in pain, so elegantly described by Elaine Scarry and historians unveiling the power of representation in creating and reproducing ideologies and social relations.[65]

But there is another side to the coin. For Mexicans, oil workers became iconic in a different way: as strikers, troublemakers, risk takers, union men.[66] They turned out bodies by the thousands onto the streets for decades. Theirs were political bodies that constructed no divide between the ideological and the material, the cultural and the economic—the workplace, the neighborhood, and the natural environment. Mexican oil workers were fierce contenders precisely because their views were complicated, because they were not afraid of contradictions, and they did not hesitate to put their bodies on the line politically. Such is the promise of integration: for working class movements as well as, in much more modest ways, for more comprehensive working class and environmental histories.[67]

NOTES

1. Letter from Andrés Araujo, Labor Inspector, Tampico, Tamaulipas, to the Department of Labor, January 13, 1928, Archivo General de la Nación (AGN), Junta Federal de Conciliación y Arbitraje (JFCA), C 21, Expediente 15/928/130.

2. Alan Knight, *The Mexican Revolution*, vol. 1, *Porfirians, Liberals and Peasants* (Lincoln: University of Nebraska Press, 1990), 406–408.

3. See Lorenzo Meyer, *México y los Estados Unidos en el conflicto petrolero* (Mexico City: El Colegio de México, 1972); Lourdes Celis Salgado, *La industria petrolera en México. Una crónica I: De los inicios a la expropiación* (Mexico City: PEMEX, 1988); Jonathan Brown and Alan Knight, eds., *The Mexican Petroleum Industry in the Twentieth Century* (Austin: University of Texas Press, 1992); Jonathan Brown, *Oil and Revolution in Mexico* (Austin: University of Texas Press, 1993); Armando Rendón Corona, Jorge González Rodarte, and Angel Bravo Flores, *Los conflictos laborales en la industria petrolera y la expropiación 1911–1932*, vol. 1 (Mexico City: Universidad Autónoma Metropolitana, 1997); and Myrna Santiago, *The Ecology of Oil: Environment, Labor, and the Mexican Revolution, 1900–1938* (Cambridge: Cambridge University Press, 2006).

4. The omission is understandable, since European and American scholars have taken the lead in the field. See Daniel M. Berman, *Death on the Job: Occupational Health and Safety Struggles in the United States* (New York: Monthly Review Press, 1978); Carl Gersuny, *Work Hazards and Industrial Conflict* (Hanover, NH: University Press of New England, 1981); Dorothy Nelkin and Michael S. Brown, *Workers at Risk: Voices from the Workplace* (Chicago: University of Chicago Press, 1984); Barbara Ellen Smith, *Digging Our Graves: Coal Miners and the Struggle over Black Lung Disease* (Philadelphia: Temple University Press, 1987); Alan Derickson, *Workers' Health, Workers' Democracy: The Western Miners' Struggle, 1891–1925* (Ithaca, NY: Cornell University Press, 1988); David Rosner and Gerald Markowitz, *Deadly Dust: Silicosis and the Politics of Occupational Disease in Twentieth-Century America* (Princeton, NJ: Princeton University Press, 1991); Claudia Clark, *Radium Girls: Women and Industrial Health Reform, 1910–1935* (Chapel Hill: University of North Carolina Press, 1997); Roger Cooter and Bill Luckin, eds., *Accidents in History: Injuries, Fatalities, and Social Relations* (Amsterdam: Rodopi, 1997); Christopher Sellers, *Hazards of the Job: From Industrial Disease to Environmental Health Science* (Chapel Hill: University of North Carolina Press, 1997); John Fabian Witt, *The Accidental Republic: Crippled Workingmen, Destitute Widows, and the Remaking of American Law* (Cambridge, MA: Harvard University Press, 2004); and Arthur McIvor and Ronald Johnston, "Medical Knowledge and the Worker: Occupational Lung Diseases in the United Kingdom, c. 1920–1975," *Labor: Studies in Working-Class History of the Americas* 2, no. 4 (Winter 2005): 63–85. In Mexico, studies of oil worker health and safety focus on the petrochemical industry. See Mónica Casalet, *Salud y bienestar de la fuerza de trabajo. Estudio de caso: Automotriz y petroquímica* (Mexico City: Instituto Nacional de Estudios del Trabajo, Secretaría del Trabajo y Previsión Social, 1982); Sylvia Vega Gleason, "Petróleo, medio ambiente y salud," in *La industria petrolera ante la regulación jurídico-ecológica en México*, ed. Jorge Muñoz Barret, Sylvia Vega Gleason, and María del Carmen Carmona Lara (Mexico City: Universidad Nacional Autónoma de México and PEMEX, 1992), 90–129.

5. Arthur F. McEvoy, "Working Environments: An Ecological Approach to Industrial Health and Safety," in Cooter and Luckin, *Accidents in History*, 59–89. See also Christopher Sellers, "Thoreau's Body: Towards an Embodied Environmental History," *Environmental History* 4, no. 4 (October 1999): 486–514; Ava Baron and Eileen Boris, "'The Body' as a Useful Category for Working-Class History," *Labor: Studies in Working-Class History of the Americas* 4, no. 2 (Summer 2007): 23–43.

6. McEvoy, "Working Environments," 60.

7. John F. Kasson, "Follow the Bodies: Commentary on 'The Body as a Useful Category for Working-Class History,'" *Labor: Studies in Working-Class History of the Americas* 4, no. 2 (Summer 2007): 45–48; Christopher Sellers, "The Dearth of the Clinic: Lead, Air, and Agency in Twentieth-Century America," *Journal of the History of Medicine* 38 (July 2003): 257–259.

8. Santiago, *The Ecology of Oil*, 221. American Progressive-Era reformers made a similar argument. See David Rosner and Gerald Markowitz, eds., *Dying for Work: Workers' Safety and Health in Twentieth-Century America* (Bloomington: Indiana University Press, 1986), xii.

9. Meyer, *México y los Estados Unidos*, chap. 1.

10. See Daniel Yergin, *The Prize: The Epic Quest for Oil, Money and Power* (New York: Free Press, 1992).

11. Compare Mexico's oil industry to others in the Americas: See Nancy Lynn Quam-Wickham, "Petroleocrats and Proletarians: Work, Class, and Politics in the California Oil Industry, 1917–1925" (Ph.D. diss., University of California, Berkeley, 1994); B. S. McBeth, *Juan Vicente Gómez and the Oil Companies in Venezuela, 1908–1935* (Cambridge: Cambridge University Press, 1983); Anamaría Varea, ed., *Marea Negra en la Amazonia: Conflictos socioambientales vinculados a la actividad petrolera en el Ecuador* (Cayambe, Ecuador: Talleres Gráficos ABYA-YALA, 1995); and Guillermo Perry Rubio, *Política petrolera: economía y medio ambiente* (Bogotá: Fundación Friedirch Hebert, 1992).

12. McEvoy, "Working Environments," 63–65.

13. Letter from Gerente General to Presidente Municipal, August 20, 1919, Archivo Histórico del Ayuntamiento de Tampico (AHAT), Expediente 85-1919; Leopoldo Alafita Méndez, "Trabajo y condición obrera en los campamentos petroleros de la Huasteca 1900–1935," *Anuario 5* (October 1986): 187–193.

14. Santiago, *The Ecology of Oil*, 177–178.

15. Aurelio Herrera v. El Aguila, Archivo General del Estado de Veracruz (AGEV), Junta Central de Conciliación y Arbitraje (JCCA), C 65, Expediente 65, 1927; Medical Report, Tampico District and Refinery Hospital, July 1919, AGN/DT, C 224, Expediente 24, 1919; Case Miguel Garcés, AGN/JFCA, C 12, Expediente 15/927/285, 1927.

16. Tomás Hernández v. Huasteca Petroleum, AGEV/JCCA, C 45, Expediente 77, 1925; Case Pantaleón Hernández, AGEV/JCCA, C 64, Expediente 114, 1927.

17. Juan D. Villarello, "El pozo de Petróleo de Dos Bocas," *Parergones* (Instituto Geológico de México) 3, no. 1 (1909): 47–49.

18. E. DeGolyer, "The Significance of Certain Mexican Oil Field Temperatures," *Economic Geology* 13, no. 4 (June 1918): 275, 296, 300.

19. Charles W. Hamilton, *Early Day Oil Tales of Mexico* (Houston: Gulf Publishing Company, 1966), 210.

20. The first text on prevention of explosions appeared in 1960: T. B. O'Brien and W.C. Goins, Jr., "The Mechanics of Blowouts and How to Control Them," *American Petroleum Institute Drilling and Production Practice*, cited in W. C. Goins, Jr., *Blowout Prevention: Practical Drilling Technology*, vol. 1 (Houston: Gulf Publishing Company, 1969), 1.

21. *El Mundo*, April 16, 1923.

22. El Aguila had a gas mask in 1919, but probably only foreigners used it. The instructions, for example, were in English. "Rules and Precautions to be observed when using the proto-self-contained breathing apparatus," AGN/DT, C. 224, Expediente 24, 1919; Arthur B. Clifford, "Extinguishing an Oil-Well Fire in Mexico, and the Part Played Therein by Self-Contained Breathing-Apparatus," *Transactions of The Institution of Mining Engineers*, 63, no. 3 (1921): 3. In 1929 Mexican professionals argued that the masks were still ineffective; see Jacobo Alvarado, "El sulfuro de hidrógeno en la industria del petróleo," *Boletín del Petróleo* 27, no. 6 (June 1929): 793.

23. A. E. Chambers, "Potrero No. 4," *Journal of the Institute of Petroleum Technologists*, 9, no. 37 (1923): 144–145; "Accidente ocurrido al terminar la perforación del pozo Cacalilao número 2," *Boletín del Petróleo* 15, no. 4 (1923): 307–308; Xavier Villegas Mora, *Petróleo, sangre, y justicia* (Mexico City: Editorial Relámpagos, 1939), 50.

24. Case Margarito Hernández, AHAT, Expediente 85-1919; Corona, Rodarte, and Flores, *Los conflictos*, 56–57.

25. Pliego de peticiones, Sindicato de Obreros Unidos de the Texas Co., Terminal de Matillas, Veracruz, 1924, AGEV/JCCA, C 40 (134).

26. Alice Hamilton, "The Growing Menace of Benzene (Benzol) Poisoning in American Industry," *Journal of the American Medical Association* 78 (March 4, 1922): 627–630.

27. Sindicato de Trabajadores del Petróleo de la República Mexicana to Jesús Silva Herzog, June 25, 1937, AGN, Archivo Histórico de Hacienda (AHH), Legajo 1857-117, Legajo 1; Donato G. Alarcón, *La tuberculosis en la República Mexicana* (Tampico, Mexico: Talleres Tipográficos "El Comercio," 1931).

28. Santiago González Cordero, "El derecho de los trabajadores huelguistas y el derecho de la nación," AGN/AHH, Legajo 1857-117, Legajo 2; Gersuny, *Work Hazards*, 20.

29. Quoted in Kasson, "Follow the Bodies," 45.
30. Santiago, *The Ecology of Oil*, 162–163, 169–171, 193–196.
31. Letter from Inspector del Trabajo de Tamaulipas to Jefe del DP, October 16, 1926, AGN/DT, C 990, Expediente 5, 1926; letter from Unión de Obreros Regionales to Gobernador, August 1926, AGN/DT, C 813, Expediente 4.
32. Santiago, *The Ecology of Oil*, 124–129, 169–171.
33. Rachel Carson popularized the idea of bodies polluted by toxins in 1962, but there is a long history of laypeople's understanding of toxicity and health. Rachel Carson, *Silent Spring* (Boston: Houghton Mifflin Company, 2002); Linda Nash, "Purity and Danger: Historical Reflections on the Regulation of Environmental Pollutants," *Environmental History* 13 (October 2008): 651–658.
34. Index of smallpox outbreaks, AGEV/G:S, Viruela (V), C 1, 1901–1904, Expediente 17-1, Letra P, Papantla, Expediente 23, Letra L, Tantoyuca; Gonzalo Bada Ramírez, interviewed by Lief Adleson, Tampico, Tamaulipas, September 30, 1978, PHO/INAH/4/91.
35. Case Florentino Alor, August 5, 1925, AGN/JFCA, C 199, Expediente 930/1419; Comité de lucha contra la tuberculosis to Secretario de Gobernación, December 2, 1931, AGN/DGG, C 71, Expediente 24, 2.017(24)10.
36. Testimony of Edward L. Doheny, U.S. Senate Committee on Foreign Relations, *Investigation of Mexican Affairs*, 66th Congress, vol. 1 (Washington, DC: Government Printing Office, 1920), 219.
37. Santiago, *The Ecology of Oil*, 188; *The Merck Manual of Medical Information*, 2nd home ed. (New York: Pocket Books, 2003), 1140.
38. Letters from Inspector Médico to Presidente Municipal, March 1, 1921, July 31, 1921, November 1, 1921, AHAT, Expediente 262-1921.
39. Corona, Rodarte, and Flores, *Los conflictos*, 71, 73.
40. Memoria de los trabajos del Consejo Superior de Salubridad, 1905, Item 1219-1221, Doheny Collection, Box/File H, Occidental College, Los Angeles.
41. See "Toxic Bodies/Toxic Environments: An Interdisciplinary Forum," *Environmental History* 13, no. 4 (October 2008): 629–703; Gregg Mitman, Michelle Murphy, and Christopher Sellers, "Introduction: A Cloud over History," in *Osiris*, vol. 19, *Landscapes of Exposure: Knowledge and Illness in Modern Environments* (Chicago: University of Chicago Press, 2004), 1–17.
42. Santiago, *The Ecology of Oil*, 232.
43. Ley Reglamentaria del Trabajo, *La gaceta oficial* 1, no. 23 (October 29, 1914).
44. 1917 Constitution, reproduced in Carl W. Ackerman, *Mexico's Dilemma* (New York: George H. Doran Company, 1918), 247.
45. Ley del trabajo del estado, *La gaceta oficial* 2, no. 92 (January 24, 1918), 1.
46. Ley sobre riesgos profesionales, *La gaceta oficial* 13, no. 58 (August 14, 1924), 1.
47. On disabled workers, see Sarah F. Rose, "'Crippled' Hands: Disability in Labor and Working Class History," *Labor: Studies in Working-Class History of the Americas* 2, no. 1 (Spring 2005): 27–54.
48. Manuel Cuevas v. El Aguila, 1927, AGEV/JCCA, C 63, Expediente 92; Vicente Arroyo v. Huasteca Petroleum, 1929, AGN/JFCA, C 89, Expediente 15/929/303.
49. José G. Ramírez v. East Coast Oil Company, 1928, AGN/JFCA, C 22, Expediente 15/928/130.
50. Letter from Esteban Sánchez to JCCA, July 1928, AGEV/JCCA, C 72, Expediente 47; Enrique Castillo v. Huasteca Petroleum, 1927, AGEV/JCCA, C 63, Expediente 94.
51. Santiago, *The Ecology of Oil*, 301.
52. Miguel A. Cruz Bencomo, "El proceso salud-enfermedad en los petroleros, 1938–1942 (notas)," *Anuario* V (July 1988): 212; Keith Wailoo, *Dying in the City of the Blues: Sickle Cell Anemia and the Politics of Race and Health* (Chapel Hill: University of North Carolina Press, 2001), cited in Kasson, "Follow the Bodies," 46. Compare to the illustration by Crystal Eastman titled "The Puddler: Valuations Put on Men in Pittsburg in 1907" in *Work-Accidents and the Law* (New York: Russell Sage Foundation, 1910), reproduced in *Labor: Studies in Working-Class History of the Americas* 4, no. 2 (Summer 2007): 22.
53. Pliego petitorio, Mexican Gulf, 1924, AGEV/JCCA, C 40.
54. Corona, Rodarte, and Flores, *Los conflictos*, 178–180, 218, 230–233, 275.

55. Pliego de peticiones, Sindicato de Obreros Unidos de the Texas Co, 1924, AGEV/JCCA, C 40, Expediente 134.

56. N. M. Farrar v. El Aguila, 1918, AGEV/JCCA, C 4, Expediente 39; Pablo Chinetti v. PennMex Fuel Co., 1918, AGEV/JCCA, C 1, Expediente 2. Employers made similar arguments about black workers in the United States. See Martin Cherniack, *The Hawk's Nest Incident: America's Worst Industrial Disaster* (New Haven, CT: Yale University Press, 1986), 3.

57. Gersuny, *Work Hazards*, 48–51; Derickson, *Workers' Health*, 175, 198.

58. N. M. Farrar v. El Aguila, 1918, AGEV/JCCA, C 4, Expediente 39; Gerente General Levi Smith, Pablo Chinetti v. PennMex Fuel Co., 1918, AGEV/JCCA, C 1, Expediente 2.

59. Collective contract proposal, 1937, AGN/DAT, C 154, Expediente 4.

60. Ibid., clauses 53–55, 76.

61. Ibid., clause 205; letter from John S. Littell, American Vice Consul to State Department, Mexico City, June 11, 1934, Record Group (RG) 59, General Records of the Department of State, Records of the Department of State Relating to Internal Affairs of Mexico, 1930–1939, National Archives, 812.5054/168.

62. Cruz Bencomo, "El proceso salud-enfermedad," 184–210.

63. Augusto Palma Alor, *Las Choapas, ayer, hoy y siempre* (Mexico City: Federación Editorial Mexicana, 1975), 48.

64. James McKinley and Elisabeth Malkin, "Accidents Reveal Troubles at Mexico's Oil Monopoly," *New York Times*, May 15, 2005, 17.

65. Elaine Scarry, *The Body in Pain: The Making and Unmaking of the World* (New York: Oxford University Press, 1985).

66. See Leopoldo Alafita Méndez, Mirna Benítez Juárez, and Alberto Olvera Rivera, *Historia gráfica de la industria petrolera y sus trabajadores (1900–1938)* (Xalapa, Mexico: Universidad Veracruzana, 1988).

67. See John Womack, Jr., "Doing Labor History: Feelings, Work, Material Power," *Journal of The Historical Society* 3 (Fall 2005): 255–296; John D. French and Daniel James, "The Travails of Doing Labor History: The Restless Wonderings of John Womack," *Labor: Studies in Working-Class History of the Americas* 4, no. 2 (Summer 2007): 95–116; Gunther Peck, "The Nature of Labor: Fault Lines and Common Ground in Environmental and Labor History," *Environmental History* 11, no. 2 (April 2008): 212–238.

Knowing and Controlling in the Developed World

3

Global Markets and Local Conflicts
in Mercury Mining

*Industrial Restructuring and Workplace Hazards at the
Almaden Mines in the Early Twentieth Century*

ALFREDO MENÉNDEZ-NAVARRO

I n 2005, as a means of protecting European citizens and their environment from mercury's highly toxic compounds, the European Commission adopted a "Mercury Strategy" calling for a reduction in mercury emissions and for measures to cut its use.[1] The new policy seriously affected the Almaden mercury mines, bringing to a close a Spanish state-owned venture that had been the world's largest mercury producer and exporter for 450 years, supplying one-third of the world's mined mercury.[2] Almaden had played an extraordinarily important role in the overall Spanish economy since the mid-sixteenth century, when amalgamation became the most widely used metallurgical technique for the processing of silver from the Americas. This led to a dramatic increase in demand for mercury and thus Almaden's monopoly of the international mercury trade.[3]

Occupational health hazards are inextricably linked to the history of the Almaden mines. Chronic mercury poisoning was the almost inevitable corollary of employment there and was responsible both for the greatly reduced life expectancy of the miners and for the shortage of workers. Mine managers traditionally tackled this problem by expansion of the labor market rather than by technical improvements in working conditions. However, this trading pattern and preindustrial management system were severely challenged by the independence of Spain's American colonies. Attempts by mine engineers since the mid-nineteenth century to introduce major technical reforms to increase productivity and reduce production costs were systematically postponed, giving the Almaden mines a growing reputation for industrial backwardness.[4]

In the early twentieth century, the Almaden mines underwent a far-reaching rationalization process that was intended to represent a definitive step forward in its economic and industrial modernization. Changes were prompted by a new international situation and inspired by the belief of political reformers that technical intervention could overcome Spanish social and economic backwardness. On the one hand, cyanide processes had progressively supplanted amalgamation since the late nineteenth century and had reduced the demand for mercury, despite an increase in its industrial applications.[5] Furthermore, the long-established primacy of Almaden in the international mercury market, severely affected by colonial independence, had been additionally challenged in the second half of the nineteenth century by changes in trading patterns and the entry into the market of mercury from other locations, considerably reducing its price.[6] On the other hand, after the 1898 Spanish-American War and the loss of its last American colonies, the Spanish government moved towards a more interventionist stance, promoting social and economic reforms. Professional elites and reformers favored the understanding of political crises in terms of technical inefficiency, presenting technical intervention as critical to the social and economic modernization of the country.[7] Following these guidelines, the state-owned company was placed under the control of a board of directors, which implemented a new managerial policy focused on technical transformation of the production process and the long-postponed intensification of workforce efficiency. This restructuring brought to an end a tradition of management that had the long-term preservation of the workforce as a primary aim.

The objective of this chapter is to complement others in the present volume by examining the ways in which economic restructuring in the mercury industry and the strategies pursued by industrial management directly affected the bodies of the mine workers who labored in these historic deposits. It is suggested here that there are clear parallels between the activities of the Almaden mines and the ways in which other large corporations exploited natural resources and processed toxic substances during the past century. This chapter demonstrates that the progress of industrial health in the Spanish mercury mines cannot be understood without a careful appreciation of the strategies that were being followed in pursuit of greater industrial efficiency and the involvement of the Spanish state with production facilities in general. The conflicts and struggles of the workforce, culminating in a series of all-out strikes at Almaden, provoked fresh controversies and policies regarding the use of medical expertise in the workplace, where the rise of laboratory science contributed to the management of workers and the resolution of labor disputes. The following section begins with a consideration of the origins of medical practices in the industry.

The Roots of Conflict: Workplace Hazards in Preindustrial Almaden

Medical historiography has traced recognition of the harmful effects of mercury vapors and identification of mercury mining as a dangerous occupation back to early modern times.[8] The environmental and human impact of early modern and modern mercury mining has also attracted attention. Authors have addressed the impact of working conditions on miners' health and the heavy toll paid by local populations, the emergence of lay and medical concerns about mercury poisoning, and the provision of health care facilities by employers.[9] Less attention has been paid to the role of unhealthy working conditions in modulating labor relations and to the strategies developed to cope with workplace hazards in these preindustrial mining settings, except for the case of Almaden.[10]

As early as the sixteenth century, Almaden mining work became recognized by medical and lay observers as unhealthy. The main occupational hazard derived from the high levels of mercury vapors present in the underground production area where cinnabar (the primary mercury ore) was extracted and on the premises where it was smelted. After a varying length of time, most workers suffered from mercury poisoning. Salivation, trembling, and other neurological symptoms were responsible for the periodic disability of miners and the shortening of their working lives. The catalogue of occupational risks was not limited to mercury poisoning. Lung diseases also afflicted face workers. Work accidents mainly derived from the use of gunpowder, from the means used to transport material and workers, and from poor underground maintenance. Besides these workplace hazards, malaria was endemic in the area during the eighteenth and nineteenth centuries and it, too, had a major impact on the local population.[11]

Occupational health hazards had traditionally been handled by widening the labor market rather than by improving working conditions. This labor market was mainly confined to the local population, who were traditionally almost exclusively employed in the mines because of the lack of agricultural employment. However, the local population showed little or no capacity for growth throughout premodern and modern times, mainly because of the health impacts of mining employment. Therefore, besides making limited use of forced labor, mine managers and Royal Treasury officials attempted to expand the local population by offering inhabitants and new workers special privileges, housing, and exemption from taxes and military service. These policies did not succeed in increasing the number of settled residents, but they were effective in converting Almaden into the destination of a large number of migrant workers during the second half of the eighteenth century, some thousand per year, whose numbers amply compensated for losses.[12]

Measures to avoid excessive biological deterioration of the employees reflected the managers' interest in ensuring the long-term preservation of the workforce, but they can also be understood as resulting from the miners' resistance to the loss of their health. Some measures became incorporated into working practice in the late eighteenth century and were even introduced into regulatory codes during the nineteenth century. They included a shortening of the mine shift (to six hours); a reduction in the number of shifts per month and year; the rotation of hand-drill workers between what they themselves identified as "dangerous" and "healthy" jobs; a decrease in activities during the summer; the rotation of workers between mining and agricultural employment; a relatively high day wage; and a progressive increase in above-ground "recovery" shifts for the miners.[13]

Finally, free health care was provided to miners, and their families, in an attempt to speed their recovery from illness or injury. Since the 1770s, the mines' health care facilities had been centered at the Royal Miners' Hospital, founded in 1752. Treatment was extended to home care by doctors' visits, the supply of medicines, and the distribution of charity to disabled miners.[14] Other methods for replenishing the supply of workers included charitable payments to miners' widows and orphans and the sale of wheat below commercial prices to limit the adverse effects of high prices for miners on inadequate wages.[15]

This overall strategy for coping with workplace hazards was challenged in the mid-nineteenth century by new difficulties in the international mercury market and by local changes that had started in the 1820s. The health care system and traditional labor market policy were apparently becoming redundant thanks to demographic growth in Almaden and to an increase in productivity due to industrial innovations. Nevertheless, the persistence of poor and unhealthy working conditions led workers to demand the perpetuation of the above-mentioned working practices, which became codified in the 1865 working regulations. These regulations established a rotation system to give miners work at the surface after a certain number of days in the mine. They furnished the mines with an expanded but less productive labor force, which averaged well over 3,300 workers by the 1880s and peaked at 4,500 in 1910. The local population increased from 7,000 inhabitants in 1857 to more than 10,000 by the early twentieth century, intensifying the conflict caused by an oversupply of labor and the need to share jobs.[16]

Framing a New Managerial Approach: Modernization and Social Reform in Early-Twentieth-Century Spain

Debates on how to modernize the country after the colonial disaster were at the core of political life in turn-of-the-century Spain. The long-term structural transformation of the Spanish economy, taking place in other European countries as well, was combined with a crisis of legitimacy, a significant rise in labor organization, and a transition to modern forms of political and social agitation. The quest for efficiency emerged as a key to national self-improvement in this scenario, alongside a drive for reform in Spanish public affairs, that led to the passing of labor and social legislation to contain unrest.[17] The modernization project was an eventually unsuccessful attempt to articulate the aspirations of new economic and social forces around a nonexplicit social agreement based on technical competence conveyed by professional elites. The aim was to provide a salutary stimulus to Spanish social life that would contribute to the development of peaceful social and economic reforms.[18] This quest for competence encompassed a wide range of initiatives—educational, social, and technical. For this purpose, different expert bodies were established within the state administration, including the Social Reform Board (1882–1902) and the Institute for Social Reform (1903–1924). These expert agencies, served by, among others, medical and industrial hygienists, acted as observation posts to identify social problems and to provide the scientific—that is, neutral—basis for interventions and reforming legislation.

Technical innovation represented the other side of the "competence" coin. Mining engineers demanded radical breakthroughs in mine management to reduce production costs and to cope with new international challenges. This new approach would also provide grounds for a rational way of dealing with social conflict and workers' unrest. Thus, in 1906, a technical commission composed of three mine engineers visited the mines with a remit from the Spanish Treasury to identify organizational shortcomings and propose urgent solutions. The commission reported the persistence of unhealthy working conditions and the underdevelopment of mining technology. This was described as contributing to excessive workforce and high production costs, which in turn reduced the resources available to improve working conditions. The commission drafted a set of "industrial restructuring guidelines": radical changes in mining and metallurgical technologies, improvements in working conditions and mine sanitation, drastic reduction in the excess workforce, and abolition of the 1865 working regulations and other paternalistic social policies.[19]

In 1910, the Drill Workers Association, the largest professional miners group at Almaden (with 500 members), called for an inquiry by the Institute for Social Reform. The main demand of the workers was for improvements in the unhealthy working conditions, considered to be the factor that most limited their work capacity and therefore their ability to earn an adequate income. Claims were also made for maintenance of the rotation system, which guaranteed access to nontoxic surface activities, and for the promotion of employment in farming "colonies" to enable recovery from mercury poisoning. The miners also demanded that workers with chronic mercury poisoning be entitled to compensation under the 1900 Law of Accidents and that the preventive measures contemplated in this law be implemented.[20]

A mining inspector and an industrial hygienist visited the mines a few weeks after the request for an inquiry. Their report, issued by the Institute, supported most of the workers' claims, focusing on the need to sanitize the mines to improve efficiency. One recommendation was for the amelioration of underground environmental conditions by ventilation as a prerequisite for overcoming the active resistance by miners to the introduction of mechanical drilling and to the replacement of gunpowder by dynamite (two of the key proposals included in the 1906 report). Another was for the implementation of mandatory initial and periodic medical examinations of exposed workers. Nevertheless, the report expressed concerns about the effectiveness of its recommendations to improve the miners' economic situation, since their positive effects on work capacity and income would be offset by the excessive size of the labor force. It proposed ending some of the historical privileges of the miners, including exemption from military service. This privilege was especially attractive given the mass call-up to put down the revolt in Spanish Morocco, a situation that had prompted a general strike and violent riots in 1909. The report criticized the miners' way of life as contributing to their health problems, especially their alcohol consumption and moral behavior, subscribing to the managers' viewpoint in this respect.[21]

Social conflict came to a head when the 1906 Commission proposals became law in 1916. The Almaden mines were put under the control of a board of directors, which implemented a new managerial policy theoretically founded on principles of industrial efficiency. The aim was to tackle the roots of the problem by technical transformation of the production process, eradication of excess labor, and increased workforce efficiency.[22] The most controversial element of the restructuring process was a new set of working regulations eventually issued in 1920. The declared aim was to improve the miners' economic situation by increasing their workload and raising wages. In fact, the regulations increased the number of working days devoted to underground production by over a third and abolished the rotation system, ending the possibility of payments for performing nontoxic and nonproductive tasks above ground. In addition, almost a third of the workforce was made redundant, and miners in poor health were dismissed with minimal compensation. The regulations were endorsed by the Royal Council of Health, the highest Spanish health authority, which declared that the new regimen was compatible with the health of workers and that the forthcoming improvements in working and environmental conditions would remove any obstacles to an increase in individual productivity.[23]

The Local Workers Federation (LWF), founded in 1917 and linked to the Spanish Socialist Union, led opposition to the new regulations, arguing that they would cause a major increase in the number and severity of mercury poisoning cases. The social conflict around these issues culminated in the first all-out strike at Almaden in 1919. The growing labor conflict persuaded the Government to strengthen scientific support for the new measures. In April 1920, a Medical Commission was appointed, chaired by the president of the Royal Council of Health. The Commission visited the mines in 1920 and 1921, between which years there was a long general strike.

In May 1921, the Commission received a list of demands from the LWF, which wanted to return to the old working regulations until workplaces were made healthy by implementation of a radical program. In 1922, the Commission published its official report, which endorsed the LWF's main demands. The report did not provide updated poisoning rates that could support workers' concerns and included only mortality records for the years 1914–1917 and 1920. The report's authors highlighted the elevated mortality rate of Almaden miners (8.1 percent per annum) in comparison to that of the general Almaden population (2.85 percent) and to that of mercury workers studied by German industrial hygienist Ludwig Hirt (3 to 4 percent), linking the excess mortality to the poor working and environmental conditions in Almaden mines. Furthermore, the mortality in 1920 (280 deaths) was 20 percent higher than that registered in the period 1914–1917 (an average of 230 deaths per annum).[24]

The political impact of the report further stimulated the search for scientific evidence to counter implementation of the new regulations. The workers' claims received support from Dr. Fernández Aldama, a local medical practitioner who campaigned in local newspapers and medical forums for chronic mercury poisoning to be scheduled as an industrial disease, allowing the possibility of compensation to sufferers. The Spanish Accident legislation had not extended coverage to occupational diseases. However, after 1903, the Spanish High Court handed down a few decisions awarding compensation to workers claiming recognition of an occupational disease under the Accident legislation. None of these claims were related to mercury poisoning, which was supposedly compensated through the paternalistic Almaden schemes.

A particular stir was caused by the contribution of Fernández Aldama to the First Spanish Congress of Work Accidents held in Saragossa in 1922, which received enthusiastic support and was approved in plenary session. Fernández Aldama confirmed a drastic reduction in the labor force to some 2,100 workers by 1922. His contribution did not offer statistical support for the supposed worsening of poisoning rates due to the intensification of working; nor did it question the 1920 regulations. Instead, Fernández Aldama focused on the minimal compensation received by miners dismissed for chronic poisoning. He presented a series of case reports on workers who suffered long-term mercury exposure and introduced in person Ignacio Cabrera, a sixty-eight-year-old Almaden miner who had started underground at the age of fourteen. He was the father of nine children, eight of whom had died at a young age, and he suffered from intense trembling that prevented him "from feeding himself." Ignacio had worked on nontoxic tasks above ground since 1915, but was retired in 1921 with negligible compensation under the 1920 regulations.[25]

"On Solid Scientific Ground": Bringing the Laboratory to the Workplace

The 1920 Commission report and the contributions of Fernández Aldama strengthened both the scientific backing of and public support for workers' demands. As a consequence, mine managers soon realized the importance of adopting a new epistemological approach to occupational health issues, incorporating laboratory analysis alongside traditional medical examinations. Managers turned to laboratory-based industrial science as the sole source of objective and neutral grounds for intervention and as a way to challenge the medical arguments used by workers. In so doing, mine managers were endorsing international trends in occupational hygiene, which showed a transition from the medical inquiry of old to the new laboratory-based approach. In the 1920s, as Sellers has convincingly argued, researchers in the Office of Industrial Hygiene in the United States developed a new format for field studies on occupational diseases, achieving a new objectivity by incorporating laboratory analysis alongside the traditional study of working conditions.[26] Symbiotic relationships between industry and "objective" academic centers have also been traced in lead-poisoning studies carried out in the United States during the 1920s.[27] Although similar experimental research was developed in the United Kingdom, its findings were rarely put into practice.[28]

In 1923, a physician with great expertise in industrial hygiene, Dr. Sánchez Martín, was recruited by the Mines Medical Service. His assignment included a large-scale health survey of workers and of environmental workplace conditions. Dr. Sánchez had long experience in occupational medicine. In 1907, he was appointed to the medical service of the Centenillo Silver Lead Mines, an Anglo-Spanish company that was at the time one of the most productive and technically developed lead mines in Spain. In common with many other practitioners who served mining companies in Southern Spain, Sánchez became familiar with laboratory work, particularly bacteriological techniques, during the campaign against hookworm disease. A sustained campaign by doctors and rural health officers (later reinforced by the intervention of the International Health Board of the Rockefeller Foundation after its agreement with the Spanish government was signed in 1922) led authorities to create a legal framework of preventive measures to be implemented by mining enterprises in 1912 and 1926. Many mining companies, such as Centenillo, established laboratories to carry out medical examinations for the parasitological screening of workers for hookworm in the early 1910s.[29] It was here that Sánchez developed his expertise, which also covered lead poisoning and pneumoconiosis, since the widespread introduction of mechanical drilling in this mining district in the late 1910s had brought public attention to this health issue in Spain.[30]

Following the guidelines established by the board of directors, the research program set up by Sánchez in Almaden was notably laboratory oriented. For the first time, clinical and functional examinations were applied to almost the entire workforce (1,917 out of 2,052 workers, or greater than 94 percent). The research confirmed the high incidence of chronic mercury poisoning, with unmistakable clinical evidence in 29.9 percent of examined miners and clinical sequelae of poisoning in 31.4 percent. Among drill workers, these rates rose to 50 and 22.9 percent, and only one out of seven drillers was free of previous or present symptoms. However, no detailed comparison with poisoning levels prior to the 1920 regulations was possible because of the lack of accurate clinical data before the regulations' implementation. For the first time, all workers were classified according to their health status into one of five categories. These categories were clinically defined but embodied a functional conception of mercury poisoning that allowed comparison with subsequent results and an assessment of the degree of worker impairment. Furthermore, Sánchez identified the susceptibility of workers on objective grounds. Individual features that made miners naturally prone to mercury poisoning were physiologically defined and linked to blood composition disorders. In this way, blood analyses could lead to the identification of apparently vulnerable workers and so to their exclusion from the labor force.[31]

The mine managers explicitly required Dr. Sánchez to determine how the period of exposure and the presence of mercury vapors in different working areas influenced the development of mercury poisoning. This task was directly intended to challenge any scientific evidence presented against the new working regulations. Well aware of the difficulties of ignoring the existence of poisoning among miners and the evidence of mercury vapors in some working areas, managers began to appreciate the utility of laboratory determinations as a means to a negotiated solution to the conflict. Sánchez performed analyses of air composition and studied oxygen and carbon dioxide concentrations, sending samples to the laboratories of the Institute of Mining Engineers in Madrid. Using equipment he designed himself, Sánchez obtained the first measurements of mercury concentration in the air, which he recorded at approximately twenty shafts and at metallurgical treatment sites. He also used a kata-thermometer to determine temperature, humidity, and airflow. His research program included rudimentary animal experiments, in which guinea pigs were placed in the galleries and exposed to mercury vapors for variable time periods.

The conclusions of his research bore little relation to the results of this unusual technological display. Sánchez was well aware of the limitations of his methods to determine mercury concentrations, and he warned that all of his findings should be regarded as underestimations. More important, quantification and standardization difficulties made any comparison or correlation with clinical examinations impossible. He concluded that increased worker efficiency would require little improvement in environmental conditions except for the ventilation systems and adaptation of mechanical drills to remove dust and mercury vapors at the source. Traditional strategies were not completely ruled out. For instance, Sánchez suggested an increase in the number of young workers used in the regular cleaning of condensers in order to reduce the length of exposure of each worker to mercury vapors. Despite the vague nature of his conclusions and, remarkably, some evidence that verified workers claims, the report issued by Sánchez in 1923 provided scientific evidence that could be used to counter the workers' arguments and support management's new policies.

In September 1923, a few weeks before Sánchez's report was issued, and taking advantage of the political situation created by the coup d'état of General Primo de Rivera, the LWF launched a new national campaign. Parliament was dissolved and political parties were banned, but the Socialist trade unions continued to operate. The LWF addressed a memorandum to General Primo de Rivera, head of the Military Directorate, attaching a "technical report" prepared by Dr. Fernández Aldama to support its demands.[32] The report largely reproduced the paper Fernández Aldama had delivered at the First Spanish Congress of Work Accidents in 1922. However, on this occasion Fernández Aldama highlighted the increase in severity and rate of mercury poisoning, which had reached well over 70 percent for drillers and

30 percent for smelters. He blamed the increase on the intensification of work, the radical suppression of nonexposed surface assignments, and the lack of improvement in working conditions. In addition to the effects of the new regulations on workers' health, the report emphasized the nonoccupational environmental dimension of the issue, using an argument related to eugenic concerns. The negative impact on the local population of mercury waste was evidenced by the increase in infant mortality and in the number of spontaneous abortions recorded in Almaden in the previous few years (well over 15 percent). The report described animal experiments in pregnant guinea pigs that demonstrated the affinity of absorbed mercury for the placenta and its pathogenic effect on the kidneys of the fetus. In addition to this memorandum, a commission of sick miners from Almaden was received by King Alfonso XIII in Madrid Royal Palace, a visit generously covered by national newspapers.

A new inspection committee was set up by the Military Directorate, which visited the mines from October to November 1923, while the LWF journal *La Federación Obrera* launched a bitter campaign against the director of the mines. The report of the inspection committee, partially reproduced in national newspapers and in the journal of the Socialist General Union, was welcomed as supporting worker demands and prompted the resignation of the board of directors.[33] In fact, however, governmental decisions after the report contributed to a definitive relocation of decision making within the realm of medical expertise, helping to break workers' resistance to the efficiency measures.

First, the Government forced the implementation of provisional working regulations to replace those established in 1920. An increase in worker efficiency would be achieved gradually while a plan to create a healthy workplace was developed. Abolition of the rotation system was seen to be impossible, but access to it was now granted under medical criteria rather than as a worker's right. Second, the composition of the board of directors was changed to include an expert in industrial hygiene who could sit alongside administrators and engineers. Indeed, this expert was responsible for designing the provisional regulations, which were clothed in the new language and concepts of the laboratory. Physiological concepts such as "health index" and "worker biological potential," rather than principles of industrial economy, provided grounds for some of the most controversial measures, including early retirement with minimal compensation for miners in their fifties and the intensification of worker efficiency. Not surprisingly, evaluation of these aspects and proposals for further amendments to regulations became the exclusive preserve of medical experts, specifically the medical member of the board and the chief of Mine Medical Services. More important, it was the cataloguing of workers' health status and environmental conditions using laboratory techniques that came to inform decision making. Regular medical examinations and determinations of mercury concentrations enabled statistical comparisons, providing a numerical and objective basis for judgment.[34]

The new strategy proved effective. The board of directors' annual report for the economic year 1925–1926 expressed great satisfaction with a doubling of mineral extraction and mercury production compared with the numbers from 1923–1924 while exploitation costs rose only by 28 percent. The report of the Mine Medical Service showed a slow decline in mercury poisoning rates. This "miracle" was attributed to technical reforms and to increased worker efficiency in a socially peaceful environment.[35]

Conclusion

This chapter illustrates how medical sciences, especially laboratory sciences, became a crucial tool for dealing with growing labor and social conflicts in early-twentieth-century Spain. In Almaden, industrial reconversion was hindered by the inertia borne of a traditional conservationist approach to the management of occupational risks and by workers' resistance to any loss of what they defended as their customary rights. The quest for industrial efficiency to reduce production costs and regain international competitiveness prompted a social conflict of unparalleled dimensions in the history of the mine. The redrawing of this conflict in medical terms created a new negotiation scenario. Both parties to the conflict were well aware of the importance of gaining scientific support for their demands. Laboratory sciences proved to be a more powerful ally than traditional knowledge based on individual experience. By classifying the health status of workers and their environmental working conditions, laboratory sciences allowed managers to regain control over workforce management, at the same time reinforcing medical expertise in the workplace.

NOTES

Acknowledgments: This research was supported by the Spanish Ministries of Education and Science and Innovation Projects HUM2006-02885 and HAR2009-07543, respectively. I am grateful to participants at the Dangerous Trade Conference for their valuable comments and to the editors of this collection for their helpful observations and suggestions.

1. Commission of the European Communities, "Community Strategy Concerning Mercury," available at http://ec.europa.eu/environment/chemicals/mercury/pdf/com_2005_0020_en.pdf (accessed July 3, 2011).

2. Lars D. Hylander and Markus Meili, "500 years of Mercury Production: Global Annual Inventory by Region until 2000 and Associated Emissions," *Science of the Total Environment* 304 (2003): 13–27.

3. Mervin F. Lang, *El monopolio estatal del mercurio en el México colonial (1550–1710)* (México City: Fondo de Cultura Económica, 1977); Rafael Dobado González, "El monopolio estatal del mercurio en Nueva España durante el siglo XVIII," *Hispanic American Historical Review* 82 (2002): 685–718.

4. Rafael Dobado González, "Labor Force and Mercury Production in Almadén, Spain, 1759–1808," in *In Quest of Mineral Wealth: Aboriginal and Colonial Mining and Metallurgy in Spanish America*, ed. Alan Craig and Robert West (Baton Rouge: Louisiana State University, 1994), 213–231; Rafael Dobado González, *Organización del trabajo y cambio técnico en las minas de Almadén, 1740–1880* (Madrid: Fundación SEPI, 2003), available at ftp://ftp.funep.es/phe/hdt2003_1.pdf (accessed July 3, 2011).

5. Lars D. Hylander and Markus Meili, "The Rise and Fall of Mercury: Converting a Resource to Refuse After 500 Years of Mining and Pollution," *Critical Reviews in Environmental Science and Technology* 35 (2005): 1–36.

6. Victoriano Martín Martín, *Los Rothschild y las Minas de Almadén* (Madrid: IEF, 1980); Hylander and Meili, "500 Years of Mercury Production," 15.

7. Esteban Rodríguez-Ocaña, "Medicine as a Social Political Science: The Case of Spain c. 1920," *Hygiea Internationalis* 7 (2007): 37–52.

8. George Rosen, *The History of Miners' Diseases: A Medical and Social Interpretation* (New York: Schuman's, 1943); Leonard J. Goldwater, *Mercury: A History of Quicksilver* (Baltimore: York Press, 1972).

9. Erna Lesky, *Arbeitsmedizin im 18. Jahrhundert. Werksarzt und Arbeiter im Quecksilberbergwerk Idria* (Vienna: Österreichischen Gesellschaft für Arbeitsmedizin, 1956); Kendall W. Brown, "Workers' Health and Colonial Mercury Mining at Huancavelica, Peru," *The Americas* 57 (2001): 467–496.

10. Rafael Dobado González, "El trabajo en las minas de Almadén, 1750–1855" (Ph.D. diss., Universidad Complutense de Madrid, 1989); Alfredo Menéndez Navarro, *Un mundo sin sol: La salud de los trabajadores de las minas de Almadén, 1750–1900* (Granada: Universidad de Granada, 1996).

11. Menéndez Navarro, *Un mundo sin sol*, 145–211.

12. Dobado González, "Labor Force and Mercury Production," 215–217.

13. Ibid., 225.

14. Menéndez Navarro, *Un mundo sin sol*, 213–299.

15. Dobado González, "Labor Force and Mercury Production," 226–227.

16. Dobado González, *Organización del trabajo y cambio técnico en las minas de Almadén*, 3–14.

17. Sebastian Balfour, "Riot, Regeneration and Reaction: Spain in the Aftermath of the 1898 Disaster," *Historical Journal* 38 (1995): 405–423.

18. Juan Pablo Fusi and Jordi Palafox, *España, 1808–1996: El desafío de la modernidad* (Madrid: Espasa-Calpe, 1997).

19. Luís M. Vidal, Ramón Adán de Yarza, and César Rubio, "Comisión de visita al establecimiento de Almadén para promover reformas, nombrada por Real Orden del Ministerio de Fomento de 27 de marzo de 1906, en virtud de Real Orden del Ministerio de Hacienda de 12 de enero de 1906" (unpublished manuscript, 1906).

20. Instituto de Reformas Sociales, *Informe sobre las minas de Almadén: Conclusiones presentadas a la aprobación del Instituto* (Madrid: Imprenta Sucesores de M. Minuesa, 1910).

21. Ibid., 24, 54–55, 64–65.

22. Consejo de Administración de las Minas de Almadén, *Su Ley-origen: Real decreto aprobando el Reglamento. Disposiciones complementarias* (Madrid: Tipografía Isabel España, 1924).

23. Consejo de Administración de las Minas de Almadén, *Reorganización del trabajo obrero en las Minas de Almadén, aprobada por Real Orden de 29 de abril de 1920* (Madrid: M. Martínez de Velasco, 1920).

24. Ángel Pulido Fernández, Leonardo Rodríguez Lavin, and Román García Durán, *Las minas de Almadén: Inspección oficial hecha por los doctores* (Madrid: Imprenta Sucesores de Enrique Teodoro, 1922).

25. M. Fernández Aldama, *Intoxicación mercurial profesional de los mineros de azogue* (Saragossa, Spain: Talleres Editoriales de Heraldo de Aragón, 1922).

26. Christopher C. Sellers, "The Public Health Service's Office of Industrial Hygiene and the Transformation of Industrial Medicine," *Bulletin of the History of Medicine* 65 (1991): 42–73.

27. Christian Warren, *Brush with Death: A Social History of Lead Poisoning* (Baltimore: John Hopkins University Press, 2000).

28. Helen Jones, "Industrial Health Research under the MRC," in *Historical Perspectives on the Role of the MRC: Essays in the History of the Medical Research Council of the United Kingdom and Its Predecessor, the Medical Research Committee, 1913–1953*, ed. Joan Austoker and Linda Bryder (Oxford: Oxford University Press, 1989), 160–189; Arthur J. McIvor, "Manual Work, Technology and Industrial Health, 1918–39," *Medical History* 31 (1987): 160–189.

29. Esteban Rodríguez Ocaña and Alfredo Menéndez Navarro, "Higiene contra la anemia de los mineros: La lucha contra la anquilostomiasis en España (1897–1936)," *Asclepio* 58 (2006): 219–248.

30. Alfredo Menéndez-Navarro, "The Politics of Silicosis in Interwar Spain: Republican and Francoist Approaches to Occupational Health," *Dynamis* 28 (2008): 77–102.

31. Guillermo Sánchez Martín, *Estudio médico del hidrargirismo de las minas de Almadén* (Madrid: Imprenta Sucesores de Enrique Teodoro, 1924).

32. "Escrito que la Federación Local Obrera de Almadén presenta al Directorio Militar," September 30, 1923, file 3094, Section: Mines of Almaden, National Historical Archive, Madrid.

33. "Minutes of the Board of Directors," book 10, Section: Board, Almaden Mines Historical Archive, Almadén.

34. Consejo de Administración de las Minas de Almadén y Arrayanes, *Memoria referente al ejercicio económico de 1924–25* (Madrid: Gráficas Reunidas, 1925); "Draft Regulations of the Almaden Mine Medical Services," February 5, 1926, file 3076, Section: Mines of Almaden, National Historical Archive, Madrid. These provisions became fully incorporated into the code of regulations issued in January 1928.

35. Consejo de Administración de las Minas de Almadén y Arrayanes, *Memoria referente al ejercicio económico de 1925–26* (Madrid: Gráficas Reunidas, 1927).

4

Trade, Spores, and the Culture of Disease

Attempts to Regulate Anthrax in Britain and Its International Trade, 1875–1930

Tim Carter and Joseph Melling

Among the dangerous trades that have injured and killed workers since the early days of industrialisation, the processing of animal parts such as wool and the manufacture of woollen products would appear to have presented few dangers. Nevertheless, this essay examines a peculiar hazard faced by British laborers engaged in wool textile work during the later nineteenth and early twentieth centuries. These laborers were identified as the first casualties of anthrax as an industrial disease in the United Kingdom during the late Victorian era. We consider the responses of successive British governments and the contribution of key activists, most noticeably those in regional and national labor movements who pressed for effective regulation of hazardous working conditions and the introduction of compensation for those injured—not by a sudden catastrophe but by a disease contracted at the workplace. It is remarkable that anthrax attracted extraordinary public interest in late-Victorian Britain, and the resources devoted to its diagnosis, detection, and eradication may appear disproportionate to the scale of the dangers it posed, particularly in comparison to other health risks known to exist in industrial occupations at this time.[1]

In seeking to explain the unusual attention given to the industrial victims of an illness more readily associated with pastoral agriculture, Bartrip recently suggested that public anxieties about the spread of anthrax can be linked to deep-seated concerns about the dangers Britain faced from imported diseases, alien intrusion, and immigration in the late Victorian and Edwardian periods.[2] However, though superficially attractive, this explanation does not accord with the known evidence that anthrax raised less alarm in the great port cities than in provincial textile centres, where migration patterns were relatively stable. Nor does it take into consideration the role of free international trade within the global capitalist economy, where anthrax created the potential for conflicts among the actors involved: manufacturers seeking to secure low-cost but high-quality wool supplies, workers exposed to risk from such wools, and regulatory arms of governments seeking to reduce the risk but limit the regulation of dangerous wools to avoid penalties on national industry in the absence of international agreements on controlling wool shipments.

This essay offers an alternative explanation for the emergence of anthrax as an industrial illness and the for decisive transformation of compensation that extended legal redress to a disease that had its origins in foreign agri-culture rather than British industry. In constructing effective explanations of illness at moments of social and political conflict, we share White's concern for locating the competing epistemologies of diseases such as anthrax within a specific historical period, and for tracing the points at which lay experience of illness connected with scientific authority.[3] We argue here that the political and cultural potency of anthrax in Britain may reflect the ways in which class relationships were changing in these years, with the growth of a politically active organised labor movement at its strongest in long established industrial areas such as those where most textile production took place. Ownership and production were more diverse in woollen, worsted, and carpet manufacture, where class relationships acquired a particular complexion from the distinct pattern of industrialisation and cultural conflict that marked the early nine-teenth century.[4] Contemporaries understood anthrax not only in class but in gender terms, associating it strongly with senior male workers who sorted the imported materials; they did not consider its absolute risk across the whole of the wool and spinning sector in which much of the workforce was female. This led to subtle but significant variations in how the disease was represented by those advocating controls.

There is an interesting comparison to be made with Blanc's study (in this volume) of poisoning from carbon disulphide during rayon production. In that case a single large manufacturer dominated production and the labor movement found a strong political voice, highlighting the impact that differ-ent constituencies and distinctive vocabularies of concern may have had on the development of occupational health policy.

In researching dangerous trades, it is important to understand the omis-sions and occlusions in policy making, including the unequal concern for different groups affected by similar hazards, because the framing of regula-tions reveals something of the structure, assumptions, and preferences of contemporary government. One notable feature of the British campaigns against anthrax was that early links between industrial risk and the wider agricultural and urban environments were lost, despite the fact that the disease threatened agricultural animals and rural workers as well as port workers and urban consumers. The political responses to anthrax reflected, in some degree, the structure of British government administration, with its peculiar division of responsibilities for agriculture, health, sanitation, and industrial safety. There were also obstacles within the ranks of experts: medical personnel in metropolitan and provincial circles were divided over the new bacteriology that played a key role in the discovery of the origins of this novel "industrial" disease. Notable doctors and medical officers generally supported greater labor protection, though laboratory science could be used to fend off and delay radical reform (as is shown in Menéndez-Navarro's essay on Spanish mining). Instead, it was often vigorous labor campaigns in regions of weak unionism that transformed debates over urban health and workplace sanitation into a fresh gospel of worker health protection and injury compensation.

We conclude that the affect of such debate and mobilisation was not (contra Bartrip) to inflate a "bacteriological bubble" into a public moral panic but rather to confine regulation to the domain of occupational hazard, monitored but rarely effectively controlled by safety rules. Because voluntary and national rules proved ineffective in the eradication of infected materials, British governments intially sought international cooperation and finally settled for an engineering solution that, again, never offered more than partial protection and was to eventually prove expensive and unpopular within industry.

Black Death or Male Plague? The Detection of Industrial Anthrax in Britain

Anthrax came to prominence in Europe during the later nineteenth century. It was not a new disease; nor did it owe its origins and impact to the lethal cocktail of mineral dusts, toxic minerals, and energy technologies that afflicted workers in other cases discussed in this volume. In contrast to many inorganic substances and sophisticated technologies that maimed and killed contemporary workers, anthrax was an organic infection that entered the manufacturing process in a peculiar and unexpected way.[5] The bacillus was identified in the 1850s as a distinctive spore-forming microorganism, clearly visible under the microscope in samples of tissue, blood, and other body fluids. Although an antiserum was developed by Sclavo at the turn of the century, treatment remained problematic and was often ineffective. Anthrax was then (and remains) a disease primarily of grazing animals, frequently persisting in remote soils and around plants for many years, infecting wild as well as domesticated animals usually through contaminated food. Humans are usually affected only indirectly and secondarily. Infected animals commonly die from septicaemia (blood poisoning), frequently termed "splenic fever." Humans who inhale the spores almost invariably develop a fatal lung infection, while contamination through skin abrasions results in black necrotic skin lesions or pustules often followed by septicaemia. The appearance of a dark ring of dead tissue on the skin of cutaneous sufferers explains something of the notoriety of anthrax, though this form is rarely fatal, with perhaps 15 percent of sufferers dying if left untreated.

Britain and North America were not confronted by endemic anthrax among wild or domesticated animals in the nineteenth century. Its arrival in these countries was primarily connected with the large-scale importation of animal products—wool, hair, hides, and bones—in the middle and later nineteenth century. Steamships had greatly extended global trade and thus increased wool imports so that by 1860 those imports overtook the home clip and by 1900 had more than doubled.[6] A wide diversity of countries and sources exported to the major centres of British woollen manufacture, based in the textiles towns of the West Riding in Yorkshire and, more particularly, the worsted capital of Bradford. Many smaller centres still used local wool, but the carpet-making town of Kidderminster in Worcestershire was a significant importer of wools well before the First World War.[7]

Some wool exports, for instance those from Australasia, were free from anthrax; however, the disease was endemic in significant areas of Asia, South America, Africa, and parts of Europe. Moreover, wool was commonly sheared from live animals, but "fallen fleeces" were sometimes taken from carcasses, including infected animals. For these reasons, the growing imports of animal products exposed increasing numbers of British workers to risk. Control of infection at the source in primitive pastoral settings of the Middle East was almost impossible.[8] The economist J. H. Clapham commented dryly that "Asia Minor is not a country in which trade runs smoothly."[9]

Wool is not a uniform product, and the grading and separation of wool fibres was never mechanized. Because fibres from different parts of a single fleece varied in quality and uses, experienced hand sorting was required[10] when the bales arrived at a mill. In Bradford, but not in Kidderminster, this was a distinct trade with skilled status. It was an apprenticeship system, in which sons often followed fathers, with an active trade union in the otherwise weakly unionised wool textiles industry.[11] Sorters were described in 1881 as "a steady, industrious and a most intelligent body of men," who received high wages and enjoyed good working conditions. This elevated status was significant in terms of the responses of workers to anthrax in the two towns. As for the isolated wool town of Kidderminster, it is possible to outline the different routes by which anthrax cases arose. Figure 4.1 illustrates anthrax cases linked to the flow of wool within a production chain, showing that human infection was by no means restricted to those handling industrial materials. Around Kidderminster liquid and solid waste disposal contributed to outbreaks in animals. It seems likely that there was a similar pattern of cases in the Yorkshire wool towns in the later nineteenth century, and it is intriguing how rapidly infections became indelibly associated with wool sorters to the exclusion of other workers at risk, such as the mainly female population in the spinning mills. Thus a disease of ruminants in distant lands became widely known not only as the "Bradford disease" but even more persistently as "woolsorters illness."

Our explanation for the association of an infection often found in grazing animals with one branch of the British manufacturing industry is centred in an interpretation of the larger material culture of an industrialised and

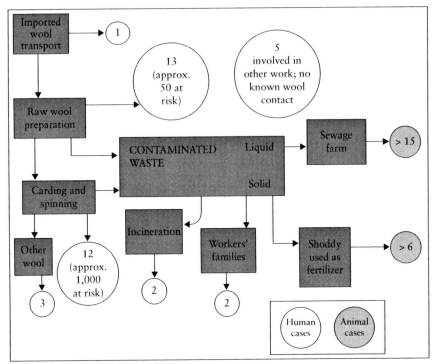

Figure 4.1 Dissemination of anthrax: the Kidderminster case, 1900–1914. (Note that the total population of Kidderminster town in this period was approximately 23,500.)

class-divided society. For it was in the industrial township of Saltaire, on the outskirts of Bradford, that a hospital surgeon first noticed (and in 1874 published a brief comment upon) the symptoms of an illness that subsequently became known as "woolsorter's disease."[12]

Saltaire was a model company "village" for workers at Titus Salt's enormous mohair mill, and the mohair and alpaca imported from South America to the mill was readily but mistakenly suspected as the source of infection. In the years that followed, letters to the *Bradford Observer* debated deaths from "blood poisoning," attributing fatalities to the handling of "foreign wools" and appealing to employers to restrict this "deadly trade."[13] From 1878 on, the national medical press carried reports on the disease affecting workers with blood, lung, and skin symptoms, while Bradford doctors such as J. H. Bell suspected that wool sorters suffered septic poisoning from wool contaminated with the same bacillus that caused splenic fever in sheep.[14] It was a death certificate Bell had written in 1880 for Samuel Firth, a mill worker, stating the death as a result of "employers' negligence," that forced the controversy into the a coroner's court, where the issues were openly aired and recorded by press and civic authorities.

The public alarm over the mysterious illnesses contracted by workers in Bradford echoed a rift within the Bradford medical community between those who supported the "foreign" germ theory of disease developed by European bacteriologists and those who opposed it. But the medical and official case for a bacterial explanation was soon established by a government report of 1881, followed by further reports on "malignant pustules" among hide, tannery, horsehair, and cattle workers.[15] The Firth inquest had set the scene for the official enquiry into the disease and for the first steps toward the regulation of sorting procedures in wool textiles.

Framing the Anthrax Hazard: Models of Investigation and Regulation

Public and professional controversy over anthrax brought the British government into the fray during the early 1880s. The first official investigations were undertaken by the Local Government Board (LGB), the department responsible for both environmental and public health and the Poor Law. Local Medical Officers of Health (MOsH) and sanitary inspectors appointed under public health regulations were ultimately accountable to the LGB, whose officials claimed expertise in animal health as well as environmental sanitation. In 1881 the LGB commissioned one of its inspectors, Dr Spear, to investigate the outbreaks at Bradford; he quickly confirmed Bell's conclusions and criticised the industry's sanitary arrangements.[16] The Bradford Town Council responded by creating a new Sanitary Committee, agreeing on voluntary regulations or "rules" in August 1884.[17] Spear was sceptical about such regulations, including the soaking of bales prior to sorting. He viewed them as a business tactic to avoid legislative controls, though he did acknowledge the value of disinfecting bloody fleeces and introducing fan ventilation to sorting benches.[18]

The progress of the anthrax controversy exposed a complex division of public health responsibilities between local authorities, monitored by the LGB, and the Home Office, which oversaw workplace hazards and safety. The potential of anthrax to galvanise political as well as industrial support for socialist campaigners is apparent in the creation of the Sanitary Committee to oversee the voluntary rules, though labor pressure forced a review of these provisions by a government Dangerous Trades Committee in 1896–1897, resulting in their statutory enforcement.[19]

Anthrax regulations for the wool textiles trade reflected changing class relationships in the West Riding during these years. Wool workers had conducted vigorous industrial and radical political campaigns during the second quarter of the nineteenth century, though these movements had been crushed or had subsided in the 1850s–1860s and trade unionism remained weak throughout the Yorkshire wool districts until the 1890s. Unionised wool sorters were a notable exception, however, engaging in collaborative bargaining with their powerful employers during this time. Political activists such as Fred Jowett continually criticised the voluntary anthrax controls at the Conciliation Board established by the Trades Council and the Bradford Chamber of Commerce in 1891, demanding manslaughter charges be brought against negligent employers.[20] The textile manufacturers persuaded labor representatives (against Jowett's advice) to extend the voluntary rules at a point in 1897–1898, while the Home Office contemplated legislative sanctions.[21] These new provisions did not deter the Trades Council from pressing for recognition of anthrax as an industrial accident and so eligible for claims under the Workmen's Compensation Act of 1897. There was no response to this until anthrax was finally included in the diseases scheduled for workmen's compensation in 1906. Paradoxically, recognition was the result principally of a legal decision in *Brintons v. Turvey* (1905) involving a fatal case of anthrax in Kidderminster, where there was no union and labor organisation was weak. The Law Lords, as the highest appeal court, ruled that anthrax was, in effect, an industrial injury eligible for compensation. The introduction of a schedule of industrial diseases in the compensation system in 1906 followed, and most anthrax cases were subsequently compensated, though the impact of these costs on any improvements in anthrax control must be doubtful.[22]

Employers responded to growing labor pressure, official concern, and legal threats merely by writing to urge suppliers and importers to pack clean bales to avoid the winding of "locks, fallen wool and skin" inside the fleeces.[23] The continuing cases of anthrax after 1900 caused friction until, in 1905, Bradford's Chamber of Commerce agreed to establish a fresh "Woolsorting and Woolcombing Rules Committee" with representatives from the workforce, the Bradford Council, and the Factory Inspectorate. This new committee created the Anthrax Investigation Board (AIB) and appointed Frederic Eurich as the bacteriologist responsible for the difficult task of eradicating infection without damaging wool.[24]

Relations on the AIB frayed as labor representatives grew disenchanted with the board and local firms used it to defend the reputation of East Indian wool imports against Home Office criticisms.[25] Conflicts at Bradford and campaigns supported by the Trades Union Congress (TUC) prompted the central government to reexamine anthrax, drawing on the expertise of notable medical civil servants such as Thomas Legge. In part this reflected the town's remarkable success in claiming anthrax as a distinct industrial malady and its own cultural property in a period when the disease remained mainly an agricultural risk and human mortality was relatively limited in comparison with contemporary endemic and epidemic disease (see Table 4.1).

Understanding government responses to anthrax in the period before the Anthrax Act of 1919 requires not only careful attention to class relations and to leading labor activists but also an explanation of the role of scientific personnel within and outside state employment. Organised businesses and workers developed distinctive connections with different organs of the state. Early initiatives were carried out by groups of practitioners and MOsH, since the latter were responsible for monitoring food quality and sewage disposal.[26] The Home Office and its Factory Inspectorate played a limited role in the early years, but by 1895 the Chief Factory Inspector reported anthrax outbreaks to the Home Secretary, who appointed a departmental committee to examine wool sorting.[27]

TABLE 4.1 ANIMAL OUTBREAKS AND HUMAN
FATALITIES FROM ANTHRAX IN ENGLAND
AND WALES, 1899–1910

YEAR	ANIMAL OUTBREAKS*	HUMAN DEATHS†
1899	393	21
1900	391	10
1901	442	12
1902	460	13
1903	502	18
1904	730	20
1905	656	24
1906	604	26
1907	678	15
1908	633	13
1909	766	15
1910	929	15

* *Report of the Departmental Committee on Anthrax: Minutes of Evidence* (London: HMSO, 1918), 274–296. Evidence from Sir Stewart Stockman, Chief Veterinary Officer, Board of Agriculture.
† Register General, *General Statistical Review* (London: HMSO, annual, 1899–1910).

The Home Office regulations of 1897 angered many mill owners, port employers, and trading brokers in commercial centres such as Liverpool.[28] Home Office initiatives were resisted within government by the Board of Trade as well,[29] and relations with the Board of Agriculture could also be uneasy. Detailed analysis of anthrax outbreaks by the board after 1900 identified bone fertiliser and imported feeds as major sources of animal infection, though import controls were thought impractical and the readiness of farmers to sell or butcher suspect animals hindered control at this level. The Home Office's 1897 report had indeed acknowledged the Board of Agriculture's work, including investigations into hide handling at the Port of London, and had discussed the extension of the Bradford Rules.[30]

The complex division of responsibilities for public health possibly delayed, but did not derail, the Factory Inspectorate's moves to take a primary role in tackling anthrax. Legge, the Medical Inspector of Factories, demonstrated his authority on the subject in his 1905 Milroy Lectures and in his contacts with Webbs of Worcester (pioneers in horsehair disinfection), which led him to introduce Sclavo's anthrax serum to Britain in 1904.[31] Legge's lectures confirmed and consolidated a medical consensus that industrial anthrax was primarily a problem "almost entirely" confined to wool working in Bradford and Worcestershire.[32] Such a view offered a rationale for his political and personal support for Eurich's laboratory research on wool disinfection at Bradford's AIB, which received significant Home Office funds in a period when governments possessed very few scientific facilities.[33]

Support for the voluntary initiatives at Bradford began to drain away before the outbreak of war in 1914, however. The leading critics were Bradford's labor activists led by Fred Jowett, who had been elected a member of Parliament in 1910 and who described the AIB as a body that "merely protected the masters' interests."[34] Calling for decisive political action to control dusty working conditions rather than further laboratory research into bloody fleeces, labor representatives withdrew from the AIB.[35] The Liberal government finally appointed a fresh departmental committee to review anthrax hazards, which continued during the war years and recommended reforms that were enacted in 1919, following a period in which unprecedented demand for military supplies and naval blockades resulted in greater use of soiled fleeces and inexperienced labor, inexorably leading to rising infection rates.[36] The solution adopted in 1919 marked a shift in policy to the disinfection of the most hazardous materials at the port of entry as a supplement to workplace regulation, with a disinfection station using the "Duckering" process of agitating raw wool in soda and then formalin established in Liverpool at that time.[37] The number of recorded human cases fell steadily in the postwar period, though when unemployment and trade decline are considered, the incidence rate for industrial anthrax probably changed little in the 1920s.[38]

As we show in the next section, the limited achievements of the 1919 anthrax legislation can be understood in the broader context of global trade patterns and limited progress in developing international disease controls during the interwar years.

International Moves to Regulate Anthrax between the Wars

The British government introduced legislation in 1918–1919 to control the immediate problem of anthrax through disinfection of the most dangerous wools used in the northern textile districts. However, cases in the industrial and agrarian districts of the Midlands and southern England were largely ignored.[39] Business groups and the Home Office also agreed that an effective solution to continued anthrax infection lay in the international control of dangerous materials passing through ports such as Constantinople.[40] The formation of the International Labor Office (ILO) offered a potential route for the regulation of international trade in dangerous industrial supplies, with Legge and others pressing for a network of disinfecting stations.[41] The 1921 ILO convention, recognising Britain as the leading reformer in the field, set up its Advisory Committee on Anthrax in London in late 1922. Surveying the treatment of hides and skins as well as wool and hair, it recommended that all hair for brush making and all wool or hair used in textiles be disinfected unless previously treated or dispatched from countries with low risk of infection.[42]

Meetings of the ILO Advisory Committee on Anthrax revealed the scale of the challenge facing regulators. Indian representatives (India was then part of the British Empire) denied any significant infection in its textile industries, pointing out the futility of investing in disinfection while cholera and plague threatened thousands with death.[43] The ILO reached somewhat anodyne conclusions that found favour among British experts but failed to secure support at the 1924 ILO convention, despite fierce protests by the

British TUC against exposure of port workers to hazardous shipments.[44] The TUC pressed the Home Office on the question as Edgar Collis (who also figures notably in Melling and Sellers' essay in this volume) criticised the ILO's lethargy in establishing an investigation committee as well as the limited progress in the disinfection of animal hides.[45]

National interest politics played a large part in weakening international initiatives to address the anthrax threat. This may be traced to the status of anthrax in each country: whether it was an endemic disease that was managed in terms of agricultural practices where these were developed—as in most of mainland Europe; whether it was, as in Britain, Australasia, and North America, largely imported; and whether, as in most developing countries at the time, it was uncontrolled. Anthrax status was associated with different standards of and expectations for enforcement, as well as distinctive agencies for control among developed and, to a very limited extent, developing countries in a period of serious commercial uncertainty regarding the international economy.[46] The creation of the ILO accelerated the emergence of an international network of scientific experts, discussed elsewhere in this volume, giving marked prominence to British expertise and practice in occupational health regulation and disease compensation.

Still, although Great Britain possessed the largest empire and a global shipping fleet, its experience with anthrax shows the persistent practical and political difficulties facing any system of multilateral supervision. Primary production of raw materials in the hands of poor graziers and contractors could not be effectively monitored, and the most advanced industrial countries in the world had little incentive to regulate agrarian anthrax where it remained a limited, and little regarded, problem within their own borders. The disease represents an early example of the limits of consensus on priorities for the control of infection across borders, even where the disease attracted disproportionate attention in the metropolitan centre of a powerful empire.

Conclusion

The essays in *Dangerous Trade* emphasise the many challenges faced by workers whose lives have been transformed by the globalisation of trade and the arrival of new hazards in the workplace. Our discussion of anthrax shares a view expressed elsewhere in this volume that we should understand the risks faced by workers, and the framing of policies to control them, as social and cultural processes rather than as merely scientific and technical responses to practical problems. Moreover, we underline the contributions made by scientists, technicians, and medical experts in these processes. Labor historians have argued for a greater understanding of how the industrial and social body is construed at distinctive moments of cultural formation. Our narrative of anthrax discovery and regulation in Britain suggests that labor activists as well as local medical practitioners played a leading role in drawing attention to the hazards faced by vulnerable workers and, in the process, illuminated and redrew the boundaries between industrial hazards and environmental pollution. The remarkable attention given to a relatively small number of fatalities among Yorkshire wool sorters helped workers to gain compensation rights and some protection at work, though labor activists turned against collaborating with the scientific agenda of the employers in favour of more urgent practical reforms. The engineering solution finally embraced after 1918 yielded little fruit in the absence of international cooperation, and it can be argued that the sharp focus on northern textile workers obscured the hazards faced by women in the largely female wool-spinning workforce and by men engaged in mainly male agricultural and port work.

This account interprets labor activism and changing perceptions of bodily hazards in relation to the class and intellectual culture of societies that were deeply industrialised by the end of the nineteenth century. Our analysis also suggests that the growth of knowledge about anthrax and the attempts to regulate it should be read in the institutional setting of the British imperial state and its internal complexities. Home Office experts such as Legge exhibited a political and personal resolve not only to gather knowledge but also to assert the primacy of industrial protection on the basis of an administrative model developed for factory inspection and civil litigation during an earlier period and for rather different purposes. The anthrax control regime was patently limited and uneven in the years before 1939, but the compromises reached sought to balance workers' welfare against commercial imperatives. A deeper understanding of the identification of the "social body" should also recognise the fundamental and continuing importance of market forces and institutional legacies.

NOTES

1. In common with animal-borne diseases such as rabies, anthrax captured the attention of both the popular and the medical press in Britain and elsewhere by the end of the nineteenth century. For a discussion of rabies, see Neil Pemberton and Michael Worboys, *Mad Dogs and Englishmen: Rabies in Britain, 1830–2000* (London: Macmillan, 2007).

2. P.W.J. Bartrip, *The Home Office and the Dangerous Trades: Regulating Occupational Disease in Victorian and Edwardian Britain* (Amsterdam: Rodopi, 2002), 249–251, 257, and passim.

3. Luise White, "Poisoned Food, Poisoned Uniforms, and Anthrax: Or, How Guerrillas Die in War," *Osiris* 19 (2004): 220–233. In this regard, White notes Balshem's study of lay responses to cancer in Philadelphia, where Polish communities were strongly inclined to attribute the disease to pollution and employment in chemical plants rather than to heavy smoking.

4. J. A. Jowett and A. J. McIvor, eds., *Employers and Labour in the English Textile Industries, 1850–1939* (London: Routledge, 1988).

5. Bartrip, *The Home Office and the Dangerous Trades*, 234.

6. D. T. Jenkins, *The British Wool Textile Industry* (London: Heineman, 1982), 184–219.

7. J. T. Carter, "Anthrax in Kidderminster 1900–1914" (Ph.D. diss., University of Birmingham, 2005).

8. *Textile Recorder* XX, March 14, 1903, 330, and August 18, 1904, 99; P. Cashmore (retired wool buyer), interview by Tim Carter, 2004.

9. J. H. Clapham, *The Woollen and Worsted Industries* (London: Methuen, 1907), 119.

10. M. L. Ryder, "Fleece Grading and Wool Sorting: The Historical Perspective," *Textile History* 26 (1995): 3–22.

11. J. Spear, *Report to the Local Government Board on So Called Woolsorters Disease as Observed in Bradford and the Neighbouring Districts of the West Riding* (first

supplement to the tenth annual report of the Local Government Board), 1880, Harvester Microfiche Local Government Board Reports, 1869–1908, 56/248; "Report on Woolsorters' Disease," *The Lancet* 2 (1881): 156–157.

12. F. M. Laforce, "Woolsorters Disease in England," *Bulletin of the New York Academy of Medicine* 54 (1978): 956–963; C. Alvin "Medical Treatment and Care in Nineteenth Century Bradford" (Ph.D. diss., University of Bradford, 1998), 277–286.

13. *Bradford Observer*, February 27, 1878.

14. "The Woolsorters Fate," *The Lancet* 1 (1878): 363; J. H. Bell, "Woolsorters Disease," *The Lancet* 2 (1879): 920–921; J. H. Bell, "On Woolsorters' Disease," *The Lancet* 1 (1880): 871–873, 909–911; W. Cunningham, "The Work of Two Scottish Medical Graduates in the Control of Woolsorters' Disease," *Medical History* 20 (1976): 169–173.

15. D. Colley, "Pathological Society Meeting Report," *The Lancet* 1 (1883): 410–411; "Anthrax at Horsehair Factories," *The Lancet* 1 (1889): 440; J. A. Fraser, "Outbreak of Anthrax in Cattle, and Five Men Infected," *The Lancet* 2 (1886): 696–697.

16. J. Spear, *Report to the Local Government Board*; W. S. Greenfield, *Supplementary Report on the Woolsorters Disease in the Bradford District, 1880*, Bradford Central Library, B614561GRE.

17. "Woolsorters' Disease in Bradford," *The Lancet* 2 (1884): 206–207, 291.

18. J. Spear, *Report to the Local Government Board*.

19. See Bartrip, *The Home Office*, 106–115, for a discussion of the limitations of "special" rules.

20. Bradford Trades Council Minutes (hereafter BTC Mins.), February 3, 1891, April 21, 1891, August 7, 1893, March 6, 1894, March 19, 1895, West Yorkshire Record Office Collection, Bradford (hereafter WYRC) 56D80/1/.

21. BTC Mins., January 19, 1897, March 16, 1897, May 11, 1897.

22. Carter, "Anthrax in Kidderminster," 149–152.

23. Bradford Chamber of Commerce Minutes (hereafter BCC Mins.), April 25, 1900; BCC Mins., February 5, 1903, WYRC, Bradford, 71D80/1/9. A letter is reproduced in *Report of the Departmental Committee on Anthrax*, vol. 3, *Summary of Evidence and Appendices* (London: HMSO, 1918), appendix 9, 136. The letter as reproduced is misdated March 1905 rather than March 1903. See Kidderminster Chamber of Commerce "Annual Meeting," *Shuttle*, 21 (March 1903), for the quotation. Kidderminster joined Keighley, Halifax, and Bradford in this appeal to suppliers.

24. Anthrax Committee (Anthrax Investigation Board), Minutes (hereafter AIB Mins.), July 17, 1905, October 30, 1905, WYRC, BCC Records, 71D80/1/66; M. Bligh, *Dr Eurich of Bradford* (London: James Clarke, 1960).

25. AIB Mins., April 23, 1906, May 2, 1906, September 17, 1906.

26. B. Luckin, "Pollution in the City," in *The Cambridge Urban History of Britain*, vol. 3, ed. M. Daunton (Cambridge: Cambridge University Press, 2000), 215.

27. *Annual Report of the Chief Inspector of Factories and Workshops 1880* (London: HMSO, 1881), 36; *Annual Report of the Chief Inspector of Factories and Workshops 1895* (London: HMSO, 1896, 30–32.

28. Home Office, "Factories Dangerous Trades—Wool Sorting and Handling of Hides and Skins, 1895–1899," October 1897, PRO HO45/10116?B12393N.

29. Letter from Board of Trade to Home Office, January 12, 1898, PRO HO45/10116/B12393N.

30. *Annual Report of the Chief Inspector of Factories and Workshops 1895* (London: HMSO, 1896); *Report of the Dangerous Trades (Anthrax) Committee* (London: HMSO, 1897).

31. T. M. Legge, "Industrial Anthrax, Milroy Lectures 1904," *The Lancet* 1 (1905): 689–696, 764–776, 841–846.

32. "Industrial Hygiene: Anthrax," *The Lancet* 2 (1905): 369–370; Legge, "Industrial Anthrax," 764.

33. AIB Mins., February 19, 1906, February 8, 1912, October 13, 1912, February 6, 1913, April 24, 1913.

34. AIB Mins., November 3, 1908, February 9, 1911. For the concern of wool sorters that the Home Office should classify East Indian wool as a dangerous material, see the National Union of Woolsorters, Minutes, December 21, 1906, Bradford Chamber of Commerce Records, WYB 111/1/2/15.

35. "Bradford Anthrax Investigation Board," *British Medical Journal* 1 (1911): 274; Anthrax Investigation Board, *Sixth Annual Report for Year Ending 31 October 1911* (Bradford, UK: Bradford Press, 1911); AIB Mins., February 8, 1912, October 31, 1912, February 6, 1913, April 24, 1913; Anthrax Investigation Board, *Annual Reports 1906–1918* (Bradford, UK: Bradford Press); Bligh, *Dr Eurich of Bradford.*

36. *Report of the Departmental Committee on Anthrax*, vol. 2, *Report of the Committee* (London: HMSO, 1918).

37. AIB Mins., June 5, 1919; CC Mins., April 29, 1921.

38. T. M. Legge, *Industrial Maladies* (Oxford: Oxford Medical Publications, 1934), 42–44; D. Hunter, *The Diseases of the Occupations*, 5th ed. (London: English Universities Press, 1975), 690–696; I. Mortimer and J. Melling, "The Contest between Commerce and Trade, on the One Side, and Human Life on the Other": British Government Policies for the Regulation of Anthrax Infection and the Wool Textiles Industries, 1880–1939," *Textile History* 31, no. 2 (2000): 223–237.

39. The cases given were Bradford and district (204), Other West Riding (55), Lancashire (33), and Liverpool (15), all separately listed. Among 48 "other" cases were 29 among the small wool-spinning population in Kidderminster.

40. BCC Mins., August 26, 1921 and March 12, 1923, for example.

41. Letter from T. M. Legge to Butler and Lloyd of ILO, March 3, 1920, ILO Archives, HY550/3/23/2, Geneva.

42. Advisory Committee on Anthrax, "Report of the Committee, 1923" (First draft of the first part of report), ILO Archives, HY550/2/14, 2–3; letter from E. W. Middlebrook to chairman of ILO, December 19, 1922, ILO Archives, HY550/2/14. The difficult problem of hide treatment was left over for further investigation.

43. Advisory Committee on Anthrax, "Minutes of First Sitting 5 December 1922," ILO Archives, HY550/2/11/1, 21. This prompted Legge's call (as technical adviser to the committee alongside Duckering) for experts to visit different countries, which was also rejected as threatening sovereignty of state control of disease.

44. Letter from Thomas Oliver to T. T. Scott, December 20, 1922, ILO Archives, HY550/2/17; Anthrax Committee, "Minority Report of Anthrax Committee, 28 June 1924," Trades Union Congress (hereafter TUC) Archive, MRC 292/144.211/6, Modern Record Centre, Warwick, UK; "Protection from Anthrax: Work of the ILO," July 23, 1924, TUC Archive, MRC 292/144.211/6.

45. Letters from E. L. Collis to Carozzi of ILO, May 14, 1925, June 24, 1925, ILO Archives, HY550/6/25/1; letter from TUC to Lord Birkenhead, July 12, 1925, and letter from Birkenhead to TUC, July 21, 1925, TUC Archive, MRC 292/144.211/6.

46. Legge, "Industrial Anthrax," 767, 772, 842–845; Christopher Sellers, *Hazards of the Job: From Industrial Disease to Environmental Health Science* (Chapel Hill: University of North Carolina Press, 1997), 120–140.

5

Rayon, Carbon Disulfide, and the Emergence of the Multinational Corporation in Occupational Disease

Paul D. Blanc

The history of "artificial silk," a man-made textile we know today as rayon, is tightly interwoven with the story of a single and singularly toxic synthetic chemical, carbon disulfide (CS_2). Between 1910 and 1930, the artificial silk industry grew exponentially to assume a major economic presence in the United Kingdom and worldwide. From the very start, it was dominated by a few large multinational firms. As these became even more interconnected, the key chemical-intensive viscose manufacturing processes they shared meant that the CS_2 hazards experienced by one factory site were present at all others. Yet despite widespread use of CS_2 and the emerging international biomedical confirmation of its toxicity in this industry, the artificial silk multinationals would not publicly acknowledge the danger, key British labor and health professionals minimized the threat, and prominent political figures practiced the art of the possible.

On March 15, 1928, in an exchange noted in the *Lancet*,[1] a British member of Parliament (MP) named William T. Kelly asked the Home Secretary whether he had received any reports of ill health among artificial silk factory employees. Sir W. Joynson-Hicks responded that "the conditions generally are satisfactory" and, without specific mention of CS_2, went on to assure the MP that this issue would "continue to receive the special attention of the medical staff."[2] By the time of this 1928 parliamentary exchange, it might be argued, the hazards of CS_2 were not widely appreciated within the biomedical community. It could also be posited that the novelty and technological complexity of artificial silk manufacturing (still an emerging industry) impeded recognition of the importance of CS_2 to this enterprise, or that it was generally presumed that new protective controls would automatically be built into the new technology, guaranteeing "satisfactory conditions" and an acceptable degree of risk. Theoretically, other barriers to a wider awareness of the carbon disulfide hazard could have come into play. The pace at which scientific knowledge was disseminated may have slowed wider recognition of the problem, in particular in foreign-language medical and technical publications for which notice in Great Britain may have been minimal. Moreover, as limited as this objective biomedical literature might have been, there was likely to have been virtually no shared contemporaneous accounting of what it meant to be a CS_2-exposed artificial silk worker in the "testimony" of these workers themselves. Finally, artificial silk manufacturing was a powerful industry. Even in the early decades of the twentieth century, it manifested elements of a traditional cartel carried over from the nineteenth century and, at the same time, of a prototypical modern multinational corporation. This was an industrial juggernaut that had a vested interest in maintaining the status quo of worker safety circa 1920. It had the will and it likely had the ways to defer, delay, or even seek to prevent altogether any external regulatory actions aimed at effective amelioration of the CS_2 problem.

This essay systematically reviews and evaluates each of these factors leading up to parliamentary debates on the subject of CS_2 beginning in 1928. Its analysis focuses on how they may have slowed recognition of the threat posed by this chemical and then, following belated acknowledgment of the hazard, blunted actions that might have been taken to abate its dangers.

Carbon Disulfide in the Nineteenth Century and the Early Twentieth Century

In order to understand the biomedical community's general awareness of the dangers of CS_2 likely in the artificial silk industry, the use of this chemical should be considered in its historical context. By the mid-nineteenth century, CS_2 was already a well-recognized toxin, particularly noted for its adverse effects on the central and peripheral nervous systems.[3] In the 1850s, its toxicity was first described in depth by a French physician, Auguste Delpech.[4] His pioneering work was quickly expanded upon by others, predominantly French neurologists.[5] The French interest in CS_2 was consistent with its use in "cold-cure" vulcanization of rubber in the production of dipped rubber objects (such as balloons and condoms), typically carried out under very poor hygienic conditions in that country. CS_2-caused disease, particularly optic nerve damage,[6] was well recognized in the United Kingdom. Through the first decade of the twentieth century, numerous medical-scientific publications documented the adverse health effects of CS_2, albeit almost entirely in rubber processing, where the chemical was most widely used. These reports focused on the pathophysiological mechanisms of toxicology, mirroring the dominant biomedical models of the period. Nonetheless, scattered case reports echoed earlier French descriptions that had emphasized the victims' complaints (in particular, sexual dysfunction).

At the turn of twentieth century, synthetic silk fiber manufacture was little more than a start-up industry, typified by small manufacturing units, much of it carried out on a prototype scale. During the decades that followed, however, the international artificial silk industry grew at an astounding rate. By 1928, viscose-process artificial silk manufacturing, based on CS_2, had become the dominant method of production.[7] The ascendancy of viscose was due to several factors: lower cost, efficiency in manufacture, and the adaptability of the final product to various commercial applications. As viscose became a very big business on a worldwide scale, Great Britain was arguably its main corporate hub. A single entity, Courtaulds Ltd., dominated the U.K. market and shared the American market with Dupont in what was referred to as a "duopoly."[8] Other exponentially expanding centers included Italy, Germany, France, the Netherlands, and Japan.[9]

From the 1920s to the present day, the fundamentals of viscose fiber manufacture have changed little.[10] Cellulose wood pulp is treated with caustic soda to break apart its long-chain polymer molecules, and then CS_2 is added. The resulting material is churned together and dissolved in additional caustic soda to form a "viscose" solution. Continuous filament can be used to make yarn for weaving into rayon textiles; rayon fleece is manufactured in a related process, and viscose-based film (that is, cellophane) uses the same feedstock. CS_2 is an essential and unavoidable process ingredient, with the potential for exposure occurring at many steps in viscose manufacture.

Even in the early years of viscose manufacturing, the role of CS_2 in the industry was widely appreciated in Britain, even if its toxicity was ignored. As early as 1913, the *Times of London* printed a descriptive piece meant for a wide audience that summarized various methods of artificial silk making, including viscose, noting the use of CS_2 in the latter.[11] In 1926, the *Times* revisited the subject, reporting on a visit to the Coventry "Viscose Silk Works" (i.e., Courtaulds).[12] Thus even a general medical practitioner who read the *Times* could have connected CS_2 with artificial silk manufacturing.

Recognition of Carbon Disulfide Exposure as a Hygiene Issue

From the earliest years of the viscose industry, medical-scientific literature in nations other than Britain recognized potential problems in the hygiene of artificial silk manufacturing, although up until 1925 such recognition was sporadic. Two key early publications (in 1904 and 1905) documented severe CS_2 poisoning among workers in a small American artificial silk factory.[13] Both reports placed the industrial poisonings clearly in the context of the substantial existing medical literature on rubber industry CS_2 toxicity. In 1912, *Il Lavoro*, the leading Italian occupational medicine journal, published a summary of a French report on the technical aspects of various artificial silk manufacturing processes, including viscose, calling attention to

CS_2.[14] The first detailed report on the potential exposure of viscose workers to CS_2, although it did not document any actual illness cases, appeared in a 1922 French industrial hygiene publication.[15]

English-language specialty textbooks from this period consistently pointed out that CS_2 exposure was likely to occur in artificial silk manufacturing, although emphasis on this point varied. A 1924 U.S. occupational medicine text noted that in such manufacturing, "The employment of carbon disulfide has given rise to a large amount of sickness in certain plants."[16] Yet the chapter on CS_2 in the same textbook barely alluded to artificial silk.[17] A contemporaneous (1923) British occupational medicine text also listed CS_2 as being used in artificial silk, but without reference to any actual cases of disease in the industry.[18] In contrast, the well-recognized industrial risk of rubber vulcanization was consistently addressed in these sources, often with emphasis on the controls introduced in previous decades that had substantially reduced this risk.

Beginning in 1925, however, new evidence of the dangers of CS_2 in the viscose industry began to accumulate rapidly outside of Great Britain. The seminal publication was an eleven-page article authored by Giovanni Loriga, the Chief Medical Inspector for the Italian Ministry of Labor, appearing in the Italian governmental publication *Bollettino del Lavoro*[19] as well as in *La Medicina del Lavoro* (formerly *Il Lavoro*).[20] Loriga noted a clinico-pathological report of a case fatality in a young artificial silk worker that had been presented earlier in 1925.[21] He also documented other CS_2-related illnesses in the Italian viscose industry.[22] Another key Italian report appeared nearly contemporaneously.[23]

German sources had begun to document viscose-related CS_2 disease in 1925 as well: an outbreak affecting five workers, one of whom committed suicide in a state of CS_2-induced mania, was reported first in 1924[24] and then again in more detail the following year.[25] Also in 1925, a Dutch labor inspector published a detailed report on exposure in two viscose factories in the Netherlands.[26] Even U.S. medical silence on CS_2 toxicity in the viscose industry was broken during that year. In the textbook *Industrial Poisons in the United States*, Dr. Alice Hamilton detailed two cases of CS_2 poisoning in a rayon plant that were presented to her in Buffalo, New York, in 1923 (two years before the textbook was published).[27]

Remarkably, this flurry of international activity bypassed Great Britain, from which no original medical reports of CS_2 disease in the viscose industry emerged during the period. However, this was not because journal editors and textbook authors in Britain (as elsewhere) did not keep a close eye other nations' medical-scientific literature. For example, the 1925 Italian pathological case that Loriga had highlighted in his groundbreaking report, together with a 1925 Italian experimental animal study, was abstracted in the British publication *Medical Science*.[28]

Underscoring the absence of native British medical reports disseminated through domestic channels, it was in an Italian journal, rather than an English one, that the earliest English medical report appeared linking artificial silk work to CS_2 poisoning. In 1925, *Il Lavoro* published a very brief notice summarizing a British report explicitly tying the two together under the title "Cause of Poisoning in the Artificial Silk Industry."[29] This 85-word notice states that Dr. Arnold Renshaw (a prominent Manchester pathologist with an interest in industrial toxicology) had presented a study of the dangers of CS_2 among artificial silk workers, specifying that "More than one milligram of carbon disulfide per liter of air produces chronic poisoning and that this limit is easily achieved even in ventilated rooms."[30] The *Institute of Chemistry of Great Britain and Ireland Journal and Proceedings* confirms that on March 2, 1925, Renshaw presented a lecture at the Manchester Literary and Philosophical Society titled "Chemical Poisoning Occurring amongst Industrial Workers," but without any abstract or content specified;[31] the meeting participants, without details of the presentation's contents, were documented in the minutes of the Manchester section of the Institute of Chemistry.[32] In contrast, the most widely disseminated British pronouncement on CS_2 of this period was made by Sir Thomas Oliver (the leading British figure in occupational medicine). In "Some of the Achievements of Industrial Legislation and Hygiene," Oliver trumpets the near elimination of CS_2 poisoning through controls in the rubber trade; however, he does not utter a word about artificial silk manufacturing.[33]

Prelude to Further Parliamentary Debate

Oliver's clean bill of health for CS_2, coupled with a lack of original local research, is all the more remarkable because of the medical information from outside the United Kingdom that had accumulated by that time and in light of the fact that in 1925 CS_2 industrial poisoning in Great Britain had become a reportable disease. As such, the *Annual Report of the Chief Inspector of Factories and Workshops* was obliged to report all instances of it. In that year's report, the Senior Medical Inspector, Thomas Legge, noted two CS_2 cases in the rubber industry, but put greater emphasis on a third, "—a very acute case, the symptoms being headache, vomiting, delirium, loss of muscular power, and almost complete anaesthesia (loss of sensation) from which he has made only slight improvement—in the manufacture of artificial silk."[34] Legge also reported symptoms of milder poisoning in twelve other artificial silk workers whose cases, remarkably, were not included in the annual report's tabulations. Legge details, "In the factory in question considerable attention had been given to the question of ventilation, but at the machines where carbon bisulphide was used this had not been sufficiently locally applied. . . ."[35] Legge does not identify the manufacturer,[36] but it is known that these cases occurred in one of Courtaulds' facilities.[37]

In the following year's annual report, the Senior Medical Inspector who succeeded Legge observed that "no case of carbon bisulphide poisoning from this manufacture has been reported" and that the importance of good ventilation is "universally recognized" by manufacturers.[38] The actual factory inspection reports of site visits to the churn room in Courtaulds' Flint factory tell a different story. In eight separate inspections of the churn room over five years through 1927, the state of ventilation was never noted, although multiple other interventions were recommended (adequate coat hooks were one concern). In other parts of the factory, ventilation was mentioned only four times over this period.[39] Inspectors subsequent to Legge do not appear to have been looking very hard. Indeed, in many ways Legge, who had close ties to the Trades Union Council, was an exceptional regulator who proved the rule of benign neglect and oversight by others who followed him.

In summary, the backstory to the parliamentary questioning in the spring of 1928, going back to 1925, was one of renewed international biomedical attention paid to the toxicity of CS_2 specific to viscose manufacturing and of solid documentation locally through labor inspectorate reports that such illness was occurring in Great Britain. Labour MP William Kelly may or may not have been aware of some of these facts when he pressed Sir Joynson-Hicks in parliament for more specifics on the health of artificial silk workers, invoking Courtaulds by name. The Home Secretary temporized: "Before I answer on definite cases, the hon. Member must give me notice."[40] Joynson-Hicks, known by the moniker "Jix," was the Conservative Home Secretary and hardly a friend to working men and women.[41] In 1926, he played a prominent role in the government's resistance to a general strike, yet, as Home Secretary, he was directly responsible for enforcement of and any legislative amendments to the British Factory Act, including factory inspections.[42]

The question posed by MP Kelly did not mark the first time that the Home Secretary had been asked about CS_2. In the previous session, James Maxton (one of the famous "Red Clydesiders" from Glasgow) had also questioned workers' health in artificial silk factories; in a written reply, Joynson-Hicks denied that there was *any* "evidence of any serious risk to health."[43] Even farther back, in December 1925, another Labour MP, W. C. Robinson (representing Elland in Leeds), had asked Joynson-Hicks how many cases of poisoning by CS_2 and other newly listed toxins had been reported in that year (as noted, the first in which such reporting was mandated). In an exchange that was reported in the *British Medical Journal (BMJ)*,[44] Joynson-Hicks replied, inter alia, that these reports included "two cases of carbon bisulphide poisoning."[45] He made no mention of artificial silk, the source of one of the *three* cases, not *two*, reported that year. Thus, his 1928 response to Kelly's question marked the third time that the Home Secretary had been queried on the same subject, demonstrating a repeated pattern of disingenuousness.

William Kelly was not only a Labour MP but also an official of the Workers' Union, and there was an artificial silk viscose plant—a Dutch-based competitor of Courtaulds, Breda Visada Ltd.—located in Littleborough, which was within his constituency.[46] In that light, it is not surprising that Kelly did not abandon his pursuit of information on artificial silk industrial hazards and even began to extend his search for answers beyond the factory door to the issue of chemical exposures in surrounding areas. He may also have seen the added matter of environmental contamination as tactically effective, providing a political wedge to help force the industrial issues that were his primary focus. Questions of neighborhood pollution were not new to the industry. In the very earliest years of Courtaulds' Coventry operations (1906–1910, during this time Samuel Courtauld & Co.), serious complaints about effluent odors had been made by adjoining factories and nearby residents.[47] Kelly may have been unaware of this earlier episode, but in 1928 neighborhood contamination from viscose was back in the news. In July 1928, the High Court of Justice granted an injunction (later stayed) abating the release of nuisance fumes from a relatively small artificial silk producer[48] and minor competitor to Courtaulds, the Rayon Manufacturing Company of Surrey.[49]

On multiple occasions in 1928, Kelly repeatedly addressed questions about artificial silk manufacturing hazards not only to the Home Secretary but also to the Ministry of Health (headed by Arthur Neville Chamberlain), the agency with jurisdiction over neighborhood exposures by virtue of the Alkali Acts covering air pollution.[50] Having been told repeatedly that any health issues inside the factories were trivial and that neighborhood issues would be dealt with in a report at some future time, Kelly, in 1929, once more took up the matter of occupational disease with the Home Secretary, receiving two written answers reiterating the absence of any ill effects beyond self-limited conjunctivitis and dermatitis;[51] this exchange was reported in the *British Medical Journal.*[52] Kelly also worked with the Trades Union Council to try to expand workers compensation coverage for artificial silk workers and, in early March 1929, was part of a deputation to the Home Secretary on these issues.[53]

Meanwhile, the health problems arising in the factories themselves were becoming more difficult to contain. In 1929, the Factory Inspectorate began a special surveillance program for conjunctivitis in artificial silk manufacturing, documenting 230 cases over only three months.[54] More ominously, the Inspectorate's 1929 annual report noted two workers "suffering from well-marked symptoms of chronic carbon bisulphide poisoning. . . . Another man, who had been employed in the churn room until three weeks previously, was also examined and found to be more seriously affected. . . . [A] man employed on the night shift . . . also exhibited marked symptoms."[55] Finally, a general inspection of the industry was made in response to this outbreak. Although no additional "definite" cases were found, there were several with "some indication of absorption" and, subsequent to that survey, another case of acute mania was reported from the same initial site.[56]

Yet despite this belated recognition, the dimensions of the problem were consistently minimized. The official registry of reportable diseases for 1929 lists only five CS_2 cases, every one a churn room operator from the same facility—none other than the Rayon Manufacturing Company of Surrey, the target of court action against neighborhood pollution a year earlier.[57] The first two cases were reported by the certifying surgeon on March 29, only a few weeks after Kelly's deputation to the Home Secretary; the symptoms of one of these included "failure of sight," which is a classic finding of CS_2-

caused toxic amblyopia. None of the hundreds of other cases of eye affliction ever appeared in the registry or were listed in any annual report table summarizing such data; a scientific journal report of the outbreak did not appear until 1936, more than a decade after the fact.[58] Equally important, none of this was ever reported directly through the voices of the workers who were made ill, whether through testimony garnered at an official inquiry (no such inquiry occurred) or through information distributed by trade unions.

Aftermath

Diminution to outright denial of any viscose-related health hazards continued. In the spring of 1929, the Alkali Acts Chief Inspector published a seven-page report wholly exonerating the industry inside (for the workers in the plants) and outside: "There is no evidence that the health of the community has suffered from the existence of these works, although the amenities of every-day life may have been in certain places interfered with."[59]

Following a Labour Party sweep on May 30, 1929, June's issue of the *British Medical Journal* carried a brief opinion piece, "Amblyopia and the Artificial Silk Industry"—a scathing critique of the continuing CS_2 hazards in artificial silk manufacturing.[60] Reviewing the history of CS_2 poisoning in this industry, it adds a key unpublished detail of one Factory Inspector case of a viscose churn sealed and under negative pressure until the poisoned worker was "compelled to put his head inside to remove the orange-coloured sticky mass." The piece concludes with the following admonition: "The artificial silk industry starts with a tremendous advantage in the experience already gained as to the effects of the toxic agents used or evolved. The day in, day out exposure to them by workpeople should never be forgotten."[61] Although unsigned, this editorial is a verbatim extract of a longer presentation by Sir Thomas Legge.[62] A few months earlier, Legge had prepared lengthy briefing materials for the Trades Union Council in regard to MP Kelley's deputation to the Home Secretary.[63] Following his earlier resignation as Chief Medical Inspector (in protest over failed lead controls), Legge continued to write about the dangers of CS_2 and even attempted to reach a broader audience: one of his last pieces published before his death in 1932 was on this subject, appearing in the *Statesman and Nation*.[64]

There may have been a new government and a more direct call for public health action, but it would be hard to argue that much had changed for the health of British artificial silk workers or their communities. The 1930s marked a period in which "artificial silk," recently having been renamed "rayon,"[65] was to witness a general worsening of working conditions in the viscose industry internationally; CS_2 disease, always endemic, became rampant worldwide. The British industry was far from the worst it this regard. The horrific conditions in the Italian viscose industry throughout the Fascist period have been well documented.[66] In areas of Nazi domination, rayon staple manufacturing depended on slave labor and those with resulting neurological disease received the same fate as those suffering from insanity.[67] In the United States, Alice Hamilton tried to follow up on reports of CS_2 illness from various viscose facilities and was stymied in her efforts by industry resistance;[68] finally, by the late 1930s, she had initiated first one state-based investigation and then a multistate study that found large numbers of U.S. workers made sick by CS_2.[69]

The viscose artificial silk industry from 1910 to 1930 can be seen as prototypical of an emerging group of multinational, chemical-intensive industries; at the same time, biomedical research was evolving into a modern international network of investigation not very different in its fundamentals from that still current today. The industry's dependence on one highly toxic chemical, CS_2, provides a case study of how such an inherently hazardous manufacturing process was addressed from a public health perspective. Increasing and widely disseminated biomedical awareness of the hazard, although it could have provided a basis for control, did not translate into effective action by the responsible labor and health agencies in Great Britain, whose inaction was accompanied by disingenuous denials at the highest governmental levels. Although there was some push-back by organized labor, this force was dissipated by the worldwide financial depression of the 1930s. Moreover, although unions spoke for their rank and file, at no time were the voices of those most affected directly heard. Absent other explanatory factors, it is most likely that the economic power and influence of the emerging multinational enterprise of artificial silk production, largely centered in Great Britain, blunted early recognition and, once belatedly acknowledged, any meaningful control of CS_2-caused illness in the rayon trade.

NOTES

1. Parliamentary Debates, 5th ser., vol. 214 (March 15, 1928), col. 2078.

2. Anonymous, "Parliamentary Intelligence: Health Conditions in Artificial Silk Factories," *The Lancet* 211, no. 5456 (March 24, 1928): 631.

3. Paul D. Blanc, "From Balloons to Artificial Silk: The History of Carbon Disulfide Toxicity," in *Occupation Health and Public Health: Lessons from the Past—Challenges for the Future*, ed. Marie C. Nelson (Stockholm: Arbete och Hälse [Ventenskaplig Skriftserie], National Institute for Working Life, 2006), 87–97. See also Paul D. Blanc, *How Everyday Products Make People Sick* (Berkeley: University of California Press, 2009), 140–149.

4. August L. Delpech, "Accidens [sic] que développe chez les ouvriers en caoutchouc: L'inhalation du sulfure de carbone en vapeur," *L'Union Médicale* 10, no. 60 (May 31, 1856): 265–267.

5. R. D. O'Flynn and H. A. Waldron, "Delpech and the Origins of Occupational Psychiatry," *British Journal of Industrial Medicine* 47 (1990): 189–198. See also Jean Marin Charcot, *Leçons du mardi a la Salpêtrière: Policlinique 1888–1889, notes de cours de MM. Blin, Charcot, Henri Colin* (Paris: Progres Médical, 1889), 43–53.

6. W. B. Hadden, "A Case of Chronic Poisoning by Bisulphide of Carbon," *Proceedings of the Medical Society of London* 9 (1886): 115–117. For an early comment in the lay British press, see Galignani (first name not stated), "Unhealthy Trades," *Times of London*, September 26, 1863, 12.

7. John Charles Withers, "Artificial Silk: A Review of the Literature," *Shirley Institute Memoirs (The British Cotton Industry Research Association)*, series A, no. 18 (1926): 293–328. (Marked "Private and Confidential. For the information of Members of the British Cotton Industry Research Association only.")

8. D. C. Coleman, *Courtaulds: An Economic and Social History*, vol. 2, *Rayon* (Oxford: Clarendon Press, 1969); E. I. du Pont de Nemours & Company, Rayon Department,

Leonard A. Yerkes: Fibersilk to Fiber "A" (Buffalo, NY: W. J. Keller, 1945); F. W. Taussig and H. D. White, "Rayon and the Tariff: The Nurture of an Industrial Prodigy," *Quarterly Journal of Economics* 45 (1931): 588–621.

9. Coleman, *Courtaulds*. For the Italian industry, see also V. Cerretano, "The 'Benefits of Moderate Inflation: The Rayon Industry and Snia Viscosa in the Italy of the 1920s," *Journal of European Economic History* 33 (2004): 233–284.

10. World Health Organization, *Carbon Disulfide: Environmental Health Criteria 10* (Geneva: World Health Organization, 1979), annex 1, figure 1.

11. "British Silk. Origin and Present State of the Industry: Magic of New Processes," *Times of London*, June 27, 1913, 41.

12. "'Frankenstein': Visit to a Viscose Silk Factory. 7 Miles of Thread a Second," *Times of London*, March 9, 1926, xiv.

13. H. D. Jump and J. M. Cruice, "Chronic Poisoning from Bisulphide of Carbon," *University of Pennsylvania Medical Bulletin* 17 (1904–1905): 193–196; A. P. Francine, "Acute Carbon Disulphide Poisoning," *American Medicine* 9 (1905): 871.

14. "Tecnica industriale. L'industria della seta artificiale," *Il Lavoro* 5 (1912): 74–75.

15. M. Chevalier, "La manipulation du sulfure de carbone dans les fabriques de viscose et de la soie artificielle viscose," *Bulletin de l'Inspection du Travail* (1922): 166–174.

16. George M. Kober, "The Button, Horn, Celluloid and Allied Industries," in *Industrial Health*, ed. G. M. Kober and E. R. Hayhurst (Philadelphia: P. Blakiston's and Son, 1924), 273–277.

17. Emory R. Hayhurst, "Carbon Disulphide Poisoning," in Korber and Hayhurst, *Industrial Health*, 360–368.

18. Edward W. Hope, William Hanna, and C. O. Stallybrass, *Industrial Hygiene and Medicine*, (London: Bailliére, Tindall and Cox, 1923), 176.

19. G. Loriga, "Le condizioni iginieniche nell'industria della seta artificale," *Bolletino del Lavoro e della Previdenza Sociale* 43, part 4 (May 1925): 85–95.

20. G. Loriga, "Le condizioni iginieniche nell'industria della seta artificale," *La Medicina del Lavoro* 16 (1925): 309–314.

21. P. Redaelli, "Sull'anatomia patologica dell'avvelenamento cronio da solfuro di carbonio," *Bolletinno d. Societa Medico-Chirurgica, Pavia* 37 (1925): 133–140.

22. Loriga, "Le condizioni iginieniche," *Bollettino del Lavoro*, 86.

23. A Ceconi, "Polineuriti," *Minerva Medica* 6 (1925): 267–284.

24. "Die Tagung der Arbeitsgemeinshaft Deutcher Gewerbärtze, Berlin," *Social Praxis* 33, no. 11. (1924): 1060–1062.

25. Wauer, "Gesundeheitsschädigungen in der Kunstseideindustrie," *Zentralblatt für Gewerbehygiene und Unfallverhütung* 12 (1925):67–71.

26. W.R.H. Kranenburg and H. Kessener, "Schwefelwasserstoff und Schefelkohlenstoff-vergiftungen," *Zentralblatt für Gewerbehygiene und Unfallverhütung* 12 (1925): 348–350.

27. Alice Hamilton, *Industrial Poisons in the United Sates* (New York: Macmillan, 1925), 368–369. Hamilton's plant visit is documented in Alice Hamilton, "Day Pocket Diary for 1923," box 1, vol. 1923, Hamilton Family Papers, Schlesinger Library, Radcliffe Institute for Advanced Study, Harvard University.

28. C. Da Fano and P Redaelli, "Sull'anatomia patologica dell'avvelenamento cronico da solfuro di carbonio," *Bolletinno d. Societa Medico-Chirurgica, Pavia* 37 (1925): 133; M. Arezzi, "Observazioni sperimentali sull'avvelenamento da solfuro di carbonio," *Bolletinno d. Societa Medico-Chirurgica, Pavia* 37 (1925): 141, extracted in *Medical Science* 12 (1925): 515.

29. "Cause di avvelenamento nelle industrie della seta artificiale," *La Medicina del Lavoro* 16 (1925): 418–420. (In 1925, *Il Lavoro* became *La Medicina del Lavoro*.)

30. Ibid.

31. *The Institute of Chemistry of Great Britain and Ireland: Journal and Proceedings, Part II* (1925): 128.

32. Royal Institute of Chemistry Manchester and District Section Minute Book, 1918–1927, Archives and Local Studies, ref: M90/1/1, Manchester, UK.

33. Thomas Oliver, "Some Achievements of Industrial Legislation and Hygiene," *British Medical Journal* (September 19, 1925): 530–531. There was a simultaneous publication (with slight editorial variants) in *The Lancet* 206, no. 5325 (September 19, 1925): 630–632.

34. United Kingdom, Home Office and Ministry of Labour and National Service and Successors, Factory Inspectorate and Factory Department, *Annual Report of the Chief Inspector of Factories and Workshops for the Year 1925* (London: His Majesty's Stationery Office, 1926), 70.

35. Ibid., 121.

36. Thomas M. Legge, *Industrial Maladies* (London: Humphrey Milford, 1934), 150.

37. United Kingdom, Home Office and Ministry of Labour and National Service and Successors, Factory Inspectorate and Factory Department, Registers of Lead, etc., "Poisoning and Anthrax Cases," British National Archives LAB 56/26.

38. United Kingdom, Home Office and Ministry of Labour and National Service and Successors, Factory Inspectorate and Factory Department, *Annual Report of the Chief Inspector of Factories and Workshops for the Year 1926* (London: His Majesty's Stationery Office, 1927), 86.

39. "Factory Inspection Reports for Courtauld's [sic] Works, Flint, 1922–1935," Flintshire Record Office, D/DM/656/1, Hawarden, Wales. Notes of churn room visits 9/7/22; 11/7/22; 8/31/23; 10/4/23; 10/31/24; 7/31/25; 10/14/26; 1/20/27.

40. Parliamentary Debates, 5th ser., vol. 213 (February 23, 1928), col. 1828.

41. H. A. Taylor, *Viscount Brentford: Being the Authoritative and Official Biography of the Rt. Hon. William Joynson-Hicks, First Viscount Brentford of Newick* (London: S. Paul, 1933).

42. William A. Robson, "The Factory Acts, 1833–1933," *Political Quarterly* 5, no. 1 (1934): 55–73.

43. Parliamentary Debates, 5th ser., vol. 214 (February 29, 1928), cols. 399–401.

44. Parliamentary Debates, 5th ser., vol. 189 (December 10, 1925), col. 642.

45. "Industrial Poisoning (Medical Notes in Parliament)," *British Medical Journal* 2 (December 19, 1925): 1206.

46. Coleman, *Courtaulds*, 265.

47. Coleman, *Courtaulds*, 160–162.

48. "High Court of Justice. Chancery Division. Nuisance Caused by Gas Fumes. Attorney-General v. Rayon Manufacturing Company (1927), Limited," *Times of London*, July 20, 1928, 5.

49. W. J. Bonner, "The Textile Industry in Surrey," *Annual of the Dorking High School for Boys O.B.A*, no. 5 (February 1927): 18–20.

50. Parliamentary Debates, 5th ser., vol. 215 (March 22, 1928), col. 545; (March 29, 1928), col. 1330; (April 3, 1928), col. 1795; Parliamentary Debates, 5th ser., vol. 216 (April 17, 1928), cols. 16–17; (April 18, 1928), col. 180; Parliamentary Debates, 5th ser., vol. 217 (May 9, 1928), cols. 252–253; (May 16, 1928), cols.1038–1039; (May 17, 1928), cols. 1184–1185.

51. Parliamentary Debates, 5th ser., vol. 224 (February 4, 1929), cols. 1418–1419; (February 5, 1929), col. 1604.

52. "Ailments of Workers in Artificial Silk (Medical Notes in Parliament)," *British Medical Journal* (February 9, 1929): 278.

53. Correspondence, Workers Union and National Union of Textile Workers including deputation to the Home Secretary, 1 March 1929 (Warwick: Warwick University, Modern Research Center, Trades Union Council Archives, MSS.292/144.54/6).

54. United Kingdom, Home Office and Ministry of Labour and National Service and Successors, Factory Inspectorate and Factory Department, *Annual Report of the Chief Inspector of Factories and Workshops for the Year 1929* (London: His Majesty's Stationery Office, 1930), 46.

55. Ibid., 77.

56. Ibid., 78.

57. United Kingdom, Home Office and Ministry of Labour and National Service and Successors, Factory Inspectorate and Factory Department, Registers of Lead, etc., "Poisoning and Anthrax Cases" (British National Archives LAB 56/30). One of these listed workers appears to match a case presented at a clinical meeting held in November 1929: F.R.R. Walshe, "Carbon Disulphide Intoxication," *Proceedings of the Royal Society of Medicine* 23 (1929/1930): 89–90.

58. David Rankine, "Artificial Silk Keratitis," *British Medical Journal* (July 4, 1936): 6–9.

59. United Kingdom, Ministry of Health, *Report on an Investigation Regarding the Emission of Fumes from Artificial Silk Works* (His Majesty's Stationery Office: London, 1929).

60. "Amblyopia and the Artificial Silk Industry," *British Medical Journal* (June 1, 1929): 1008–1009.

61. Ibid.

62. Thomas M. Legge, *Shaw Lectures on Thirty Years' Experience of Industrial Maladies: Delivered before the Royal Society of Arts, February and March, 1929* (London: Royal Society of Arts, 1929), 16–17

63. Correspondence, Workers Union and National Union of Textile Workers including deputation to the Home Secretary, 1929 (Warwick: Warwick University, Modern Research Center, Trades Union Council Archives).

64. Thomas M. Legge, "An Industrial Danger," *Statesman and Nation*, new series 2, no. 25 (August 15, 1931): 190.

65. "Name Committee Meets Thursday," *New York Times*, April 15, 1924, 28; "Retailers to Adopt 'Rayon,'" *New York Times*, April 26, 1924, 24.

66. Francisco Carnevale and A. Baldesseroni, "La lotta di Mussolini contro le malattie professionali (1922–1943): I lavoratori e il primato Italiano nella produzione di seta artificiale," *Epidemiolgia e Prevenzione* 27 (2003): 114–120.

67. Emil A. Paluch, "Two Outbreaks of Carbon Disulfide Poisoning in Rayon Staple Fiber Plants in Poland," *Journal of Industrial Hygiene and Toxicology* 30 (1948): 37–42.

68. Alice Hamilton, *Exploring the Dangerous Trades* (Boston: Little, Brown, 1943), 387–394. See also Barbara Sicherman, *Alice Hamilton: A Life in Letters* (Cambridge, MA: Harvard University Press, 1984), 357–359, 437 n5.

69. Department of Labor and Industry, Commonwealth of Pennsylvania, *Survey of Carbon Disulphide and Hydrogen Sulphide Hazards in the Viscose Rayon Industry* (Occupational Disease Prevention Division Bulletin No. 46, Harrisburg, PA: Commonwealth of Pennsylvania, August 1938); Alice Hamilton, *Occupational Poisoning in the Viscose Rayon Industry* (U.S. Department of Labor Bulletin No. 34, Washington, DC: U.S. Government Printing Office, 1940).

PART II

THE MIDDLE TO THE LATE TWENTIETH CENTURY

New Transfers of Production

6

Shipping the "Next Prize"

*The Trade in Liquefied Natural Gas
from Nigeria to Mexico*

ANNA ZALIK

Since 2004 a range of North American community and environmental organizations have successfully opposed liquefied natural gas (LNG) infrastructure on the East and West coasts. From California and British Columbia to Rhode Island, Baja California, and the Canadian Atlantic, these popular movements center attention on the hazards of LNG.[1] In California not a single proposed LNG terminal has proceeded, in sites as diverse as the northern college town of Arcata and the Los Angeles suburb of Long Beach. In early 2010 groups in Oregon and Washington State announced their victory against the proposed Bradwood LNG project when the project's financial backer withdrew its support. These movements advance a combined set of arguments against LNG projects, including their environmental consequences, the security and safety risks posed by possible accidents at facilities, and LNG's promotion of a nonrenewable energy future dependent on distant supplies of gas.[2]

LNG development forms part of the rush to natural gas as the "greener" hydrocarbon of the twenty-first century—"The 'Next Prize." Indeed, over the past ten years, the oil and gas industry has placed a major emphasis on the creation of LNG facilities as well as infrastructural connections between those facilities and domestic power supplies. LNG terminals—the locations at which the liquefied gas arrives and is regasified—are frequently run by private multinationals such as Shell, although national oil companies are also major players.[3] LNG is employed where terrestrial pipelines are not possible; overseas shipment of gas requires its liquefaction at extremely cold temperatures, of –260°F (127°C). This reduces its volume by 600 percent, after which it is transported in special tankers to terminals where it is made available to domestic power grids.[4]

Successful opposition to LNG in North America is illustrative of the growing role of fenceline residents and environmental advocates in shaping facility siting in the latter part of the twentieth century and the early twenty-first. In North America, the environmental justice movement has demonstrated the disproportionate burden of industrial hazards on race- and class-marginalized populations, and a range of work under the rubric of political ecology examines these tendencies globally.[5] As underscored by the recent BP spill, certain categories of bodies are much more likely to be subject to facility risks than others. In this chapter, a successful and recent North American LNG siting decision on the Mexican Gulf Coast, for importing LNG from Nigeria, indicates how histories of regional and social inequality influence potential opposition to facility installation.[6]

This was Mexico's first operational LNG terminal, opened in 2006 as a Shell project in Altamira, Tamaulipas State, on the Gulf Coast, that sources its shipments from the Nigerian Liquefied Natural Gas Facility on the coast of the Nigerian Niger Delta.[7] Via this Mexican location, Shell established itself where domestic subsidies to infrastructure were available and the lucrative North American market readily accessible. By constructing the terminal on Mexico's Gulf, Shell partially sidestepped protest against LNG on the Californian and Mexican Pacific Coast, while claiming to remediate the problem of gas flaring, a practice for which the Nigerian oil industry—and Shell in particular—has been harshly criticized. Flaring is the practice by which the gas that is extracted alongside oil (known as "associated gas")—is burned as a waste product. In the Nigerian setting, this flaring is often seen as huge surface flames, much of the time in close proximity to Niger Deltan villages.[8] Among Nigerians and globally, this has stirred ecological justice and conservationist concerns about the oil industry's presence. Shipping LNG out of Nigeria invests in a future for that country's LNG industry that centers on export rather than the construction of costly domestic gas infrastructure. In Nigeria such infrastructural investment, while needed, is perceived as highly risky for the transnationals. The industry thus avoids the opposition it has come to face in the Nigerian operating environment, and the violent relations that its policies have shaped, while claiming to adopt a cleaner practice through liquefying, rather than burning, gas.[9] All told, this facility siting and the shipment of gas from Nigeria to Mexico demonstrate how the trade in LNG exemplifies what David Harvey refers to as a "spatio-temporal" fix, where capitalism seeks to resolve some of its socio-environmental contradictions by expanding its territorial reach.

By illuminating the range of local protests shaping multinational practice in the early twenty-first century, this story of Shell's siting decision also challenges ecological modernization (EM) theory. EM theory offers a social and scientific explanation of demands for environmental protection. It holds that greater economic development may result in social demands for environmental protection and ultimately lead to the adoption of more "ecologically sound" and often more costly technologies.[10] While the LNG protests on the California coast would seem to follow this dynamic, it fails to account for the extent to which industrial activities, as they have increasingly concentrated in the Global South, have also stirred ecological protests. Shell's decision about where to site its latest LNG plant involves a more complex navigation than that which EM theory indicates.[11] As suggested by the author's fieldwork on the California and Baja California coast, both elite and grassroots mobilization, as well as the corporate energy scandals in California at the turn of the millennium, shaped social resistance to proposed LNG terminals.

Nigeria and Mexico in Comparative Perspective

Conventional definitions of industrial development would place the national economies of Nigeria and Mexico in somewhat divergent categories. Nigeria represents the ravages of the "resource curse," where dependence on extractive revenues and accompanying ecological degradation erode social cohesion and impede national industrial development.[12] Mexico provides a model of a developing oil exporter that, despite ecological impacts, has managed to "avoid the worst impact of the resource curse."[13] This is largely due to Mexico's history of nationalization during the 1930s, when the foreign oil industry was expropriated, as discussed by Santiago in this volume. In taking over its own oil industry, Mexico was able to fuel domestic industrialization and subsidize national consumption in ways that Nigeria was not.[14] Yet because Nigeria became such a target for exploitation by foreign oil companies, the activities of those companies stirred a more powerful late-twentieth-century opposition to the presence and operations of Shell in that country.

Royal Dutch Shell's "first mover" position in the Niger Delta, as the first company to sink a well in the 1950s, endowed it with an economic edge over competing multinationals. For many years Royal Dutch operated in conjunction with British Petroleum in Nigeria, but BP's share in this venture was formally nationalized in 1971 in part because of its infringement on the embargo of apartheid South Africa. Although thereafter the Nigerian National Petroleum Company held a majority share in the oil industry, in practice operations remained largely under control of transnational companies, with Shell (SPDC Nigeria) the leading operator onshore. At the time of its initiation in the 1980s, the Nigeria Liquefied Natural Gas (NLNG) terminal on Bonny Island was a joint venture between the Nigerian National Petroleum Company, Shell, ENI (Agip) Italy, and Total. The NLNG saw its first shipment to Europe in 1999.[15] Today, the role of LNG projects as a "spatial fix" is deepening through the extension of Clean Development Mechanism (CDM) financing for them. This is the World Bank's subsidy for so-called carbon sequestration projects under the Kyoto Protocol.[16]

As referenced above, the turn toward liquefaction and export of natural gas provided a first solution to the Nigerian oil industry's problem of gas flaring, and to the opposition it aroused. Gas has been burned by Delta oil operations at rates that are the highest in the world.[17] Flaring in the Niger Delta occurs at a rate of more than 20 billion cubic meters per year (some sources argue 2.5 billion cubic feet per day), with many riverine villages "never knowing a dark night." Shell Nigeria is the largest single flarer. Since the rise to international notice of the Ogoni movement in Nigeria in the 1990s, gas flaring in the Delta has become a major target for global environmental justice advocates and for domestic lawmakers. Ken Saro-Wiwa is often memorialized with his fist up in protest and an enormous surface flare at his back. Condemned by Ogoni, Ijaw, and other Nigerian "oil minorities" as a violation of indigenous rights, flaring in the Delta is read as a clear manifestation of environmental racism, or "global apartheid," as applied to the exploitation of natural resources. Despite the profits extracted from the area, a population of some millions in the Niger Delta's creeks remains disconnected from a road network and electricity, able to access state capitals only by boat. In protest against these conditions, in 1999 Ijaw youth declared "Operation Climate Change," whose aim was to "extinguish the flares." However, the Nigerian military's suppression of youth movements and the ongoing infrastructural marginalization of the Delta is now responded to in a diffuse insurgency. Today those excluded from formal employment are armed and engage in kidnappings of oil workers, attacks on facilities, and trade in contraband oil. The scale of domestic and transnational concern regarding this insurgency has led to considerable global action and domestic pressures. Goodluck Jonathan, an Ijaw from Bayelsa State in the central Delta, became Nigerian president in 2011, assuming that position as vice president upon the death of President Yar Adua. Ten years ago this would have been unthinkable. In part, Jonathan's rise expresses the role of the Niger Delta in Nigeria's global reception and the view that his national role will help de-escalate the Niger Deltan "crisis."

The global boycott of Shell that arose in the 1990s because of the company's activities in Nigeria, as well as the threatened dumping of its Brent Spar platform in the North Sea, pushed the company toward an image makeover. It made itself a leader in global "corporate social responsibility" at the end of the 1990s. The NLNG project at Bonny Island, and the public affairs programs it has advanced, were intended to illustrate corporate "best practice," employing industry-community models that depart from the divisive "host-community" policies that stoked intercommunal conflict in Nigeria's oil fields.[18] On Bonny Island itself, an ecologically protected area at Finima was established as a requirement of the Environmental Impact Assessment for the Nigerian LNG and is administered by a Nigerian environmental NGO. Challenging the tenets of "Ecological Modernization," the administering NGO has often found discarded pipes and industrial waste on the site. Territorial conflict over the industrial area has been violent at Bonny. In addition to intercommunal disputes over ownership of this land, insurgent youth sympathetic to the Movement for the Emancipation of the Niger Delta have succeeded in invading the facility on a number of occasions.

The spatial "fix" offered by the transfer of LNG from Nigeria to Mexico thus emerges from the historical legacy of environmental hazards of the oil industry and the social protests they stirred. The LNG industry in general and the flaring it claims to remediate have already shaped deteriorating eco-systems, the impacts of which are not erased when the resource is transferred overseas.[19] This is manifest in declining human health, deteriorating liveli-hoods and agrarian systems, and sociopolitical violence. In contrast to this social mobilization in Nigeria and, as we will see, on the Pacific Coast the Mexican Gulf's history of oil extraction demonstrates not only how indus-try has been central to shaping the deteriorating ecology of the extractive region—now imprinted on the minds of the general public in the images of the 2010 BP accident in the U.S. Gulf—but also how its political and eco-nomic conditions make it relatively socially *amenable* to LNG infrastructure.

The Mexican Terminal and Its History

Mexico's first regasification plant, the Shell facility at Altamira, had been operational for four years as of 2010.[20] Located just south of Altamira is the port city and capital of Tampico, Tamaulipas, the historical pivot in the his-tory of Mexican labour struggles for control of the oil industry.[21]

The particular nationalized history of its oil and gas industry distin-guishes Mexico from many other oil exporters. First run by private operators, Mexico's oil industry exacted a heavy environmental toll on the Gulf Coast states. The Huasteca region of Tamaulipas and the northern Veracruz States, as described by Santiago in this volume(and later the Tabasco wetlands and the Isla del Carmen, Campeche State), suffered considerable ecological and health consequences from the relatively unregulated extraction that occurred in the late nineteenth and early twentieth centuries. The ravages of foreign, privatized control over oil extraction were challenged via the expropriation of the foreign-controlled oil industry on the eve of World War II; the 1938 nationalization was the culmination of oil workers' struggles to implement progressive sections of the 1917 revolutionary constitution.[22] As Santiago demonstrates, demands for resource conservation on the Gulf Coast and oil worker struggles for health and safety constituted one of the most powerful labour sectors in twentieth-century Mexico. Indeed, the relationship between the petroleum workers union (STPRM—the Union of Oil Workers of the Mexican Revolution, literally translated) and the postrevolutionary state in Mexico held foreign participation in the industry at bay for fifty years and, on a per-barrel basis, ensured a much higher level of employment in PEMEX than in any other oil company in the world—ten times higher, according to some estimates.[23] This relationship also entrenched both national industry's and organized labour's interest in the survival and expansion of the oil and gas sector.

South of Tamaulipas and Veracruz, the state of Tabasco has been the major land-based site of PEMEX activity since the boom of the 1970s, although, in terms of oil production, offshore development in Campeche Sound has surpassed it since the 1980s. Even prior to the entry of PEMEX, Tabasco's natural environment—once popularly referred to as an "eden"—had undergone an "ecological modernization" with negative consequences. Tabasco's wetlands and rain forest had seen a major transformation by the middle of the twentieth century through the industrialized agriculture of banana plantations—geared at export—which was accompanied by destruction of the rain forest to create pasture for cattle grazing. The rain forest was further disrupted by PEMEX's installation of a road network to facilitate extraction.[24] Ongoing ecological deterioration in the waterways profoundly affected both farming and fishing livelihoods in the Gulf region. This prompted ongoing protests, including a host of rural movements for payment of ecological damages from the 1970s and what is described as a "claims industry" around the oil industry, in which fishermen were accused of oiling their nets so as to demand compensation from PEMEX.[25] In the 1990s Andres Manuel Lopez Obrador, who would later become the Mayor of Mexico City and 2006 presidential candidate, led protests of both peasants and workers laid off under neoliberal policies seeking to break the patrimonial PEMEX union. Indeed, many fishermen and campesinos had been PEMEX workers, so agrarian and oil worker mobilization coincided.[26] Agrarian residents sought funds from PEMEX and a cleanup of its operations, but not its privatization or denationalization. As put by a key ecologist working on these issues in the 1990s, on the issue of privatization/denationalization:

> During all the years I was fighting against Pemex I never lost faith that one day it would be a clean company, with responsible executives—a patrimony of the nation. Never in my wildest dreams did I think they would sell off the industry.[27]

Today, the Mexican LNG projects exemplify the creeping privatization and denationalization of the country's energy sector since the late 1980s.[28] The current government of President Calderon has pursued privatization of the oil industry but has met considerable opposition, given the role of a nationalized PEMEX as a symbol of Mexican sovereignty from imperial power (wielded by the United States and Great Britain and now transnational capital in general). Nationalist groups in Mexico, recognizing how LNG serves foreign energy interests, critique the new foreign-operated LNG projects as unconstitutional. Independent PEMEX staff associations have challenged these projects in the courts.[29] Although privately run LNG projects in Mexico have been officially justified by the government as "non-extractive" and aimed at the domestic energy market, is it well known that the LNG terminals are sited in the North of the country for proximity to the United States.[30]

Gas as Hazard/Lubricant: Contention at the Terminal

Less overtly, the siting decision for the Altamira LNG terminal occurred against the backdrop of sustained protests surrounding LNG facilities in

California and Mexico's Baja California.[31] Unlike the long history of oil industry investment on the Gulf Coast, social interests in these regions do not see a future tied to hydrocarbons. The coalitions opposing LNG stress its volatility and argue that large storage quantities pose hazards to coastal populations and ecologies. One public interest group based on the West Coast points out that "no other energy infrastructure brings together the four major risk factors that are associated with LNG marine receiving facilities: 1) high energy density, 2) very large inventories, 3) unusual release dynamics associated with extreme cryogenic temperatures, and 4) very large potential impact zones."[32]

According to official U.S. sources, ten serious LNG accidents have occurred since the 1940s worldwide but with few fatalities. For that reason Congress gave LNG land terminals a relatively safe rating in a 2003 report.[33] However, these safety ratings are contested. A critical report on the U.S. Federal Energy Regulatory Commission's (FERC) description of LNG, titled *Public Safety and FERC's LNG Spin: What Citizens Aren't Being Told*,[34] argues that "for a variety of significant reasons, past operating records do not provide an appropriate perspective for the analysis of LNG risks. Overemphasis on past operations to predict future failures is a characteristic of poor risk management techniques, particularly for such complex systems."[35] As a rallying point for local mobilization, public health and safety have broad popular appeal in the North American context. As opposed to promotional material portraying LNG as "methane[36] that is colorless, odorless and non-toxic," environmental groups stress that LNG includes contaminants like ethane and propane. Although official discourse has put LNG as not at all explosive in its liquid state, critics point out that this applies to most flammable liquids. LNG's flammability varies since it is held at unnaturally cool temperatures. In seeking the cancelation of the Chevron Islas Coronado project in Baja California, Greenpeace Mexico cited accidents at Staten Island in 1975 with a death toll of 45, a gas cloud in Boston in 1988, and an accident in Algeria—the second largest exporter of LNG globally—that killed 23, not to mention a spill in Cleveland in 1944 that resulted in a fire that killed 128 people.[37] Accordingly, the U.S. Energy Information Administration identifies "NIMBY" ("Not in My Backyard") as one of the key "uncertainties" facing LNG projects.

In Mexico, just over the border from California, a Marathon Oil and Conoco project near Tijuana was canceled in 2004 because of public opposition. The Chevron Islas Coronado terminal near Ensenada was canceled in 2007, following public opposition from a range of groups. The islands provide a habitat for a vulnerable marine bird, the Xantus, on which basis a case was taken to NAFTA's Committee on Environmental Cooperation in 2005.[38] In the nearby state of Sonora on Mexico's western coast a proposed project is unlikely to proceed. However, a Shell/Sempra project at Costa Azul has advanced, to the chagrin of a somewhat surprising coalition of California surfers and Mexican housewives against it.[39] In an interview, Shell Mexico's manager indicated that Shell's reentry[40] prospects in Mexico benefit from the fact that the "company does not suffer from the negative press in Mexico that it does in Nigeria."[41]

In contrast to the U.S. and Mexican Pacific Coast, where a broad-based coalition against LNG terminals emerged, the Gulf states of both the United States and Mexico have been less socially contentious, offering an "in-between" space for the facilities.[42] Here the varying industrial/environmental histories of the California and Gulf coasts are important. The political economy of Mexico's Gulf region, not unlike the U.S. Gulf to its north, is strongly connected to oil extraction. In Mexico judicial opposition to trans-national controlled projects such as that at Altamira was initially prompted by sovereigntist sectors associated with PEMEX workers as opposed to deriving from any antihazards movements. This differs from Mexico's Baja California coast, where the tourism, real estate, and fishery sectors are strong. Freudenberg and Gramling identify the parallel tendency on the U.S. coastlines. In their comparative analysis of public reception to offshore oil development in California and Louisiana, they identify a number of reasons that Lousiana accepted these developments and California rejected them: (1) the historical moment at which offshore industrial development was initi-ated in each of these regions; (2) the relative socio-environmental sensibility, including California's history as the "birthplace" of the Sierra Club; and (3) the political economy of the interest groups involved with marine devel-opment in California, where tourism and real estate are significant sectors.[43] Support for tourism often goes hand in hand with the wealth associated with "ecological modernization" so that consumers of wilderness may also have an interest in leisure developments.

These variations between the West and East coasts play themselves out in the strength of contemporary anti-LNG movements. A hundred-year his-tory of oil and gas development, and the corporate-state-labour alliances associated with it, make the Gulf states relatively receptive to coastal indus-try, although clearly the recent BP spill alters these conditions. Ecological degradation resulting from hydrocarbon extraction has *already* occurred (making tourist development less likely), local industries are *already* reliant on an extractive economy, and a labour force equipped for and interested in working in this sector is *already* readily available.

LNG and Its Contradictions

Liquefied natural gas offers business both a strategic opportunity to "trans-fer" the reputational and ecological externalities of gas flaring out of Nigeria and a conveniently "green" hydrocarbon with which to reenter the Mexican oil and energy industry (proximate to a prime energy market in the United States). The pollution and social protest associated with the Niger Delta oil industry is partially skirted through the funneling of some quantity, albeit small, of formerly flared gas into LNG—suggestive of a longer-term commit-ment to liquefy all currently flared gas. Indeed, the oil industry has claimed that these projects offset carbon emissions and should thus be eligible for

Global Environmental Facility (GEF) funding through the World Bank, but this claim has been strongly contested by some environmental nongovernment organizations and critics of carbon trading.[44] The marketing of the LNG, in turn, serves as an outlet to recycle natural capital, as per Harvey's "spatio-temporal" fix.

In Nigeria, the infrastructural and social marginalization of the Delta region and the country as a whole makes the Nigerian domestic energy sector unappealing for investors, despite a considerably underserved domestic market for natural gas. Shipping the gas overseas is thus a more lucrative and, apparently, a more secure option for industry. The violence and environmental erosion shaped by the activities of the key multinationals operating in the Delta, particularly Shell, are partially evaded through LNG transfer, even as the company's earlier history in Mexico is masked. In this way, transfer of LNG allows capital an opportunity to engage in a kind of "spatial fix" for overexploitation of society and nature even while it produces more of the same.

In moving LNG from Nigeria to Mexico, the oil industry benefits from the latter's stability as well as its proximity to the largest domestic market in the world. By siting plants in Mexico rather than in the United States, the LNG industry also avoids the "ecologically modernized"—that is, wealthier—areas that resist industrial development while benefiting from the lesser environmental restrictions on LNG just over the border. Despite the supposed technological fix it offers, LNG thus entails a set of contradictory[45] outcomes. Simultaneously in Mexico, fossil fuel dependence and reliance on foreign companies for LNG technology is deepened. These tendencies have facilitated the creeping privatization and blatant erosion of labour power, as employees contracted by private companies in Mexico make a fraction of the wages of unionized PEMEX oil workers and must sign contractual clauses that they will not attempt to unionize against harsh working conditions— thus countering the relative advantages offered to a somewhat protected, although patrimonial, labour organization under PEMEX. These tendencies have only deepened in the 2009–2010 period in Mexico, when two major electricity and mining unions were harshly repressed by the Calderon government. The Nigeria-Mexico transfer indicates how the spatial movement of LNG is only a partial and stopgap "fixative" for socioeconomic and ecological consequences of industry, which contributes to a neoliberal weakening of Mexican labour solidarity that demands safer conditions at facilities. Tracing LNG's transglobal shipment thus demonstrates that so-called "ecological modernization" is a process that benefits certain populations over others. As a consequence of long-distance transport to, and socio-ecological impacts at, terminal sites, LNG is accompanied by a new set of global and local hazards.

NOTES

Acknowledgments: I thank Fernando Rouaux for research assistance; Sergio Chavez for guiding this research in Baja California; and Rory Cox, Chris Sellers, and Jo Melling, as well as participants in the 2007 conference "Dangerous Trade" at SUNY Stony Brook, for helpful comments on this paper.

1. See http://lngpollutes.org.

2. For background information on these movements, see the Pacific Environment website http://lngpollutes.org.

3. LNG has been used in the United States since the 1940s, times of high demand for pipeline supplies. Its imports were initiated in the 1970s but in 2002 amounted to only 1 percent of consumption, although 50 percent of U.S. energy consumption is via natural gas and LNG import is projected to increase. In Japan, LNG supplies 90 percent of domestic gas. Today natural gas represents 50 percent of U.S. energy consumption. See P. Parfomak. *Liquefied Natural Gas (LNG) Infrastructure Security: Background and Issues for Congress* (Washington, DC: Congressional Research Service/Library of Congress, 2003).

4. D. Yergin and Michael Stoppard, "The Next Prize," *Foreign Affairs* 82, no. 6 (2003): 103; G. Bridge and A. Wood, "Geographies of Knowledge, Practices of Globalization: Learning from the Oil Exploration and Production Industry," *Area* 32, no. 2 (2005): 199–208; Gavin Bridge "Gas, and How to Get It," *Geoforum* 35 (2005): 395–397; Michael Klare, "The Geopolitics of Natural Gas," *The Nation*, January 23, 2006, available at http://www.thenation.com/article/geopolitics-natural-gas.

5. The now extensive literature on global political ecology includes N. Peluso, N. Watts, and M. Watts, *Violent Environments* (Ithaca, NY: Cornell University Press, 2001).

6. Robert Vitalis, *America's Kingdom: Mythmaking on the Saudi Oil Frontier.* (New York: Verso, 2009).

7. The Nigerian National Petroleum Corporation is the majority shareholder in the NLNG, but the construction and launch of both the Nigerian and the Mexican LNG plants were Shell projects. Minority shareholders in Nigeria are Total Gas (France) and ENI (Italy).

8. See Friends of the Earth, "Media Briefing: Gas Flaring in Nigeria," October 2004, available at http://www.foe.co.uk/resource/media_briefing/gasflaringinnigeria.pdf.

9. Ike Okonta, *When Citizens Revolt: Nigerian Elites, Big Oil and the Ogoni Struggle for Self-Determination* (Trenton, NJ: Africa World Press, 2008); E. Osaghae, "Managing Multiple Minority Problems in a Divided Society: The Nigerian Experience," *Journal of Modern African Studies* 36, no. 1 (1998): 1–24; M. Watts, "Resource Curse? Governmentality, Oil and Power in the Niger Delta, Nigeria," *Geopolitics* 9, no. 1 (2004): 50–80; E. Osaghae, "The Ogoni Uprising: Oil Politics, Minority Agitation and the Future of the Nigerian State," *African Affairs* 94, no. 375 (1995): 325–344.

10. For a discussion of this literature, see A. Mol, "Ecological Modernisation and Institutional Reflexivity: Environmental Reform in the Late Modern Age," *Environmental Politics* 5, no. 2 (1996): 302–323; and Riley E. Dunlap, Frederick H. Buttel, Peter Dickens, and August Gijswijt, *Sociological Theory and the Environment: Classical Foundations, Contemporary Insights* (Lanham, MD: Rowman and Littlefield, 2002). For a recent critique, see K. I. MacDonald, "The Devil Is in the (Bio)Diversity: Private Sector 'Engagement' and the Restructuring of Biodiversity Conservation," *Antipode* 42, no. 3 (2010): 513–550.

11. N. Castree, "The Nature of Produced Nature: Materiality and Knowledge Construction in Marxism," *Antipode* 27, no. 1 (1995): 12–48.

12. Michael Watts, "Collective Wish Images: Geographical Imaginaries and the Crisis of National Development," in *Human Geography Today*, ed. D. Massey, J. Allen, and P. Sarre, 85–108 (Boston: Polity Press, 1999); C. Ake, "Political Ethnicity and State-Building in Nigeria," in *Global Convulsions: Race, Ethnicity and Nationalism at the End of the Twentieth Century*, ed. Winston Van Horne (Albany: State University of New York Press, 1997), 299–314.

13. Jose Eduardo Beltran, *Petroleo y desarrollo: La politica petrolera en Tabasco* (Villahermosa, Mexico: Gobierno del Estado de Tabasco, 1988); Nancy Birdsall and Arvind Subramanian, "Saving Iraq from Its Oil," *Foreign Affairs* 83, no. 4 (2004), available at http://www.foreignaffairs.com/articles/59923/nancy-birdsall-and-arvind-subramanian/saving-iraq-from-its-oil.

14. Lorenzo Meyer, *Mexico and the United States in the Oil Controversy 1917–42* (Austin: University of Texas Press/El Colegio de Mexico, 1972); J. Brown, Jonathan Knight, and A. Knight, *The Mexican Petroleum Industry in the Twentieth Century* (Austin: University of Texas Press, 1992); Myrna Santiago, *The Ecology of Oil: Environment, Labor*

and the Mexican Revolution, 1900–1938. (Cambridge: Cambridge University Press, 2006); Judith Teichman, Policymaking in Mexico: From Boom to Crisis (Winchester, MA: Allen and Unwin, 1988); Lorenzo Meyer and I. Morales, Petróleo y nación: La política petrolera en México (1900–1987). (Mexico City: Fondo de Cultura Económica, 1990).

15. Initiated in 1985, the project was implemented in the 1990s. O. Omole and M. Eghre-Oghene, "The Economics of the Nigerian Liquefied Natural Gas Project," OPEC Review 23 (1999): 304–340.

16. For a critique of these projects, see http://carbontradewatch.org.

17. Nigeria's gas, extracted alongside oil, is flared because of the lack of processing infrastructure. The NLNG reports that 80 percent is flared, the highest rate in the world. In 2006 the U.S. EIA indicated that 43 percent was flared, stating that Nigeria accounted for about 20 percent of the world's total flared gas. "The [NLNG] facility is currently supplied from dedicated (non-associated) natural gas fields, but it is anticipated that, within a few years, half of the input natural gas will consist of associated (currently flared) natural gas from existing oil fields." U.S. Department of Energy, Nigeria Country Analysis Brief (Washington, DC: U.S. EIA, 2006), 6.

18. A. Zalik, "The Peace of the Graveyard: The Voluntary Principles on Security and Human Rights in the Niger Delta," in Global Regulation: Managing Crises after the Imperial Turn, ed. Libby Asassi, Kees vander Pijl, and Duncan Wigan, 111–127 (London: Palgrave, 2004); A. Zalik, "Labeling Oil, Contesting Governance: LegalOil.Com, the GMOU and Profiteering in the Niger Delta," in Violent Conflict in the Niger Delta, ed. Cyril Obi, Siri Camilla, and Aas Rustad, 184–199 (London: Zed, 2011).

19. David Harvey, The Limits of Capital (New York: Verso, 2006); B. Mommer, Global Oil and the Nation State (Oxford: Oxford University Press, 2002); J. W. Moore, "Environmental Crises and the Metabolic Rift in World-Historical Perspective," Organization and Environment 13, no. 2 (2000): 123–157.

20. Israel Rodriguez, "Llega el primer buque-tanque de GNL para regasificadora de Altamira," La Jornada, August 18, 2006, available at http://www.jornada.unam.mx/2006/08/18/index.php?section=economia&article=035n3eco.

21 Jonathan Brown, Oil and Revolution in Mexico (Berkeley: University of California Press, 1993); Nora Hamilton, The Limits of State Autonomy: Post-Revolutionary Mexico (Princeton, NJ: Princeton University Press, 1982).

22. Articles 27 and 123 deal with public ownership of land and resources and protection of labour, respectively.

23. David Shields, Pemex: Un futuro incierto (Mexico City: Editorial Planeta Mexicana, 2003).

24. A flood in 2007 left 80 percent of Tabasco's capital, Villahermosa, underwater, suggesting the negative outcomes of forced "modernization" of the wetlands. Fernando Tudela, La modernizacion forzada del tropico: El caso de Tabasco (Mexico City: UNRISD/Colegio de Mexico, 1989); Rodolfo Uribe Iniesta, La transicion entre el desarrollismo y la globalizacion: Ensamblando Tabasco (Cuernavaca, Mexico: Centro Regional de Investigaciones Multidisciplinarias, 2003); Ramón Martínez Bebaraje, Moisés Frutos Cortés, and Esther Solano Palacios, "El impacto social, productivo y ambiental de las actividades petroleras en el sureste Mexicano: Tabasco y Campeche (1970–2008)," presented at 13 Encuentro Nacional sobre Desarrollo Regional en México of the Asociación Mexicana de Ciencias para el Desarrollo Regional (AMECIDER), Aguascalientes, Mexico, October 27–31, 2008; S. Ridgeway, "Monoculture, Monopoly, and the Mexican Revolution: Tomás Garrido Canabal and the Standard Fruit Company in Tabasco (1920–1935)," Mexican Studies 17, no. 1 (2001): 143–169.

25. Lorenzo Bozada Robles, El subdesarrollo pesquero y acuicola del estado de Tabasco (Villahermosa, Mexico: Asociacion Ecologica Santo Tomas, 1999); A. Zalik, "Re-Regulating the Mexican Gulf" (working paper, Center for Latin American Studies, University of California, Berkeley, 2006).

26. Andes Manuel Lopez Obrador, Entre la historia y la esperanza: Corrupcion y lucha democratica en Tabasco (Mexico City: Grijalbo, 1995); Andrés Manuel López Obrador, La gran tentación: El petróleo de México (Mexico City: Grijalbo, 2008).

27. Statement by Bozada Robles in Joel Simon, "Mexico's Giant Polluter: Will Privatization Force Pemex to Clean up Its Act?" Pacific News Service, November 1, 1995.

28. Fabio Barbosa, *El petroleo en los Hoyos de Dona*, ed. Instituto de Investigaciones Economicas (Mexico City: Miguel Angel Porrua/UNAM, 2003).

29. Jaime Veloz, "Izquierda y frontera norte (apuntes para un programa)," *La Jornada*, October 14 2005; see also http://www.cnee-sur.net/portal/.

30. California Energy Commission 2010 West Coast proposed LNG facilities; see http://www.energy.ca.gov/. Three other projects in Northern Mexico were canceled because of public opposition, including the Chevron project discussed here and the proposed Marathon Oil and Conoco Philips Terminals, all in Baja, California.

31. See "Mexico LNG Proposals Face Political, PR Battles," *Oil and Gas Journal*, February 9, 2004, 27–28.

32. Richard Kuprewicz, Clifford Goudey, and Carl Weimer, *Public Safety and FERC's LNG Spin: What Citizens Aren't Being Told* (Bellingham, WA: Pipeline Safety Trust, 2005).

33. See P. Parfomak, *Liquefied Natural Gas (LNG) Infrastructure Security: Background and Issues for Congress* (Washington, DC: Congressional Research Service/Library of Congress, 2003).

34. The FERC argues that the relative safety of LNG ships versus other tankers results from "double-hulled" vessels less likely to spill than those that normally transport crude oil. In response, the Pipeline Safety Trust notes that these "newer, economical designs" involve "thin stainless alloy backed with plywood and insulated with foam. In many of the ships this foam is flammable" (Kuprewicz, Goudey, and Weimer, *Public Safety and FERC's LNG Spin*, 5).

35. See Kuprewicz, Goudey, and Weimer, *Public Safety and FERC's LNG Spin*, 3.

36. (Unburned) methane emissions are weighted at four times CO_2 as a greenhouse gas.

37. Greenpeace Mexico, "With Liquefied Natural Gas Plant, Mexico Accepts Risks that the U.S. rejects," press release, May 24, 2004 (translated from Spanish).

38. In a 2004 briefing, a business source suggested that Mexican congressional opposition to the Chevron Islas Coronado project, twenty miles off shore, was based on the argument that "foreign multinational companies will end up having control of Mexican sovereign waters." Haynes and Boone LLP, "Mexico's Gas Markets," HG.org, August 16, 2004, available at http://www.hg.org/articles/article_410.html.

39. This was initially a Shell project but is now executed by Sempra without Shell's "public presence," although Shell had conducted initial community meetings in 2003. Personal interviews, San Diego and Tijuana, 2005.

40. Shell has sold bulk petrochemicals in Mexico since 1954 but, as a foreign company, is prohibited from advertising.

41. In an interview with the author (2004), a senior representative described Shell as the country's "most ambitious" foreign operator.

42. Of note is that East Coast LNG projects have also been canceled because of protests, including one in Rhode Island.

43. W. Freudenburg and R. Gramling, *Oil in Troubled Waters: Perceptions, Politics, and the Battle over Offshore Drilling* (Albany: SUNY Press, 1994).

44. See, for instance, http://carbontradewatch.org.

45. Elmar Altvater, "The Social and Natural Environment of Fossil Capitalism," in *Coming to Terms with Nature: Socialist Register 2007*, ed. Leo Panitch and Colin Leys (New York: Monthly Review Press, 2007).

7

New Hazards and Old Disease

Lead Contamination and the Uruguayan Battery Industry

Daniel E. Renfrew

The Old and New Hazards of Lead

A versatile heavy metal, lead has been mined and used by humans for over six thousand years, and its toxic effects were identified in writing almost twenty-five hundred years ago.[1] Though one of the world's oldest known occupational and environmental diseases, lead poisoning remained a mostly silent epidemic in Uruguay until 2001, when a neighbors group responded to the realization that perhaps hundreds of children of Montevideo's La Teja working-class neighborhood had been poisoned. The group crystallized into the nation's largest-ever environmental movement, the Live without Lead Commission (Comisión Vivir sin Plomo, CVSP), sounding the alarm of lead poisoning through the mass media. Responding to popular pressure, the state formed an inter-institutional commission that directed policy interventions, including opening the nation's first pediatric lead poisoning clinic, conducting limited environmental and epidemiological studies, and initiating housing relocation for families living in highly contaminated squatter settlements. Studies identified lead as a multisource pollutant affecting Montevideo and other cities, from industrial factories, landfills, automotive emissions, cottage industries, and various consumer products. In a period of several months, lead poisoning had been collectively redefined from an obscure occupational hazard into a ubiquitous pediatric and environmental disease.

From the early days of the issue, the principal media, governmental, and activist focus was on lead poisoning as a pediatric illness, affecting children of the poor neighborhoods and squatter settlements of western Montevideo. The first case of lead poisoning was identified by a pediatrician examining a La Teja child with severe anemia and bone and joint pain. Following this first diagnosis, concerned parents in the neighborhood identified similar symptoms in their own children, and the alarm spread throughout the area. The pediatric focus also responded in part to the fact that children are more susceptible than adults to the neurological and developmental damages of lead poisoning, even at low levels of exposure. Because children serve as potent symbols of innocence and vulnerability, they were in this way "objectified" by activists, officials, and the media alike in the ensuing political battles over regulation and remediation efforts. However, often lost in the public debates about lead was the story of Uruguayan workers, who for decades had toiled in lead industries and suffered the noxious effects of occupational exposure.

Under a paternalistic system of factory control, within a limited national tradition of environmental, occupational, or public health, the dangers of lead for these workers, as for Uruguayans in general, had been and remained hidden from view. Though officials, activists, and scientists often understood the Uruguayan lead poisoning epidemic as having somehow "fallen from the sky," there had been growing calls for attention to the hazards of lead exposure, not just internationally but in Uruguay itself. And lead had been a feature of the Uruguayan environment for still longer, with industrial workers having for many years confronted it as an occupational hazard.[2]

Analyzing Uruguayan lead contamination through the lens of battery production offers a novel avenue into this longer history of Uruguayans' contentions with lead. It situates the epidemic of 2001 at a rich intersection, not of just past with present but of the domestic with the transnational and of a formal with an informal economy. In many ways the epidemic was part of the socio-environmental fallout of, at once, mid-twentieth-century nationalist development practices and late-twentieth-century neoliberal transformations. Prevailing work on the social and environmental repercussions of neoliberal globalization on developing countries often highlights the negative and unidirectional impacts of multinational corporations and "toxic imperialism" on local populations. This chapter instead analyzes a "neoliberal" disease rooted in both "new" and "old" processes of environmental contamination, with a complex articulation at work between national and transnational modes of capital, formal and informal labor practices, reconfigured forms of social vulnerability, and new movements for social change. It parallels Henry's argument in this volume that a broad societal "environmental turn" served to spark and channel public interest in occupational disease, redefining the problem of industrial hazards while reinvigorating movements for workplace safety. The present case also demonstrates that the transformative power of environmental movements is not a phenomenon confined to the developed Global North, though in the Global South this form of environmentalism may arise to contend with a very different set of industrial issues.

The present chapter is divided into three sections. The first analyzes battery production during the mid-twentieth century, which was dominated by Import Substitution Industrialization (ISI), a state-led development strategy that attempted to reduce dependency on foreign imports by substituting them with domestically produced consumer products. The resulting battery industry fostered dismal working conditions and widespread environmental contamination that went under-recognized. The second section looks at the international as well as domestic transformations associated with neoliberalism and their consequences for the battery industry and its lead exposures. As a political economic theory promoting free-market-oriented development, mandating the radical restructuring of the Uruguayan state and its productive system through Structural Adjustment Programs (SAPs), neoliberalism introduced foundations for the material intensification of lead contamination and exposure risk. Multinational corporations made their entrance into, among other places, the Uruguayan battery industry. As the informal economy and illicit forms of production and trade also burgeoned, informal battery-smelting enterprises grew apace. The resulting contamination, revealed in 2001, was what Uruguay's new environmental movement arose to address. The chapter concludes with a discussion of this new environmentalism in relation to the dilemmas faced by workers caught between occupational and socio-environmental security, and the strategies workers and activists have employed in transcending this apparent dichotomy.

"A Miniature Auschwitz": ISI–Period Battery Production

The Import Substitution Industrialization (ISI) period in most of Latin America followed the global economic depression of the 1930s. In the ISI model, economies were restructured toward state-led, inward-oriented industrialization for the provisioning of domestic consumer markets.[3] The goal was to promote economic sovereignty and reduce dependency on the vicissitudes of powerful economies to the North. Because of high tariffs on imported goods and machinery, domestic industries turned to innovative and often makeshift solutions in an attempt to cover all phases of the production process. The storage battery industry was one of the pioneers of ISI-modeled production in Uruguay.

Decades of storage battery production and the dumping of lead acid battery waste from the Radesca S.A. factory have produced some of the gravest known cases of lead contamination in Montevideo. The health of the Radesca workers and their families has been devastated, and the environmental conditions around the factory, in the surrounding community of Peñarol, and along the areas where most of the waste was dumped, including an extensive shantytown bordering the Miguelete River, are abysmal. Longtime Radesca worker Enebé Linardi smelted lead for two decades. He was also placed in charge of dumping lead waste at various locations in Montevideo, leading ultimately to an environmental disaster. Though he has survived to an older age, he admitted, "At 76 years I've buried a lot of friends much younger than me . . . from cancer [of] the liver . . . and the men just keep dying."

When Mr. Linardi joined Radesca, he went, as he said, "straight to the oven." During the 1960s, in Uruguay's first attempt at domestic battery production, the Radesca family developed a pioneering smelting and lead recovery system with the help of the Asturian González brothers, owners of a Montevideo smelting facility. In part because of the smelter's "homemade" and improvised character, the workers who ran it faced grave occupational hazards that they only partially understood.

To break up the batteries and retrieve the lead, the workers used plant-made axes. By hand they would dump the contents into a large open oven to be melted down. The lead then went through a two-step process of purification. After the first round, the lead-laced tailings (*escoria*) that floated to the top were simply discarded and later dumped at various sites around Montevideo or on the plant grounds, or they were sold as landfill. The "cleaner" substance would then be resmelted, with the tailings again discarded, until the lead became sufficiently pure to use in assembling new storage batteries.

When the plant needed pure (or soft) lead oxide, it would resort to a separate oven and a "froth flotation" process,[4] where caustic soda was used as an agent to separate the antimony from the lead. Everything was performed by hand in the first years. When a truck was bought to dump the lead mixtures into the ovens, explained Mr. Linardi, "a large cloud of [lead] oxide" would fill the air. He and his co-workers would stand next to the open oven, pushing the lead in with long iron rods in order for it to melt uniformly. The workers never used protective facial masks, and hand protection in the early years consisted of rubber mittens made at the plant itself.

The workers were given half a liter of milk per four-hour shift, ostensibly to counter the negative health effects of lead exposure. When they saw the company doctor, he usually assured them that everything was fine. "He was a son of a bitch," Mr. Linardi concluded bitterly. The workers were examined for their health card every two years, though Mr. Linardi did not remember any other times that he was tested for anything. He said that workers never saw the results of health exams, but once in a while they were sent to the social security hospital for days of "de-intoxication." Mr. Linardi himself was hospitalized once, though it was never explained what was wrong with him. Workers at the time could rarely speak out against these practices, as the paternalistic system of factory control combined with the repressive context of Uruguay's military dictatorship (1973–1985), turned labor activism into a matter of life and death.

Mr. Linardi did not realize the true dangers of lead exposure until the La Teja lead contamination discoveries:

> The truth is that it was then when I began to find out that [lead contamination] is truly bad. Because I could see the factory, the filth of the factory, yes. But I've worked in other filthy factories too. The

NEW HAZARDS AND OLD DISEASE / 103

pig slaughterhouse for instance. . . . I'd come out much filthier from the slaughterhouse than from [Radesca]. I was used to working in all kinds of places. I didn't know it was as dangerous to health as it actually was.

The Radesca company employed a strategy of worker control through the direct and selective recruiting of employees. Mr. Linardi said that he could not think of another worker like himself who was from Montevideo. He was offered the job through the connections of a cousin, but all of the other workers came from remote areas of the Uruguayan countryside. They were offered low-cost housing near the factory and were taken care of paternalistically. Though Mr. Linardi insisted that he was "too communist," he was nevertheless a loyal worker who won the trust of the Radesca management. His loyalty was rewarded with delivery jobs, usually between Montevideo and the small company farm (*chacra*) in the countryside, where managers went to relax. The most infamous tasks Mr. Linardi was asked to perform, however, were the dumpings of lead tailings and other waste around various parts of Montevideo. One of the primary sites was along the Miguelete River, where squatter settlements sprang up years later.

Mr. Linardi said that factories from all over Montevideo dumped in this and other areas: "It wasn't just us. . . . I remember a chocolate factory [would too], and the kids would go there to pick out chocolate." The most toxic dumping spot, however, was the factory itself. Mr. Linardi said that there was already a huge pile of lead waste when he entered the factory, and it grew exponentially during his twenty years there. The pile, he emphasized, was "bigger than this house."

Workers and neighbors were not the only ones to suffer from the factory's contaminating practices. José Radesca is the nephew of the original factory owners. His father was the foreman there, and Mr. Radesca was essentially born and raised within the factory. In an interview, he claimed that he could identify a period during his youth when he began his intellectual and physical decline, coinciding with the opening of the lead smelter and chimney. The opening of the smelter signaled the beginning of in-house operation of virtually every phase of the battery production process. Mr. Radesca referred, dramatically, to his childhood home as a "miniature Auschwitz."

As a child, Mr. Radesca and his friends played marbles with homemade balls of lead. He said that he always had a sweet taste in his mouth, which he would neutralize by chewing asphalt or natural rubber. He showed me pictures of the early days of the factory, with plush gardens, fruit trees, grape vines, and thick wooded areas. A picture taken twenty years later depicts a desolate and defoliated landscape. Mr. Radesca said that he could not keep pets because either they would die or the cats would "attack" him. He claimed that his mother used to raise chickens until they literally began dropping dead on the ground, promptly devoured by pigs.

The widespread media and political attention given to lead in 2001 catalyzed Mr. Radesca and Mr. Linardi to organize surviving workers and families through the creation of an NGO and a "clearinghouse" of lead-related information, as well as through the filing of a lawsuit for health and environmental damages. "If these people [of La Teja] have lead, then we're the kings of lead," Mr. Radesca stated. Their efforts never gained much traction, however, in part because of inexperience in collective organizing following years of paternalistic factory control and in part because of the burnout and lack of will to fight of several of the workers and widows. The former workers also faced the negligible precedence of environmental and occupational health litigation in Uruguay. Public officials, meanwhile, remained largely indifferent to their suffering.

"Greening" Uruguay: Lead Poisoning as a Neoliberal Disease

At the time of the 2001 lead discoveries, Uruguay was reeling from decades of economic decline, the progressive dismantling of a once-strong welfare state, and the socio-spatial fracturing of a country once lauded as the democratic and prosperous "Switzerland of South America." The economic recession that began in 1999 led to a dramatic increase in poverty and reached its peak in 2002, fueling the fall from grace of the Colorado Party that had ruled for most of Uruguay's modern history and that had first implemented the advanced social democratic reforms that distinguished Uruguay in the region.[5]

The Colorados had throughout the early to mid-twentieth century forged Uruguay's system of Keynesian welfare capitalism. The system began stagnating in the late 1950s, coinciding with the eclipse of the ISI model, as was the case throughout most of Latin America. Industrialization during the ISI period was still dependent on foreign capital inputs, fueling trade deficits exacerbated by the influx of petrodollars in the 1970s and leading to the regional debt crisis and the hyperinflation of the 1980s, known as Latin America's "lost decade" of development.[6]

Latin America's debt crisis and its dependence on newly restricted private bank credits led the economies of the region to turn to the IMF and the World Bank for desperately needed loans. Structural Adjustment Programs (SAPs) were imposed as loan conditions, introducing a period of neoliberal economic policies. Under neoliberalism, the state serves as guarantor of the conditions making market freedoms possible, most often through deregulation and the privatization of former state-run enterprises or services. Neoliberal economic restructuring mandated, among other measures, the reduction of the state's role in social spending, public-sector employment, and public subsidies, as well as wage restrictions and labor "flexibility" and tariff reductions to allow foreign imports.[7]

The discovery of lead contamination in Uruguay and its framing as an urgent public health issue exemplifies the creative destruction of neoliberal globalization. Following the insular period of military dictatorship and coinciding with the international growth of an environmental regime of conservation and regulation, new environmental laws and constitutional reforms during the 1990s set up a legal framework for environmental policy and regulation.[8] New Uruguayan environmentalist movements emerged during the 1980s and 1990s, mostly organized around issues of urban industrial pollution. Environmental paradigms in science and medicine, furthermore, slowly began to gain a foothold through international academic exchanges in universities emerging from dictatorial repression. This "greening" of Uruguayan society was largely a product of neoliberalism's generative role in opening up political, institutional, and ideological spaces for recognition of and engagement with environmental problems. Neoliberal globalization, in this way, created possibilities for the recognition of lead as an occupational and environmental hazard, as an object of scientific and medical analysis and of bureaucratic interventions, and as a basis for rights talk and political claims.

The new environmentalism, on the other hand, also responded to newly configured environmental problems and challenges produced by the neoliberal economic system itself. Neoliberalism brought about sharp changes that introduced new pathways for and sources of lead exposure in Uruguay.[9] Reduced tariffs and economic restructuring during the late 1980s opened up the economy to an influx of imported consumer goods, as well as to new export industries and manufacturing technologies, some of which intensified lead exposure. During the 1990s, new industries such as plastics and electronics provoked an increase in the overall use of lead.[10] A boom in new automobile sales in the 1990s increased urban vehicular traffic and the emission of leaded gasoline. Decades of leaded gasoline use (banned only in 2004), in addition to other consumer and infrastructure sources such as lead paints and lead water pipes, significantly contributed to the urban population's long-term lead exposure. Though epidemiological studies have been limited, it is likely that the urban population had a baseline blood lead level in the 1990s and early 2000s that approximated the World Health Organization (WHO) and the Centers for Disease Control (CDC) threshold for lead poisoning.[11]

Since the late 1980s, growing unemployment and poverty and a sharp reduction in housing credits have forced unprecedented numbers of people out of formal housing arrangements in the city center and into makeshift squatter settlements in the urban peripheries. These settlements (or *asentamientos*, as they are called in Uruguay) have experienced explosive growth since the 1999 recession. Many of them were built on marginal and contaminated lands, including the areas in which Mr. Linardi had dumped lead on behalf of the Radesca company. Finally, the recent growth of the informal economy has included highly contaminating cottage industries. Informal battery and metals recycling, as well as "cable burning," or the smelting of stolen electrical and telephone cables to extract and sell their copper and lead, is often conducted in residential areas and lots, thereby endangering families and communities.

Neoliberal restructuring and socioeconomic decline in Uruguay, then, has resulted in both new and intensified lead exposure for the general population, with children, pregnant women, and the poor facing heightened and unequal risk and vulnerability. The declining quality of health care and services to low-income families increases the risk for vulnerable subpopulations for which poverty and malnutrition have conditioned and limited their ability to mitigate the impacts of toxic exposure.[12] The increased material exposure and social vulnerability to lead contamination have combined with a new environmental vision that has allowed workers and grassroots and institutional actors to recognize lead's hazards.

"Cemeteries of Scrap": Battery Production and the New Environmentalism

Along with gasoline combustion, the production, disposal, and recycling of storage batteries were the most prevalent sources of lead contamination in Uruguay, according to a 2002 parliamentary report.[13] Between 800,000 and 1,000,000 kilos of lead were handled through battery recycling each year, the report states, most of which ended up as contraband smuggled to Brazil.[14] Figures from 2006 indicate that Brazil at the time acquired most of its lead through domestic and imported recycled sources, and up to 80 percent of its own storage batteries were recycled.[15] These figures reflect formal production, however, with the net worth of contraband smuggling not factored into the estimates. Brazil is a party to the 1989 Basel Convention on the Transboundary Movement of Hazardous Wastes and its 1994 amendment banning the export of hazardous waste for the purpose of recycling. Moreover, it has instituted a national ban on lead acid battery imports. A Greenpeace investigation in 1997, however, revealed that Brazil had illegally imported 5,000 tons of used lead acid batteries from the United States from January to June of that year.[16] Uruguay also ratified the Basel Convention, but enforcement remains a major issue in that country, despite the expressed knowledge of high-level authorities concerning the ongoing illicit trade. Uruguayan Environment Ministry Director Andrés Saizar expressed to me in a 2005 interview, for instance, that up to 80 percent of Uruguayan used car batteries at the time were being sold as contraband to Rio Grande do Sul state in Brazil. An unknown number were recycled in Uruguay itself, with highly toxic lead oxide waste dumped illegally across the territory and the metals resold either domestically or internationally.

"Jorge," a worker at a battery manufacturing plant that subcontracts to a multinational corporation, explained that dealers request that customers exchange their old batteries when purchasing new ones. At his factory, the old batteries are piled high in a warehouse. "Every once in a while," said Jorge, "some trucks come and take the batteries away." Given the absence of a battery-recycling system in Uruguay, Jorge is certain that most of these batteries are sold to dealers in Brazil, despite laws banning the practice.[17] Battery contraband, in sum, is a practice sanctioned by the directors of a multinational company's subcontractor, widely acknowledged by local officials, and an open secret to everyone involved in the business.

Workers found themselves in a difficult position in early-twenty-first-century crisis-hit Uruguay. When they spoke out against unsafe or unhealthy working and environmental conditions, they faced the threat of being fired. While worker repression is not new to Uruguay, the relative position of organized labor vis-à-vis management weakened under the neoliberal trends of outsourcing and part-time hiring.[18] As one oil worker said, workers are forced to confront the realization that "if I work I get contaminated," but "I need to work."

Unionization proved difficult at small factories, particularly under the neoliberal mandates of a "flexible" labor force. Workers were often hired for less than the three-month period necessary to obtain formal legal status and rights. They were then fired and left with the burden of occupational disease. One battery worker in 2004 told me about some of the shiftiness involved in lead controls at the revamped Radesca factory. Echoing the practices of ISI-period Radesca, he said that workers were still given lead examinations only once a year. They were typically scheduled for Mondays, after workers had had an entire weekend for their bodies to eliminate toxins. The workers never saw the results of the tests, and simply got a "pass" or "fail" as fit for work. Another worker, "Juan José," noted all of the informal metals smelting conducted in Montevideo. He said that sometimes, when metallurgic or battery workers were laid off, they applied their metals-working skills to cable burning and lead smelting for the contraband economy so they could "put food on their families' tables."

The Fanaesa battery factory in Rosario, Colonia Department, operated for almost twenty years before shutting down in 2002, leaving an environmental and health disaster in its wake. The local environmental group Modear denounced the premature deaths of twenty-four Fanaesa workers because of deplorable work conditions and considered the city of Rosario a "time bomb" of environmental contamination.[19] None of the Fanaesa workers passed sixty-five years of age, and, according to one workers' leader, the average life expectancy reached only fifty-five years.

Industrial hazards and contamination in twenty-first-century Uruguay have been increasingly contested by the grassroots environmental movement. Groups like the CVSP and Modear have brought together current and former industrial workers, families, citizens, and professionals to confront the dual assault on decent jobs and a safe and clean urban environment. The collective anxiety provoked by the precariousness of life under neoliberal times both fuels engagement in these social movements and enables widespread public support and sympathy. These politically savvy groups have proven adept at working both against and within the political system and at drawing commercial and community media exposure and public interest. They organize protests, hold public informational meetings, engage in media outreach, and host or participate in "social encounters" that draw together a broad range of social, political, and academic actors to reflect upon experiences of lead contamination and to engage in political strategizing.

The language and practice of environmentalism has historically been negligible within Uruguayan working-class ideology and militancy, as across much of the developing world. Nevertheless, the lead issue dovetails with a broader consciousness and valorization of the environment, presenting new possibilities for an integration of working and environmental concerns, and of workplace and community health.

In a speech at a 2001 May Day labor rally, longtime industrial worker and CVSP leader Carlos Pilo stated, "We are fed up that the neighborhoods of the poorest become garbage dumps, where no road is ever constructed or paved, or where they never clean a gutter." The punishment of being poor, Pilo continued, is "contamination, the lack of sanitation, of water." The squatter settlements proliferate each day across Montevideo, said Pilo, who referred to the "Men and women who are forgetting, who are made to forget, what it was to work." Neoliberal policies, he concluded, are "converting the factories into cemeteries of scrap."[20]

Pilo's speech linked neoliberal policies, deindustrialization, poverty, and the loss of jobs and decent working conditions to the degradation of the urban environment and its health consequences. The health of the community is compromised by multiple attacks, from job insecurity and environmental contamination, and by the weakened ability to withstand environmental toxins because of poverty and its associated suffering. Political mobilization against lead poisoning has made possible a new awareness of broader environmental problems and workplace and community health issues. In this way, environmental activism has enabled and empowered factory workers to revisit the effects of both previous and ongoing exposures to workplace lead and other industrial hazards.

Conclusion

The documented 2,500-year global history of lead poisoning is continuously made and remade, forgotten and reinvented.[21] Lead contamination in the contemporary world is facilitated by the complex global articulation of production and consumption practices under neoliberal globalization, including the demands for cheap labor and cheap commodities; the "maquiladora" model of export-led growth; the driving down of wages; the erosion of labor, health, and environmental conditions; and the intensification of social vulnerabilities. A comprehensive understanding of lead poisoning (and, indeed, of environmental toxins generally), should take into account the multiplicity of sources in both the Global North and the Global South, through both "legacy" pollutants and ongoing forms of contamination. In particular, this approach necessitates careful attention to the complicit and uneven webs of power, knowledge, and political economy linking South to North, with similar patterns of vulnerability structuring lead poisoning risk throughout the world.

In twenty-first-century Uruguay, the pollution of both factories and informal labor practices has served as a powerful metaphor of betrayal and decline, symbolizing the loss of a proud working-class tradition and the once protective and "benevolent" Uruguayan state. As the lead issue coincided with the peak of the economic crisis, it added a potent symbolic dimension to this struggle. The intensification of long-term practices of industrial pollution and environmental degradation suddenly became unacceptable, a crime to society, its children, and its workers. A result of both objective changes in exposure vectors and rates, and in part linked to the greening of Uruguayan society, occupational and environmental hazards took on a public face, becoming collectively visible for the first time.

Lead contamination in Uruguay became a vector and a means to denounce both previous and ongoing forms of industrial hazard. Though lead poisoning there is still largely defined as either a pediatric illness or a disease of poverty, workers and activists have been able to connect occupational, pediatric, and environmental perspectives, presenting lead contamination anew as a generalized public health hazard. Workers have reevaluated their individual afflictions by forging meaningful alliances with community and environmental health activists, coming to understand lead poisoning as a form of "social suffering."[22] In this way workers have taken important steps towards denaturalizing their contaminated and objectified condition, using their bodies as "sites of resistance" and as a means of subjective empowerment.[23] They do so, however, while facing continued uncertainty and precariousness in labor and housing. What is demonstrated in this case, at the very least, is a blueprint of possibility for innovative alliances and a reinvigorated movement for workplace and environmental justice.

NOTES

Acknowledgments: This research was funded by the International Institute for Education's Fulbright Program, the Wenner-Gren Foundation for Anthropological Research, and a Rosa Colecchio Dissertation Enhancement award from Binghamton University, State University of New York. I am grateful for the editorial direction and insightful comments of Chris Sellers on previous drafts and would also like to thank Jo Melling and participants of the "Dangerous Trade" conference for feedback on earlier manifestations of this work. A modified version of this paper was presented as part of the Social Sciences Speakers Series at the University of Wisconsin-Stout. Many thanks to Tom Pearson and the UW-Stout Department of Social Sciences. Any and all remaining errors are my sole responsibility.

1. Sven Hernberg, "Lead Poisoning in a Historical Perspective," *American Journal of Industrial Medicine* 38 (2000): 244.

2. There were at least two community outbreaks of lead poisoning in Uruguay during the 1990s and a handful of published clinical pediatric and occupational cases prior to 2001. Several international agencies, including the United Nations Environmental Programme, the United Nations Development Programme, UNICEF, and the World Bank, made international calls for the elimination or reduction of lead hazards and the mitigation of childhood lead poisoning during the 1980s and 1990s. In 1992, the Uruguayan government's environmental report, jointly issued with the Organization of American States and the Inter-American Development Bank, warned of future environmental and health hazards associated with urban pollution, including lead exposure from automotive emissions, paints, and water pipes. OPP-OEA-BID, *Uruguay:Estudio ambiental nacional* (Montevideo, Uruguay: OPP-OEA-BID, 1992). These warnings failed to galvanize public or media attention, however, evidenced by the fact that only eight articles related to lead contamination or poisoning appeared in the Uruguayan print media during the decade of the 1990s, according to a

Parliamentary study. Ramón Legnani, *En Uruguay con plomo en tu cuerpo: Fundamentos para efectuar determinación sistemática de niveles de plomo en sangre niños, embarazadas y trabajadores* (Montevideo, Uruguay: Cámara de Diputados, República Oriental del Uruguay: Imprenta La Canasta, 2002), 10–11.

3. William L. Canak, ed., *Lost Promises: Debt, Austerity, and Development in Latin America* (Boulder, CO: Westview Press, 1989); Thomas Perrault and Patrick Martin, "Geographies of Neoliberalism in Latin America," *Environment and Planning* A37 (2005): 191–201.

4. On froth flotation, see Bruce Lanphear, Paul Succop, Sandra Roda, and Gerry Heningsen, "The Effect of Soil Abatement on Blood Lead Levels in Children Living near a Former Smelting and Milling Operation," *Public Health Reports* 118 (2003): 83–92.

5. Despite being the founders of Uruguay's modern welfare state, the Colorado Party (in coalition with the Blanco Party) openly embraced neoliberal economics by the 1990s. The center-left Frente Amplio (FA) coalition gained national power in 2004 for the first time, ending over a century of two-party rule. The FA ran on a largely anti-neoliberal platform and during the 1990s repeatedly opposed privatization measures, backing several popular referenda and plebiscites against neoliberalism. See Carlos Santos, Sebastián Valdomir, Verónica Iglesias, and Daniel Renfrew, *Aguas en movimiento: La resistencia a la privatización del agua en Uruguay* (Montevideo, Uruguay: Ediciones de la Canilla, 2006).

6. Canak, *Lost Promises*; John Gledhill, *Neoliberalism, Transnationalism and Rural Poverty: A Case Study of Michoacán, Mexico* (Boulder, CO: Westview Press, 1995).

7. Marc Edelman, *Peasants against Globalization: Rural Social Movements in Costa Rica* (Stanford, CA: Stanford University Press, 1999), 83–84; Sarah Radcliffe, "Neoliberalism as We Know It, but Not in The Conditions of Its Own Choosing: A Commentary," *Environment and Planning* A37 (2005): 323–329; Daniel Renfrew, "In the Margins of Contamination: Lead Poisoning and the Production of Neoliberal Nature in Uruguay," *Journal of Political Ecology* 16 (2009): 87–103.

8. Renfrew, "In the Margins."

9. An overview of the increase in urban lead exposure in Uruguay is also discussed in Renfrew, "In the Margins."

10. Sindicato Médico del Uruguay (SMU), *Contaminación por plomo: Informe elaborada por la Comisión de Salud Ocupacional Sindicato Médico del Uruguay* (Montevideo, Uruguay: SMU, 2001), 2.

11. The Centers for Disease Control (CDC) lead poisoning "action" threshold since 1991 has been 10 µg/dl (micrograms of lead per deciliter of blood). A recent study (A. Z. Cousillas, N. Mañay, L. Pereira, C. Alvarez, and Z. Coppes, "Evaluation of Lead Exposure in Uruguayan Children," *Environmental Contamination and Toxicology* 75 (2005): 629–636) indicates an average blood lead level of 9.4 µg/dl in "uncontaminated" zones and 11.8 µg/dl for "contaminated" areas of Montevideo, with 30 percent and 59 percent of children under fifteen years of age in each respective area exceeding 10 µg/dl. The most comprehensive toxicological study in Uruguay was conducted in La Teja in 2001. Of 2,700 children tested for lead, 65 percent exceeded 10 µg/dl, with 7.6 percent over 20 µg/dl (Virginia Matos, "El caso de la contaminación por plomo," in *Políticas ambientales en Uruguay*, ed. Eduardo Gudynas [Montevideo, Uruguay: Coscoroba, 2001], 147). By 2004, over 700 children with blood lead levels over 20 µg/dl were being treated at the national lead poisoning clinic. The highest recorded levels of pediatric lead poisoning in Uruguay included several cases falling in the range of 60 to 70 µg/dl (Dr. Elena Queirolo, personal communication).

12. For example, a malnourished child who does not ingest adequate amounts of iron and calcium will absorb lead more quickly, and the heavy metal eventually replaces calcium in the bones. It is for this reason that children with severe lead poisoning in Uruguay are given baskets of fortified food.

13. Legnani, *En Uruguay*, 13.

14. Ibid., 14.

15. International Lead and Zinc Study Group (ILZSG), "Lead and Zinc Statistics," available at http://www.ilzsg.org/static/statistics.aspx?from=1.

16. Greenpeace, "U.S. Exports of Lead Acid Batteries Poisoning Brazil," August 4, 1997, available at http://archive.greenpeace.org/majordomo/index-press-releases/1997/msg00276.html.

17. In 2003 President Batlle passed a decree (373/003) for the regulation and recycling of car batteries, but it has yet to be implemented or enforced.

18. See Daniel Olesker, *Crecimiento y exclusión: Nacimiento, consolidación y crisis del modelo de acumulación capitalista en Uruguay (1968-2000)* (Montevideo, Uruguay: Ediciones Trilce, 2001).

19. "Ecologistas alertaron al gobierno por contaminación con plomo en Rosario," *La República*, October 21, 2002, available at http://www.larepublica.com.uy/comunidad/95300-ecologistas-alertaron-al-gobierno-por-contaminacion-con-plomo-en-rosario.

20. "Uruguay: La Marcha histórica de los barrios obreros Cerro-La Teja," *Red-Libertaria*, May 6, 2001, available at http://www.red-libertaria.net/noticias/modules.php?name=News&file=article&sid=560.

21. Didier Fassin and Anne-Jeane Naudé, "Plumbism Reinvented: Childhood Lead Poisoning in France, 1985–1990," *American Journal of Public Health* 94 (2004): 1854–1863.

22. Arthur Kleinman, Veena Das, and Margaret Lock, eds., *Social Suffering* (Berkeley: University of California Press, 1997).

23. Ana Baron and Eileen Boris, "'The Body' as a Useful Category for Working-Class History," *Labor: Studies in Working-Class History of the Americas* 4 (2007): 23–43.

New Knowledge and Coalitions

8

Objective Collectives?

Transnationalism and "Invisible Colleges"
in Occupational and Environmental Health from
Collis to Selikoff

JOSEPH MELLING AND CHRISTOPHER SELLERS

> *It was a guy named Irving J. Selikoff who first told*
> *me that occupational health is an inherently conflic-*
> *tual field—smile—and unwittingly you have put your*
> *finger on a tender spot.*
>
> J.C.A. DAVIES TO IRVING SELIKOFF, JUNE 7, 1989

In 1978 the New York Academy of Sciences listened to one of its distinguished members, Irving Selikoff, explain how he and his peers had recently achieved a deeper understanding of diseases caused by asbestos. New scientific research into this toxic mineral and its health hazards had yielded advances that were, in Selikoff's view, the fruits of collective rather than individual genius. The formation of an "invisible college" of experts had enabled hundreds of scientists to communicate, integrate, and disseminate key information, establishing the study of asbestos as an "active special area in science."[1] Those productive personal interchanges, outside the walls of a single academic institution, had provided a powerful social motor for scientific innovation. In speaking of an "invisible college," Selikoff supplemented a long and distinguished tradition of practitioners offering a historical context for his analysis of workplace and environmental health. But he did so in a manner peculiar to his own time and his own place. We have borrowed the term "invisible college," from Robert Boyle's celebrated description of England's early Royal Society, so recently resuscitated among American sociologists of science.[2] Selikoff's appropriation suggested a fortuitous match between the practices, preferences, and rivalries that prevailed in a transatlantic field of occupational and environmental health during the 1960s and 1970s, and in the American sociology of science. But it also suggested something more. It pointed to a generational shift in the way some experts in this field, their societies' most influential arbiters of environmental health realities, thought and talked about knowing.

In drawing on contemporary sociological discourse so reflexively, Selikoff and his collaborator E. Hammond were not just seeking to explain and validate their own enterprises; they were also prescribing a new standard of scientific professionalism. In deliberate contrast to the professionals who had long claimed jurisdiction over industrial hazards, which in the United States meant an entire generation of "industrial hygienists," they proposed to link technical objectivity with more explicitly social thinking as well as new notions of responsibility. In helping to build an "invisible college" of like-minded scientists during the previous decade and earlier, Selikoff, Hammond, and their colleagues marshaled allies beyond the United States, particularly in the United Kingdom. This essay seeks to recount this passage of interlinked British, American, and other experts from one generation of socially and publicly engaged investigators to another. Starting in the 1890s, movements arose to establish a scientific understanding of dangerous trades that crossed national boundaries, as the essays by Carter and Melling and Blanc in this volume indicate.[3] Leading figures in this earlier generation of transnational experts and publicists included gifted bureaucrats such as Thomas Legge and Edgar Collis, who matched American state- and university-based authorities such as Alice Hamilton and David Edsall. Conscious of their membership in a cross-national enterprise, these experts forged a standard of objectivity conceived not just as technical but as explicitly social, drawing upon a distinctive contemporary vocabulary of social as well as medical science.

The historical impacts of such groups have varied across time and place, and have remained dependent on the changing receptiveness as well as understanding of the experts themselves. Social historians of labor have emphasized the role of workers, community groups, and other nonexpert citizens in building knowledge and effecting change concerning industrial hazards.[4] But the focus on nonexpert mobilizations alone may obscure a long-term transition, over the middle of the twentieth century, in the expert identification of industrial dangers as subjects of knowledge and controversy. While earlier scientists such as Collis displayed a keen social awareness in discussing silicosis or asbestos, they commented little on the carcinogenic properties of asbestos, which became a subject of passionate concern for Selikoff. Some obstacles to later knowledge were physiologically built in, in the decades that could separate cause from cancer-causing effect. But they were also social, as Selikoff and like-minded scientists came to recognize. It was with good reason that the study of industrial hazards remained, in Selikoff's words, an "inherently conflictual field," and questions about their own allegiances and scientific qualifications frequently provided a "tender spot" of debate.[5] These inherent conflicts were resolved differently in different countries, each of which had its own distinctive professions of medicine and science, political and legal systems, and industrial and cultural fabrics. Claims to scientific neutrality were inevitably contested in the struggle between capital and labor; they also intensified in adversarial legal systems where experts appeared as witnesses in courtrooms, before compensation boards, and even in legislatures. A transnational "invisible college" might well bolster the impact and aspirations of factions of experts within their own nations, though the bridges built across a variegated geography of historical legacies often proved unstable. Such frailties remain apparent even as we accentuate the larger and longer rhythms that characterized the struggles of experts not only in the parallel histories of different nations but in the cross-national mobilizations of such specialists.

By comparing transnational groups of British and American scientists across two different and distinct periods of modern health history, our essay highlights longer-term changes in expert knowledge and professionalism in two industrialized nations, and it pinpoints links to different lay groups. The narrative is organized around two pan-national conferences, each providing insights into British-American networks during a specific period, and the transition of values, methods, and conclusions that was then under way. The first is the conference on silicosis (and related pneumoconioses) convened by the International Labor Organization (ILO) in Johannesburg in 1930. Here, we can see the fruit of the social thinking and network building of an earlier generation of experts, acutely aware of the politics of the "labor question." Emerging models of professionalism and state-based regulatory systems were already supplanting this earlier "autodidact" generation of experts with another that was more concerned with technical and administrative structures. This resulting professionalism, especially in the American context, would become a target for those networks that came together at a second, pivotal conference, in 1964 at the New York Academy of Medicine. Convened by Selikoff's team in conjunction with their British allies, this conference highlighted the asbestos-cancer link. But its consequences were much broader: a solidifying challenge to mid-century models of professionalism and regulatory practice. It reflected how, particularly on the American scene, not just unions but new environmental and consumer groups had joined the fray.[6]

These two moments of transition highlight another, and longer, process that is noted in many essays in this volume. This is the shift from a focus on specifically occupational diseases characteristic of the early twentieth century, toward a rising concern by the 1960s and 1970s, with industrial hazards beyond the workplace and with more preventive or "precautionary" strategies. Left-leaning scientists such as Selikoff helped to define the new era of social and environmental sensibility, stressing an approach to disease investigation that encompassed a moral economy not only of labor but of consumer and environmental rights. Experts' communities during and after Johannesburg excluded laypeople, including labor unions, from many vital discussions. By the 1970s Selikoff and others were, in some respects at least, seeking to harness the representatives of those excluded from power and bring their voices into the discussion.

Silicosis in 1930 Johannesburg: From Social to Technical Professionalism

The origins of Johannesburg's 1930 silicosis conference can be traced to the dust-laden industrialization of the late nineteenth century, when international trade as well as new technologies transformed the workplace in Britain, America, and elsewhere. Advanced power tools generated a dense, unprecedented fog of dust in mines, workshops, and factories, which attracted the early attention of industrial health experts appointed by national governments, including pioneers such as Thomas Legge and Alice Hamilton. Along with other notables such as Edgar Collis, Legge and Hamiliton participated in what Daniel Rodgers has called "Atlantic crossings," through which ideas and advocates for reformist investigations and laws traveled between Europe and North America at this time. Their posts and the gravitas accorded to their work owed much to pressures from organized labor movements and to the revelations of insurance actuarial statisticians.[7] In contrast to the laboratory specialists who later rose to prominence, these earlier luminaries appear as amateur polymaths whose methods of investigation consisted almost entirely of field surveys and clinical exams, often drawing on their experience in the politics or administration of public health to combine an experimental understanding of a specific problem with a detailed awareness of legal and bureaucratic remedies.[8] In their forays into the hazards of factory life, they carried with them experiences from the crowded quarters that housed the industrial populations of Birmingham, Dundee, and Chicago.

It appears paradoxical that the "labor problem" so widely discussed in the late nineteenth and early twentieth centuries should have become so narrowly circumscribed in the hands of public health experts as primarily a matter of workplace hazards. One factor was the experts' consciousness of historical precedents that fixed administrative and legal rules regarding contractual obligations of employer and employee. Early occupational health scientists were especially concerned to isolate dangers specific to the workplace. This concern to narrow etiology arose in part from a recognition of formidable difficulties in distinguishing illness caused by, say, dust in the workplace from the host of respiratory ailments that could readily be associated with domestic and communal life. New bacteriological tests and X-rays helped to better discriminate which respiratory disease was due to mineral dusts, though the symptoms of diseases such as silicosis continued to be overlain and obscured by tuberculosis infections, which were also widely dispersed in industrial and urban populations. Collis's Milroy lectures of 1915 provided an authoritative British account of silicosis. Though Collis insisted that coal dust posed few problems for the workforce with proper preventive measures, he expressed deep sympathies with injured workers and their unions in South Wales and other regions. Diagnostic questions about silicosis posed ethical issues that preoccupied Legge and his fellow medical inspector Collis throughout the first two decades of the century. Experts insisted that diagnoses for compensation purposes must combine scientific technique with direct clinical observations of the patient's impairment.[9]

Collis's synthesis of existing knowledge of dust-related diseases also gained him a reputation among the emerging 1920s network of international experts. These included many who assembled around the International Labor Organization (ILO), a companionate organization to the League of

Nations. Expert committees in Geneva worked to accumulate and coordinate knowledge and to influence member nations by disseminating current scientific understanding through its conferences and conventions and by recommending that best practice be given legal force.[10] Many ILO conventions were supported by Anglo-American industrial health pioneers, though their enthusiasm was not always shared by their political masters. Hamilton promoted ILO's ban on white lead, though the ban was never passed into law by any American state; Legge resigned in frustration on the same issue. Compensation for industrial diseases, pioneered in Britain in 1906, was widely adopted after ILO endorsement, though again no American state was compensating workers for dust-related illnesses by 1930, and Britain as well as the United States proved less energetic than South Africa's mining sector in developing preventive screening for silicosis.[11]

Continuing controversy over workers' compensation for silicosis and other work-related diseases prompted fresh efforts to consolidate expertise on disease. Britain's Medical Research Council (MRC), along with the U.S. Public Health Service, encouraged new experimental styles of clinical science in the medical academy as well as an industrial epidemiology relying more heavily on diagnostic X-rays and laboratory tests. More specialist and laboratory- or instrument-centered experts also began to challenge the "public sphere" engagements and "radical" politics of earlier noted authorities.[12] Many but not all "industrial hygienists" came to see their authority as resting on the objectifying power of their tools and technology rather than on public pronouncements. This changing of the scientific guard in Britain and the United States can be detected in the delegations sent to the ILO's Johannesburg conference of 1930.

Johannesburg represented the first international gathering of accredited experts assembled by the ILO to discuss a single industrial disease. We might class South Africa as a developing nation, though its strategic production of global gold supplies and its imperial dominion status help to explain the fostering of a health model and the adoption of a pattern of technological innovation forged in the United Kingdom. Albert Thomas, chief of the ILO, acknowledged that the conference drew together a "unique collection of material" concerning silicosis that should be made "internationally available."[13]

In moves that reflected the regard for established, older authorities on silicosis, as well as for his instrumental role in the scientific diplomacy that sustained the ILO's Industrial Health Committee, Collis, along with Britain's current Chief Inspector of Factories, was invited to Geneva to assist in planning and organizing the ILO event.[14] However, the selection of delegates soon exposed a harsher realpolitik that registered changes under way in British and American health politics and in their respective responses to industrial hygiene issues. Britain's Home Office and the MRC firmly resisted Collis's nomination as an invited expert. They questioned whether he possessed sufficient expertise to "represent Great Britain at an international meeting on this question," insisting that an experimental pathologist closely associated with laboratory-centered investigations and another scientist experienced in the adjudication of compensation should represent the United Kingdom.[15] American choices of participants also reflected a growing emphasis on laboratory experimentalism and the Public Health Service (PHS) style of clinical epidemiology over Hamilton's shop floor surveys.

The 1930 conference wove together from national institutions and professional factions a transnational patchwork of expertise that would set a "universal" standard for the understanding and prevention of occupational disease. The Johannesburg discussions were to prove a seminal moment in the formation of transnational expertise, affirming much of the agenda of an earlier generation of industrial health researchers in Britain and the United States, while also marking the ascent of a more rigorously technical style. Labor unions played little part in the deliberations, and the sessions dealt only minimally with legislation. Such issues could be taken for granted partly because South Africa (like Britain) had adopted many dust suppression measures recommended by ILO. Instead, the conference papers ranged across established medical, engineering, and administrative questions: from causation, diagnosis, and pathology to compensation, and from mine engineering to dust control.[16] Front and center in their discussions, participants dedicated their energies to recommending further work on "uniform standards as a basis for research," including international standards in the utilization and interpretation of X-rays in diagnosing silicosis.[17] The emphasis was on finding "technical fixes" for complex practical problems. Such solutions would be identified and delivered by experts capable of understanding and using technology to cope with hazardous conditions.

Many cross-national collaborators continued to see their task as mediating between the sectional interests of worker and employer in the older tradition, but the 1930 conference in Johannesburg demonstrated the limits of the broadly "reformist" agenda in which earlier pioneers had understood their roles. A social understanding of industrial hazard investigation steadily gave way to deliberations on impersonal tools—administrative techniques, diagnostic and dust-measuring standards, and animal experiments—fostered via the exchange of knowledge among experts. In the era of Selikoff and his contemporaries, this technical style of industrial hygiene and the pioneering spirit of conciliation espoused by early reformers appeared sociologically naïve, neglecting or ignoring the biases of its employers and benefactors. It was in regard to a hazard mentioned briefly at Johannesburg—that of asbestos dust—that a new science and a fresh sociological understanding of science itself would arise.

Asbestos and Cancer in 1964 New York: Precautionism and the Return of the Social

In the years that followed the Johannesburg conference, new technologies posed fresh hazards while biomedical professionals in Britain and the United States saw their discipline transformed as the terms, methods, institutions, and politics involved in the investigation of industrial health hazards shifted. Classic occupational lung diseases such as silicosis may have increased in developing and less regulated countries, but in the developed world occupational criteria widened to include more controversial diagnoses (such as brown lung) and the dangers posed by asbestos dust. Industrial health experts in the United Kingdom and the United States extended their vision of hazards and health beyond workplace interiors to wider environments. This shift arose, in part, from evidence of persistent toxic seepages beyond factory confines and from a plethora of new substances to which industry was turning, whose chemical and physical properties ensured that they traveled well and were highly profitable. Asbestos in particular became a defining cause of industrial lung disease in the second half of the twentieth century, a development that the conference convened in New York by Selikoff in 1964 clearly foreshadowed. It also reveals how a transatlantic "invisible college" was used by Selikoff and his colleagues to build a fresh understanding of asbestos hazards, involving collaborations as well as conflicts.

Priming American and British investigators to investigate the threats that asbestos posed beyond the workplace was their growing appreciation of air pollution, which had begun turning up in graphic and novel forms in less likely locations such as Donora, Pennsylvania. Pollution worries in both countries heralded new directions for health researchers. Experts were also aware that classical infectious diseases of cities were being eclipsed by "degenerative" illnesses, including lung and other cancers and coronary disease. American and British researchers debated the contribution of air pollution and smoking to this rise in pulmonary carcinomas, while British investigators emphasized as well the possible impacts of asbestos and other occupational exposures.[18] Methodologies devised for such workplace studies, including atmospheric measurements of dust and toxins developed in investigations of silicosis and lead poisoning, contributed to basic advances in pollution surveys. These methodologies similarly relied on "threshold limit values" (TLVs) devised by American industrial hygienists (and others) during the 1940s. TLVs posit aerial exposure levels below which, workplace epidemiologists had shown, no clinically significant poisoning or dust disease "normally" occur. Analysis of pollution problems was likewise encouraged by environmentalist or consumerist groups, who had pioneered anticorporate and anti-industrial campaigns in the United States before most European countries. Environmental groups were rooted in organizations of homeowners and hikers, as well as consumer advocates, and enjoyed few links with organized labor.[19] The influence of these movements and the sympathies of fresh generations of experts became evident in the growing scrutiny applied to American and British industrial hygiene incidents, including controversies over asbestos that attracted noticeably different stakeholders from those involved in prewar silicosis battles.[20]

Asbestos was to provide a momentous field on which fresh forces of citizens advanced against entrenched corporate interests. Not only did the social backdrop of the asbestos debates differ; so did the track of asbestos contamination and effect. The footprints of asbestos turned up outside factories and mines, and its biology proved more lethal than pneumoconiosis. An early British investigator of 1935 implicated asbestos in cancer—a disease beyond the contemplation of American architects of TLVs.[21] Two decades later, asbestos was linked to lung tumors, and the rare cancer mesothelioma (which invades the pleural lining of the lung) appeared among asbestos mine workers and, disturbingly, among nearby residents. During the 1950s a contingent of researchers who established these links gathered at the MRC Pneumoconiosis Unit in Wales, headed by John Gilson, securing the center's reputation as an authority on coal dust research and early social epidemiology that proved critical to Selikoff's work.[22]

Selikoff himself studied medicine in Britain before working at New York's Mount Sinai Hospital in the 1950s, entering asbestos research only after Gilson's unit was established. His engagement with industrial hygiene grew quickly in the early 1960s, when he undertook a study of asbestosis among insulation workers with cancer statistician Hammond and pathologist J. Churg. By the time of the 1964 conference at least, and probably earlier, Selikoff had become convinced of the superiority of British approaches to occupational and environmental health and sought to emulate them in his work. To underpin support in the United States for similar studies, he pressed for a 1964 asbestos conference, to coincide with a meeting of the International Union against Cancer (UICC). Selikoff lauded Gilson's MRC Unit as "the leading research group concerned with dust diseases of the lungs in the world," inviting Gilson to collaborate in the selection of participants and offering him a keynote position in the gathering.[23] Conscious perhaps of a pivotal conference at Lyon earlier that year, Selikoff presented New York's event as "the first to so broadly approach the problems associated with human exposure to asbestos."[24] He might have added that he and his allies were assailing many assumptions and methods laid down by America's founding industrial hygienists.

The assault had begun with Selikoff, Hammond, and Churg's study of neoplasia among insulation workers, foreshadowing their major studies of asbestos-related diseases. Drawing on union records to examine the deaths of six hundred workers, the three concluded that "light and intermittent exposure to asbestos dust" resulted in much higher proportions (40.4 versus 5.5 percent) dying from cancers than from asbestosis, including a number (3.3 percent) from the rare mesotheliomas.[25] Possibly to deflect the ire of earlier researchers who missed these effects, the authors speculated that improvements in dust levels and antibiotic treatments for tuberculosis permitted workers to survive until tumors struck. Because British, American, and South African researchers had detected mesothelioma among patients whose occupational exposures were minimal or absent, the 1964 conference broached fundamental and controversial questions about effects from extra-workplace exposures, including consumer products such as asbestos-insulated automobile brakes. Searching questions were posed about asbestos TLVs that had been set by the American Conference of Government and Industrial Hygienists (ACGIH): based on a 1938 asbestosis study, these standards had taken no account of chronic disease effects such as cancer. Gilson himself joined in these criticisms of asbestos TLVs (also known as "MAC"), pointing out that deaths of workers from bronchial and other tumors, without intervening asbestosis, must have "very important implications in connection with a MAC for asbestos."[26]

The social composition and technical focus of the 1964 asbestos conference appeared to epitomize the industrial hygiene approach that had been registered at the 1930 silicosis event. Speakers made few references to wider values and legal issues, including compensation policy. The technical vision of industrial hygiene was reflected in commonplace assumptions that TLV assessments of tolerable risks for workers should be exclusively decided by experts. While dependent on labor union support, Selikoff's team invited no union representatives; in contrast, invitations were offered to spokespeople for corporations such as Johns-Manville, the asbestos-dependent automobile parts company. Such business voices chided the conference for its "air of pessimism" regarding cancer links.[27] Following the 1964 event, as the implications of their debates and scientific findings became evident, Selikoff and like-minded colleagues undertook alternative forms of institution building. These efforts were given greater impetus by surging environmental and consumer lawsuits in American courts and by a political ferment that transformed the legal milieu in which industrial and extra-workplace hazards were addressed. The federal government acquired new powers of oversight, through the Environmental Protection Agency (EPA), founded in 1970, and the Occupational Safety and Health Administration (OSHA), founded in 1972.

Selikoff and his allies seized the opportunity to build new kinds of professional organization for their field. Their American Society for Occupational and Environmental Health (ASOEH) forged a fresh vision of professionalism in workplace and environmental hazards, in marked contrast to that of the ACGIH, the American Academy of Occupational Medicine (AAOM), and the American Industrial Hygiene Association (AIHA). ASOEH recognized extra-workplace or "environmental" influences on health, articulating a research ethos of scientific objectivity in coexistence with values of social inclusiveness. Union leaders as well as industrialists were invited to join an initial "committee of 100," the Selikoff group seeking not an unqualified advocacy but rather a means of institutionalizing a broader dialogue between stakeholders where professional experts corresponded not only with corporate representatives but also with "all important concerned groups, such as Labor."[28] In one sense at least, they sought a return to the strategic thinking apparent during the 1920s as preparations were made for Johannesburg, where health experts advised an assembly of officials from different countries, along with business and labor representatives. Long absent from such deliberations in the United States, labor groups were invited back to the table of professional expertise and policy advice.

While dependent on British allies such as Gilson at the beginning of this quest for a reconfigured scientific objectivity, by the 1970s Selikoff and his group were moving in directions with which Gilson felt less comfortable. As a leading figure in the International Agency for Research on Cancer (IARC), Gilson invited Selikoff's participation at Lyon in 1972 but resisted efforts to crown New York's achievements at a subsequent New York asbestos conference.[29] Tensions surfaced when Selikoff was quoted in a *New Yorker* report claiming that two or three asbestos fibers per cubic centimeter (TLV was 5) resulted is "a very great increase of death due to cancer and to asbestosis." Gilson was not only skeptical but appalled that he should first read such bold conclusions in a magazine rather than in a scientific journal. Mount Sinai was ready with its ammunition in reply—they had undertaken the studies, and published their results, albeit in a relatively obscure journal.[30] Dwindling correspondence between Selikoff and Gilson registers the divide that opened between them in the 1970s. Beneath these polite debates lay deep rifts over the scientific culture that each espoused: Gilson was particularly concerned to preserve the "purity" of science, with British research remaining more firmly "occupational" in interest and in its analysis of asbestos. In contrast to ASOEH, no similar British network added "Environmental" to its title.

American protagonists were clearly responding to opportunities and demands emerging in a peculiarly American context: one shaped by OSHA and EPA as well as by "environmental," consumer, and union interests. These forces and strategic considerations nurtured but also recast the model of scientific rigor guiding research. In discussions of science's role in regulating and compelling preventive action, Selikoff's group was vocal in embracing what would be termed the precautionary principle. Selikoff wrote to the Ford Foundation in 1975, "There is a wide chasm between the accumulation of scientific knowledge in occupational health and its applications. We can ill-afford this; our data are scant enough, the problems to which they refer are of increasing urgency."[31]

The follow-up New York conference on asbestos, which Gilson had discouraged, came in 1978. As Selikoff spoke about "invisible colleges," many other trends came to fuller fruition. While half the papers addressed workplace exposures, a third considered extra-occupational or "environmental" causes of asbestos-related diseases. Participants discussed acceptable standards for industrial uses of asbestos and directly addressed questions of compensation and product liability alongside those regarding asbestos abatement and waste disposal.[32] As Selikoff envisaged, the health science, law, and policy surrounding this industrial hazard came to be discussed side by side in an academy of science. By the late 1970s, "objectivity" in occupational health returned in some form to models of the early twentieth century. Its meanings in scientific, legal, and policy arenas were in active dialogue. Moreover, with the support of advocate experts, lay representatives of those most affected had won places at a higher table.

Conclusion

Over the last century and more, in a world that that was shaped and reshaped by international as well as intra-national forces, by mobilizations of capital as well as of laypeople, communities of experts in industrial hazards themselves crafted and then recrafted what they take scientific objectivity to be. In Britain, America, and other parts of the developed world, transnational networks of experts or "invisible colleges" emerged. Their scientific gaze expanded the field of occupational health from workplaces to wider human environments. This "environmental turn" required not only scientific endeavor, by brilliant research opportunists such as Selikoff, but also new social movements and collective action, which widened demand for, and receptiveness to, the new science. We suggest that there was a reciprocal and reflexive relationship in the formation of new kinds of knowledge: the rigor that Selikoff and others brought to studies of industrial cancer spurred new groups of environmental and consumer activists to push for more evidence and accountability. The cumulative result, most apparent in the United States by the 1970s, was a thorough reconfiguration of both the law and the science of industrial hazards. By shifting the methods and conceptions of hazard, and asserting a new precautionism, the revisionists mapped out not just new knowledge but a higher moral ground. While union strength helps explain the persistence of occupational models in British studies of industrial health, the greater sway of environmental and consumer groups over his American counterparts caused Selikoff's erstwhile British ally, Gilson, increasing discomfort.

Our conclusions more broadly confirm Mary Douglas's suggestion that institution building is necessarily both a practical and a normative exercise in naturalizing knowledge, involving political and intellectual labor.[33] The similarities in social-mindedness among later and earlier twentieth-century experts in this field of knowledge indicate a broader point regarding the proliferation of social thinking: that it was encouraged especially in the earliest or most formative stages of institution building and less so later on as their legal and other authority stabilized. As historians, we must also emphasize how irretrievable earlier institutional solutions were to prove. Earlier boundaries between the occupational and the environmental eroded through a new understanding of industrial hazards as well as through corrosive changes in the political climate. Selikoff's and Hammond's accomplishments have recently been too easily and prematurely celebrated as victories for democracy while asbestos and similar threats have proliferated beyond the horizons of the affluent world. Today, a still more robustly transnational standard for objectivity is in order, through which progressive curtailment of hazards in one nation does not so easily allow their export to other parts of the globe.

NOTES

Acknowledgments: The research on which this essay is based was funded, in part, by the Wellcome Trust. We warmly acknowledge the commentaries of Barry Castleman, Geoff

Tweedale, and others at the "Dangerous Trade" conference, as well as the assistance received from the archivists at the ILO in Geneva and from Valerie Josephson, archivist at the Department of Community Medicine, Mount Sinai Hospital, New York City.

1. Irving Selikoff and E. Cuyler Hammond, "Foreword," in Irving Selikoff and E. Cuyler Hammond, eds., "Health Hazards of Asbestos Exposure," *Annals of the New York Academy of Sciences* 330 (1979): ix.

2. Derek de Solla Price, *Big Science, Little Science* (New York: Columbia University Press, 1963).

3. Bruno Latour, Pandora's Hope: Essays on the Realities of Science Studies (Cambridge, MA: Harvard University Press, 1999), esp. 172–173. See also Michael Worboys, *Spreading Germs: Disease Theories and Medical Practice in Britain, 1865–1900* (New York: Cambridge University Press, 2000).

4. See our Introduction in this volume and its citations as well as chapters throughout.

5. On labor/capital divides, see, for example, Theo Nichols, *The Sociology of Industrial Injury* (London: Mansell, 1997), 43, 47–48, 55–58; David Rosner and Gerald Markowitz, *Deadly Dust: Silicosis and the Politics of Occupational Disease in Twentieth Century America* (Princeton, NJ: Princeton University Press, 1991); Alan Derickson, *Black Lung: Anatomy of a Public Health Disease* (Ithaca, NY: Cornell University Press, 1998). On postwar influences of consumerism, see Lizabeth Cohen, *A Consumers' Republic: The Politics of Mass Consumption in Postwar America* (New York: Alfred A. Knopf, 2003). On environmentalism, see Christopher Sellers, *Unsettling Ground: Suburban Nature and Environmentalism in Twentieth-Century America* (Chapel Hill: University of North Carolina Press, forthcoming).

6. David Rosner and Gerald Markowitz, "Industry Challenges to the Principle of Prevention in Public Health: The Precautionary Principle in Historical Perspective," *Public Health Reports* 117 (November-December 2002): 501–512. See also other articles in this issue.

7. Rosner and Markowitz, *Deadly Dust*, 28, 73, 79; Daniel Rodgers, *Atlantic Crossings: Social Politics in a Progressive Age* (Cambridge, MA: Belknap Press, 1998).

8. See Christopher Sellers, *Hazards of the Job: From Industrial Disease to Environmental Health Science* (Chapel Hill: University of North Carolina Press, 1997), chap. 3.

9. Edgar Collis, *Industrial Pneumonoconioses with Special Reference to Dust-Phthisis* (London: HMSO, 1919); Rosner and Markowitz, *Deadly Dust*, 31–33.

10. Among the many works on ILO history, see B. L. Lowe, *The International Protection of Labor: International Labor Organization, History and Law* (New York: MacMillan, 1935); Gerry Rogers, *The International Labor Organization and the Quest for Social Justice* (Ithaca, NY: Cornell University Press, 2009).

11. John Heitmann, "The ILO and the Regulation of White Lead in Britain during the Interwar Years: An Examination of International and National Campaigns in Occupational Health," *Labor History Review* 69 (2003): 167–284. On Hamilton and the white lead ban, see P.W.J. Bartrip, *The Home Office and the Dangerous Trades: Regulating Occupational Disease in Victorian and Edwardian Britain* (Amsterdam: Rodopi, 2002), 201, 210–212, 216; compare M. W. Bufton and J. Melling "A Mere Matter of Rock: Organised Labour, Scientific Evidence and British Government Schemes for Compensating Silicosis and Pneumoconiosis among Coalminers, 1926–1940," *Medical History* 49 (2005), 155–178.

12. Alan Derickson, *Black Lung*, 23, 64, 81,115, 101–103; for doctors and others, see 43, 134, 153; Sellers, "A Prejudice Which May Cloud the Mentality: The Making of Objectivity in Early Twentieth-Century Occupational Health," in *Silent Victories: The History and Practice of Public Health in Twentieth-Century America*, ed. John Ward and Chris Warren (New York: Oxford University Press, 2007), 230–250.

13. International Labor Organization, *Silicosis: Records of the International Conference Held at Johannesburg 13–27 August 1930* (Geneva: International Labor Organization, 1930), 11.

14. Letter from Collis to Carozzi, May 14, 1925, Archives of the ILO, ILO HY550/6/25/1, Geneva; letter from N. B. Butler to Delevingne, December 28, 1928, Archives of the ILO, ILO HY1000/34/1/2/25; "International Conference on Pneumo-Coniosis (Silicosis) Johannesburg 1930: Correspondence with Great Britain: July 20, 1928," Archives of the ILO, ILO HY1000/34/1/2/25.

15. Letter from Delevingne to Butler, October 17, 1929, Archives of the ILO, ILO HY1000/34/1/2/25.

16. Jock McCulloch, Paul-André Rosental, and Joseph Melling, "The Road through Johannesburg: Silicosis as a Transnational and Imperial Disease (1900–1940)," in *Silicosis: The First World Disease*, ed. P. A. Rosental (Berkeley: University of California Press, forthcoming).

17. E. L. Middleton, *Report on the International Conference on Silicosis Held at Johannesburg in August 1930* (London: Home Office, 1931), 11, 16.

18. Robert Proctor, *Cancer Wars: How Politics Shapes What We Know and Don't Know about Cancer* (New York: Basic Books, 1995); Christopher Sellers, "Discovering Environmental Cancer: Wilhelm Hueper, Post-WWII Epidemiology, and the Vanishing Clinician's Eye," *American Journal of Public Health* 87 (1997): 1824–1835.

19. Samuel Hays, *Beauty, Health and Permanence: Environmental Politics in the United States, 1955–1985* (Cambridge: Cambridge University Press, 1987); Richard Andrews, *Managing the Environment, Managing Ourselves: A History of American Environmental Policy* (New Haven, CT: Yale University Press, 1999).

20. Irving Selikoff, "Opening Remarks," *Annals of the New York Academy of Sciences* 312 (1965): 8.

21. K. Lynch and W. Smith, "Pulmonary Asbestosis III: Carcinoma of Lung in Asbesto-Silicosis," *American Journal of Cancer* 24 (1935): 56 (first mention of two lung cancer cases).

22. R. Doll, "Mortality from Lung Cancer in Asbestos Workers," *British Journal of Industrial Medicine* 12 (1955): 81ff; J. C. Wagner, C. Sleggs, and Paul Marchand, "Diffuse Pleural Mesothelioma and Asbestos Exposure in the North Western Cape Province," *British Journal of Medicine* 17 (1960): 260.

23. Letter from Selikoff to J. C. Gilson, August 3, 1965, Mount Sinai Hospital Archives, Selikoff papers, Gilson file, New York.

24. Irving Selikoff, "Opening Remarks," in "Biological Effects of Asbestos," I. J. Selikoff and J. Churg, *Annals of the New York Academy of Sciences (ANYAS)* 132 (1965): 7–8.

25. E. C. Hammond, I. J. Selikoff, and J. Churg, "Neoplasia among Insulation Workers in the United States with Special Reference to Intro-Abdominal Neoplasia," *Annals of the New York Academy of Sciences* 52 (1965): 519–525; Muriel Newhouse and Hilda Thompson, "Epidemiology of Mesothelial Tumors in the London Area," *Annals of the New York Academy of Sciences* 52 (1965): 579–588.

26. E. L. Schall, "Present Threshold Limit Value in the U.S.A. for Asbestos Dust: A Critique," *Annals of the New York Academy of Sciences* 52 (1965): 317; J. C. Gilson, "Problems and Perspectives: The Changing Hazards of Exposure to Asbestos," *Annals of the New York Academy of Sciences* (1965): 702.

27. K. Smith, "Trends in the Health of the Asbestos Worker," *Annals of the New York Academy of Sciences* (1965): 689.

28. Letter from Selikoff to Mazzocchi, August 8, 1972, Mount Sinai Hospital Archives, Selikoff papers; "The Society for Occupational and Environmental Health (Occupational Health Society) Minutes of Inaugural Meeting, November 12, 1972," Mount Sinai Hospital Archives, Selikoff papers.

29. Letter from Gilson to Selikoff, July 5, 1973, Mount Sinai Hospital Archives, Selikoff papers.

30. Letter from Gilson to Selikoff, January 8, 1974; letter from William J. Nicholson to Gilson, February 8, 1974, Mount Sinai Hospital Archives, Selikoff papers.

31. Letter from Selikoff to Ford Foundation, March 11, 1975, Mount Sinai Hospital Archives, Selikoff papers, Ford file.

32. Irving Selikoff and E. Cuyler Hammond, eds., "Health Hazards of Asbestos Exposure," *Annals of the New York Academy of Sciences* 330 (1979): 611–619.

33. Mary Douglas, *How Institutions Think* (London: Routledge and Kegan Paul, 1987), 45; David Bloor, *Wittgenstein, Rules and Institutions* (London: Routledge, 1997), 7–11.

9

Bread and Poison

Stories of Labor Environmentalism in Italy, 1968–1998

STEFANIA BARCA

This chapter tells the story of the encounter between a generation of Italian experts in industrial hygiene (physicians and sociologists) and factory workers, and how that encounter translated into new forms of knowledge and political action. The chapter aims to highlight the material relations existing between occupational, environmental, and public health as they were experienced by subaltern social groups, who knew industrial hazards through their bodies and through the environments where they worked and lived. This material reality—the organic relationship between humans and nature through work—has been politically obscured by dominant social forces and by the divide between the labor and environmental movements. The case of labor environmentalism in Italy, however, shows how, in particular places and at particular times, the possibility emerged for a reunified consciousness of industrial hazards, one that challenged alienating forms of scientific knowledge and political-economic power.[1]

The experience of labor environmentalism in Italy began when what I call "militant science"—the new Italian industrial hygiene born out of the 1968 student movement—interacted with the knowledge of environmental hazards embodied by factory workers. During the seventies, starting from a platform of health grievances based on a mix of scientific and lay expertise, the Italian labor movement drew up a comprehensive strategy of struggle for occupational, environmental, and public health. That early coalition of labor with "militant" industrial hygiene in Italy eventually produced legislative reforms of great social and environmental significance, such as the Labor Statute (1970) and the national public health system (1978). Yet, as this chapter also shows, the actual impact of those institutional reforms on workers' bodies, work environments, and local landscapes came to be biased by a history of political-economic differences.

In dealing with workers and the environments around them, I aim to contribute to the building of an "embodied" and environmentally conscious working-class history. I start by showing how, during the transformation of the country into a highly industrialized economy (1958–1978), workers' bodies bore the marks not only of capital but of the Industrial State, especially in the petrochemical sector. At the same time I emphasize how, once they joined with "militant" experts, those same bodies (and minds) openly challenged and counteracted dominant ways of knowing and regulating industrial hazards.[2]

The Economic Boom and Its Social Costs

Between 1955 and 1970, roughly four million people from southern Italy migrated to the northern industrial regions, searching for factory jobs. From the 1960s onward, they found work in the fast-growing petrochemical, steel, and mechanical industries. By the end of that decade, and during the 1970s, the Italian government implemented a new policy of transfer of industrial jobs to the South by locating a number of publicly controlled companies, mainly in the petrochemical sector, along the shores of the southern regions.[3]

In consequence of such massive changes, the country experienced the epidemiological shift typical of advanced industrial economies—namely, from infectious to degenerative diseases, especially those correlated with environmental poisoning from mercury and benzene hydrocarbons. Research in industrial hygiene began to be sponsored by the INAIL (the Workers' Compensation Authority) and by the European Community for Coal and Steel, but it was mainly focused on risk insurance and clinical pathology rather than on prevention in the work environment. Facing an impressive worsening of work conditions and a steady increase in occupational accidents, the Italian unions adopted a defensive strategy, mainly based on the attempt to increase compensation and strictly enforce it. Compensation law, however, was a major obstacle to the prevention of industrial hazards, for the same law sanctioned the total nonliability of employers in the matter of both workplace accidents and long-term health risks.[4]

Expertise and Militancy: The "Environmental Club"

This typically market-oriented approach to workers' safety was to be abandoned and completely revised during the 1960s—a period in which union confederation was particularly strong politically—and gradually led to the passage of a very advanced piece of legislation, the Labor Statute of 1970. Coming after a decade of tremendous changes in the cultural and political climate of the country, the statute granted workers the right to exercise direct control over working conditions. This principle was revolutionary in the sense that it emancipated employees from the oppressive control of "company doctors," whose behaviour was strongly conditioned by their being on the company payroll. Furthermore, the Labor Statute introduced a radically new conception of workers as assigners of physicians' services and thus entitled them to control over employers' choices. To enforce this right, workers were allowed to bring independent experts into the workplace to test its environmental conditions and to examine the workers' exposure to risks.[5]

Those "experts," on whom workers relied for their empowerment in the workplace, were mostly young physicians and labor sociologists, coming from a student movement that in Italy was strongly hegemonized by the radical left and considered itself—in Gramscian terms—an intellectual army at the service of the working class. During the 1968 university protests, students and researchers in industrial hygiene were invited by union representatives to collaborate with the union confederation in breaking a history of subordination of medical doctors to employers. "Socialising Culture," the slogan of the student revolt in general, became particularly meaningful in the case of workplace injuries and diseases. Medical students neglected their university courses to study in the factories, learning from workers' testimonies.[6]

This was the golden age of the movement for workers' health in Italy. A permanent workshop, formed by sociologists and "new" industrial hygienists under the political hegemony of the union confederation, elaborated a new scientific paradigm for the work environment based on the translation of complex analysis into a few simple principles of political action. These were embodied, mainly, in the slogan "Health is not for sale" and in the principle of nondelegation in the matter of health issues, implying the workers' direct control over knowledge and practices regarding the workplace. Soon renamed the "Environmental Club," this group helped to redefine the new confederate political strategy for safety and health. Meanwhile, at its thirty-sixth congress held in 1972, the Italian Association of Industrial Hygiene officially recognised the "objective" value of the workers' experience and the utility of a "participative" methodology for the collection and recording of environmental and biostatistical evidence at the work group level. This was a methodology on which the Environmental Club had been working for a few years, based on the direct production of knowledge within the workplace through a series of practical measures that workers could carry out during their workday—such as monitoring noise, dust, temperature, and so forth.[7]

Between 1969 and 1972, unions' grievances directly regarding safety and health grew from 3 to 16 percent. Most interesting, however, is that this struggle did not concern the work environment only: it was directed toward broader reform in national health policies, since unions and the left parties were calling for a new system of public health services directly controlled by the State. A series of industrial accidents occurring during the seventies, mainly in the petrochemical sector—and particularly the Seveso disaster of 1976—were instrumental in keeping public opinion focused on the relationship of industrial hazards to environmental and public health. Risk prevention, cancer epidemiology, exposure standards, right to know, and participatory decision making became widespread ideas, leading to the formation of the organisation Medicina Democratica—a grassroots action/research movement that was to become instrumental in a number of occupational and environmental health controversies in the following decades.[8]

The importance of this particularly positive period of struggle and social alliances can be seen in its major accomplishment, the Public Health Reform Bill passed in 1978. This legislation mandated locally based public health services (USL) that would supervise both environmental and health quality within factories and communities. With it the principle of the internal relationship between workers' and citizens' rights to health obtained institutional recognition at the highest levels. The most important meaning of the workers' health struggle, therefore, was as a primary test for broader social reform, affecting the whole of Italian society. By struggling for a redefinition of pollution-related diseases, factory workers not only sought greater safety for themselves but also aimed for more comprehensive sanitary protection for their families and the entire national community. This story represents in some way the success of what unions, and the political left in general, defined as "the political strategy of class alliances and solidarity."

The Italian public health system was born at the end of a long battle for occupational health and represented that battle's most significant victory. At the core of the fight was a new consciousness about the material and political unity of work, environment, and public health—or labor environmentalism—that had first been tried on the shop floor.

Health Struggles North and South

The encounter between labor and environmentalism in Italy began at the heart of the country's most industrialized area, between Torino and Milano, in the core years of the Italian economic boom and in the middle of a revolutionary cultural transformation related to the student protests of 1968 through 1977. Where the joining of occupational with environmental and public health produced its most advanced results was the province of Milano in the period 1972 through 1977—with the experience of the SMALs, which is the topic of the following paragraph. The chapter then moves through space and time toward a rural area of the South—Manfredonia, Apulia— where a very different scenario of labor environmentalism took form.

Milano: Reforming from Below

In 1972, the regional government of Lombardia instituted SMALs—Servizi di Medicina per gli Ambienti di Lavoro (Medical Services for the Work Environment), giving it the task of supporting the implementation of the fifth and ninth articles of the Labor Statute, which concerned workers' right to control the enforcement of safety and health measures in the workplace. At the demand of the "factory board" (a union representative committee),

SMAL physicians entered the workplace to investigate the health conditions of the workers by measuring levels of hazard and compiling and updating "environmental data" registers and personal sanitary journals for each worker. On the basis of their research, they made nosological inquiries in collaboration with public health agencies, and instructed employers regarding compulsory risk prevention measures. Most important, both the results of the SMAL physicians' research and the countermeasures they proposed were formally discussed with workers, through a "health committee" overseen by the factory board. The SMALs were a public health service mandated by law with the purpose of integrating the work of existing public health services (namely the Labor Inspectorate and INAIL), as these agencies had proved ineffective in halting the worsening of workers' health during the previous two decades.

The creation of the SMALs gives us an idea of the extent to which the action/research methodology elaborated by the Environmental Club since the late sixties had become culturally hegemonic and politically feasible. We might consider them a successful example of what science scholar Sandra Harding defined as the philosophy of "strong objectivity"—that is, a research method that intentionally assumes the standpoint of victims and marginalized others. Supported by physicians and labor clinicians from the University of Milano and overseen by local and regional administrations, the SMALs were granted authority based on scientific rationality, and unions could use their findings as a solid basis for labor disputes.

In fact, the SMALs were a form of "militant' science." Their methods reversed the traditional industrial hygiene approach: now it was not workers as guinea pigs for occupational medicine, with scientists reading their bodies to extract "scientific" data from them; it was the other way round, as workers themselves solicited the experts' intervention to give scientific support to their empirical observations about health hazards on the shop floor. But workers could only realize this in an organized way, through their factory boards. It was the factory boards—that is, the unions—that called for a SMAL intervention and finally decided what initiatives to carry out on the basis of the SMAL's recommendations. The control of the unions over all SMALs activity is clear: they had pressed local administrations to create the SMALs and had lobbied for the passage of the regional bill; they organized courses and training activities for would-be SMAL physicians, selected candidates, and put them in contact with workers; and they set the SMALs' agenda and coordinated their activities at the regional level.[9]

It was not just a practical and political hegemony, however. The language of the SMALs' reports shows how physicians fundamentally shared with the unions a militant conception of knowledge as a form of empowerment, as well as a militant conception of health as part of the broader conflict between labor and capital. The SMALs interpreted their relationship with employers not in a defensive, but in a counteractive, way. They entered the structure of production, starting at the plant level, and discussed the scope and regulation of technological change that is the very core of industrial production.

In the SMAL vision, in line with the insights of the "new" industrial hygiene and the "Environmental Club," technical progress and economic growth had produced in Italy, as in other advanced industrial countries, not a general improvement in health conditions but a shift in disease patterns. The types of pathology had changed, not their social incidence. This was true within the factory, where the classic distinction of risk factors (dust, chemicals, and physical conditions) was to be aggravated by new factors, such as rhythm and position of work, standardisation, repetition, and automation. Furthermore, given that most occasional illnesses tended to become chronic, "the opinion that any health professional felt to give about the dangerousness of some work environment," according to a SMAL document, "would be deficient and partial if not confronted with the opinion of those who live there eight hours a day."[10] The workplace was to be seen as an (unnatural) environment, and workers were the ones who knew it best.

The SMALs' self-conception as militants is also shown by their behaviour as rank-and-file activists rather than as impartial, disinterested science professionals. In Cinisello Balsamo, for example, the local SMAL dealt with a complex social conflict, fostering local opposition to the Terzago steel plant because of a noise issue. It proved in this case to be much more than a health professionals' service, instead acting as an intermediary in an environmental conflict while also accomplishing its task of mandating stricter health and safety measures. SMAL physicians quickly connected the noise pollution issue in the community with the existence of a serious health hazard within the workplace, and acted to eliminate both at their source. That was not an easy task, however, because the situation was exacerbated by the factory owners' response to citizens' protests—forcing workers to close the plant's windows and thus aggravating the effect of the noise on workers' ears and the lack of ventilation in the plant. Furthermore, in this small-scale factory the union's presence was weak, so SMAL intervention had been called for by the local public health official responding to the demand by a citizens' anti-noise committee. The physicians' official entrance into the workplace as a bureaucratic agency could have upset the employees, who were worried about the employer's threat of shutting the plant down.

This case clearly shows the internal contradictions in the relations between workplace and environment and between labor and community in the matter of health. These contradictions led to a kind of intervention that was scientific and political at the same time, that was able to reconnect the two fundamental loci of the struggle (within and beyond the factory gates), and that was able to act at different material and political scales. Reassuring the workers and looking at ways of eradicating the noise problem required the SMAL physicians to adopt a militant vision of their institutional and professional task: it required them to accomplish tasks not strictly inherent in their mandate, such as setting up a series of community-worker meetings with the participation of experts from the Otolaryngology Clinic of the University of Milano and members of the local government.

In their final report, the SMAL physicians diagnosed partial deafness in 30 percent of the workers and chronic acoustic shock in another 36 percent, mostly women. These results, based on "objective" audiometric measurements and international standards, could not be denied by the employer. The SMAL intervention, though, did not stop at the workers' health conditions; the physicians sought the collaboration of "democratic technicians and engineers," as they wrote in their report, meaning the voluntary support of external experts in solving the interrelated problems of vibration and transmission of acoustic waves. As a result, the SMAL was finally able to suggest a whole variety of technical solutions for limiting noise and preventing future injuries, at the same time resolving the community/workplace conflict.[11]

Another case, that of Metal-Lamina, a metal-mechanical plant in Assago, illustrates further the interconnections between the work environment, worker health, and community health. In this case, too, SMAL intervention had been demanded by public officials at the local level, starting with the Municipal Ecology Service, on the grounds of complaints coming from workers in a neighboring plant about Metal-Lamina's discharges of smoke. The SMAL physicians found that the presence of lead dust within the workplace was ten times the legal standards and ordered the immediate hospitalization of eight out of thirteen smelters. The workers reported that five dogs had died in the plant in the course of one year, probably by the ingestion of lead dust deposited on the ground.

The stopping of the foundry blocked production, and management threatened to shut down the plant; eventually, however, the company decided to implement all of the SMAL's requirements and those of local public officials concerning the abatement of lead dust and smoke, and it installed a water purification system. The managers also asked the SMAL experts to become the company's consultants in the matter of health and safety regulations.[12]

This case opens up the question of managerial and entrepreneurial behaviour. The only reported cases of continued opposition to the SMALs' work are those involving the plants owned by Montedison, the most important partially State-owned chemical corporation in the country, producing synthetic fibres and pharmaceuticals in a number of plants. Montedison had merged with the ENI group (the State Agency for Hydrocarbons), forming Enichem, a powerful petrochemical company that came to own a number of plants for the production of fertilizers and plastics spread along the Italian coast. Its behaviour was representative of the particular contradictions that marked the Italian experience in the matter of worker and environmental health. In opposing the entry of SMAL experts into its plants, the Montedison management claimed the protection of workers' health as their exclusive business, accomplished by its medical service. The existence of such a company service and its partial control by the State were, in management's view, sufficient reasons to present the company's workers as a privileged category, which did not need supplementary oversight.[13]

The idea of the Montedison-Enichem workers as a privileged group was grounded in the State's involvement with the petrochemical sector, which was perceived as strategic production in the Italian economy. It was also the result of the power relations between unions and the State, which allowed Italian workers in public companies to have permanent, secure jobs. This complex mix of conditions gave the petrochemical industry in Italy immense social power, as we will see in the next case, concerning an Enichem plant in Manfredonia. Here the entrepreneurial State dealt with a rampant internal conflict of interests and functions, centred on the problem of risk definition and distribution of social costs.

Manfredonia: State Chemicals

The ENI group first arrived in Manfredonia—a fishing town on the Adriatic coast—in the late sixties, under the name ANIC (Azienda Nazionale Idro-genazione Combustibili, State Company for the Hydrogenation of Carbons) to explore the methane layer in the area with the intention of building a plant for the production of urea and ammonium sulphate (used as fertilisers) and caprolactam (a raw material for synthetic fibres).[14]

From 1972 onward the ANIC plant saw a series of accidents, which had the long-term effect of changing the collective local psychology and trans-forming residents into citizens of the "risk society." These accidents allowed Manfredonians to see and clearly perceive—by their noses, ears, and hands—what was being produced within the factory besides salaries and income. Ammonia, arsenic, nitrous acid, sulphuric acid, and other pollutants were visibly released in a series of fallouts amounting to several tons each, provoking collective intoxication, mass escapes, and panic. The most serious fallout occurred on a Sunday morning in September 1976 (two months after the more famous Seveso accident), when an explosion in the arsenic column caused the dome-shaped roof to blow off the plant, falling on a shed on the opposite side. Soon after, people walking downtown could see a wide brown cloud coming from the plant and moving toward them, followed by a yellow slush that gently fell like snow all around. That snow was arsenious dioxide, and it was later calculated that some thirty-two tons of it had fallen on the town.[15]

The symptoms of widespread contamination soon became apparent: the day after the explosion, many barnyard animals died and large quantities of arsenic dust were found on leaves. In the following hours, the first one hundred people were hospitalised with strong symptoms of arsenic intoxication. These were mostly workers from the plant and residents from the Monticchio neighbourhood, a former rural area surrounding the factory that had become a crowded settlement of 12,000 poorly housed people who had migrated from the countryside in search of jobs. The management of the ANIC denied the existence of any risk and put the employees back to work as if nothing had happened. The only action it took was sending in a special team of maintenance workers, to clean up, who were given no protection and had no idea of what they were handling. These workers swept away the arsenic dust day and night so that the plant could resume regular operations the following Monday. Soon after the accident, in October 1976, six top managers from the ANIC plant were investigated for "negligent slaughtering," but the preliminary inquest did not even get to the courtroom. In fact, the slaughtering was not evident, yet it would become so only a couple of decades later, when a number of workers who had entered the factory in the early seventies came to suffer illness and death by a variety of serious ailments related to the acute arsenic intoxication of 1976.

The Manfredonia accident occurred when the golden age of labor environmentalism in Italy was coming to an end; moreover, it happened in the South. There was no SMAL in Manfredonia nor any public health officials, students, or even unions willing to counteract ANIC's overwhelming contamination of both human bodies and social values. The politics of "deceit and denial" were easily implemented in this case; in fact, the Manfredonia accident is still mostly unknown in the international literature and even to the Italian public. The existence of a well-consolidated knowledge/power assemblage connected to the Italian State was materially experienced by the victims of the 1976 accident in the form of delayed and misinterpreted data coming from laboratory tests and the deliberate manipulation of scientific standards with the aim of altering test results. Well-known and respected industrial hygienists, at the Labor Clinics of both Bari (the closest city) and Milano—all employed as consultants on ENI's payroll—denied public access to test results for nine precious days, then revealed levels of urine contamination from arsenic that were twenty to fifty times the maximum standard for several hundred cases. Local hospitals, however, were not able to receive so many people at once, and a number of victims were sent home having received no care. Company doctors decided to arbitrarily raise the levels of allowable urine contamination by one hundred and two hundred times so as to declare most of the employees "able to work."[16]

The 1976 accident gave rise to no wide or significant reaction from the community. The attempt to minimise hazards, by delaying test results and by recalling almost all of the workers to work, had the effect of reassuring a population still largely unaware of the real consequences of the contamination. Only a radical left, grassroots organization, Democrazia Proletaria (DP), attempted to keep public opinion alert to the "lock on information" enacted by the government in Manfredonia—a practice already manifest in the Seveso experience. A few hundred people participated in a public demonstration set up by the DP some weeks after the explosion. The participants were not mere observers but people directly affected by the environmental consequences of the ANIC operation. These protests did not represent the voice of isolated and elitist environmentalists, but came from the world of work. Factory employees denounced having been sent to work with high levels of arsenic in their urine and no protection against the environmental contamination within the plant; local fishermen—a group that in the past had been strongly representative of the community identity and that continued to produce a significant part of the town's income despite the growing threat to their livelihoods from the ANIC plant—claimed that the Harbour Office had kept evidence of marine pollution in the bay area secret in order not to create alarm and disturbance in the local economy. Most interesting, however, are the voices that came from the Monticchio neighbourhood, where a Citizens' Committee for the Defence of Health was created and where a march of more than ten thousand on City Hall began on October 17. Nevertheless, DP was not a powerful organization with thousands of affiliates, nor could its social influence grow much given its clearly declared loyalty to the extra-parliamentary Marxist left.

Other political forces, including the left parties, were largely absent from the social construction of community opposition to the plant, on this as well as later occasions. In understanding such a position, the "job-versus-the-environment" discourse is probably the most relevant explanation: no party or union wanted in fact to be identified as contesting an agency offering employment, even if only 850 people effectively worked in the plant in 1976 and the total number in the following decades would never exceed a thousand.[17] Even more deafening—for what concerns us here—was the silence of the unions in Manfredonia. No SMAL was mobilized to assess the effects of the 1976 accident or the long-term effects of urea and caprolactam production on ANIC workers and their families in the surrounding area. Such a striking difference between the politics of the union confederation North and South is still in need of a historical explanation, hopefully achieved by future research.

Nevertheless, the lack of initiative on the part of (male-led) unions left open the possibility for another agency to come to the fore: women. It was a group of forty local women, those most affected by the accident's fallout while living in proximity to the plant and the wives of its workers, who mobilized. Embracing an ecofeminist approach, they formed a Womens' Citizen Committee and succeeded in bringing the ENI group to court. Not the Italian court, though, but the European Court for Human Rights in Geneva, which, hearing the Manfredonia case in 1988, eventually came to rule against the company in February 1998. The court declared Enichem guilty of moral damage by highlighting the relations between the toxic wastes and emissions from the plant and the women's private/family life. The ruling was centred on the "right to know"—that is, the idea that the plaintiffs were entitled to access to information strictly concerning their own and their relatives' properties (house and body) and that the company had illegally withheld that information. The court also declared the Italian State guilty for not protecting the plaintiffs from the violation of their privacy. The "right to know" theory, however, does not imply the liability of a company (or the State) for the direct consequences of production. While the women of Manfredonia had asked for a huge, collective settlement for "biological damage," the court granted each plaintiff an individual sum as compensation for "moral damage," for a total amount of one-fiftieth of the original request. Even more striking, the court rejected the request of the plaintiffs that the Italian State be compelled to clean up the area, to establish an epidemiological study of the entire Manfredonian population, and to open an enquiry into the environmental impact of the Enichem plant.[18]

And yet something happened in Manfredonia that again set up the possibility for industrial hazard to translate into social, and legal, action. In 1995, a disabled and retired worker from the Enichem plant, Nicola Lovecchio, casually met a physician at the Labor Clinic of the University of Bari, Maurizio Portaluri, for a routine medical check. At the time Lovecchio was already suffering the consequences of the strategy of denial played by company doctors from 1976 onward: he had lung cancer that, had it been diagnosed a couple of years before when it was already visible by an accurate X-ray, could have been effectively treated. Lovecchio, instead, was declared "able to work" until the cancer was widespread, and he died at age forty-nine, twenty-one years after the accident of September 1976.[19]

Portaluri represented the "democratic physician" the movement for workers' health in the seventies had called for, being allied with the workforce against employers and company doctors. Some years before, he had read a dossier filed by the organization Medicina Democratica about another Enichem plant located in Porto Marghera, near Venice. The dossier documented the investigation that another worker, Gabriele Bortolozzo, had started against management detailing the criminal responsibility of the company doctors for the death and disability of many workers from various forms of cancer, all related to the production of vinyl chloride (VCM) and polyvinyl chloride (PVC), as well as for environmental devastation in the Venetian lagoon (noted in Barbara Allen's essay in this volume). Bortolozzo's investigation had opened up a new possibility for labor environmentalism in Italy, one that may be termed "workers' epidemiology." This led Portaluri to think that something similar could, and indeed should, be done in Manfredonia. Together, the physician and Lovecchio, before his illness overcame him, decided to carry out a bottom-up investigation: Portaluri asked for help from the "militant" experts of Medicina Democratica (medical doctors, biologists, engineers), while Lovecchio interviewed his colleagues (and their widows), collecting memories of the 1976 Manfredonia accident and any relevant data concerning the work environment; he also solicited his fellow workers to ask the company for their clinical files. The final result of this research was a trial, involving hundreds of plaintiffs, a number of organizations, the town of Manfredonia, and the Italian State, which, sadly enough, was concluded in March 2011 with the dismissal of all charges against the company.[20]

Conclusion

The stories told in this chapter offer particular insights into the historical agency of labor in environmental matters. As well, it meets the call of scholars for an "embodied environmental history."[21] First, by combining with union action for the recognition of the objective value of workers' knowledge about industrial hazards, the militant new industrial hygiene of the seventies translated into political change with general social, and environmental, impacts. Many improvements in occupational and environmental health, and even the encounter between Portaluri and Lovecchio at a public hospital in

Apulia and all that came afterward, would not have been possible without that extraordinary season of Italian labor environmentalism, creating both the cultural and the material conditions for a public health system and for the enforcement of workers' right to know about the hazards of production.

Second, and equally important, is the great historical significance of the workers' (bodily) knowledge of industrial hazards and the ways in which this could translate into political action beyond (and even possibly against) that of labor organizations. The case of Manfredonia, in particular, shows how the encounter between militant science and this embodied knowledge, and thus the possibility of socio-environmental change, is not necessarily confined to the context of organized labor or even to the political hegemony of the unions, for it can arise from the initiative of individuals. Predicated by the Italian left in the seventies, and then abandoned under the pressure of economic recession, the Gramscian strategy of class solidarities became itself embodied in the story of a personal encounter: that between Lovecchio and Portaluri in the impoverished and heavily polluted Manfredonia of the mid-nineties.

One final point of methodological significance for an environmentally conscious working-class history emerges from the chapter. Environmental historian Arthur McEvoy once suggested that workers' bodies be seen as meta-texts on which the political ecology of industrial societies has been written—and in many ways this perspective is reflected in the stories told in this chapter. But the chapter has also shown workers as self-reflective agents of environmental change and workers' bodies not simply as biological machines but as historical actors endowed with cultural and symbolic tools and producing not only commodities but knowledge and political agency as well. In the Italian case, the knowledge of work/nature relationships embodied by factory workers has become a powerful lever of environmental consciousness and action. In association with militant expertise, working-class people North and South, men and women, have historically acquired the ability to read the work environment and their own bodies, and take action for a stronger science and a more just society.[22]

NOTES

Acknowledgments: This chapter summarizes a longer paper, originally presented at the Agrarian Studies Colloquium of Yale University and at the Tenneco Lectures Seminar of the University of Houston, both in April 2006. I thank Jim Scott and Martin Melosi, Barbara Allen, Chris Sellers, and Jo Melling for their insightful comments on previous drafts.

1. On the relationship between labor and the environment (especially in the United States) see, for example, Richard White, "'Are You an Environmentalist, or Do You Work for a Living?' Work and Nature," in *Uncommon Grounds: Rethinking the Human Place in Nature*, ed. William Cronon (New York: W. W. Norton, 1996), 171–185. See also Scott Dewey, "Working for the Environment: Organized Labor and the Origins of Environmentalism in the United States, 1948–1970," *Environmental History* 1 (1998): 45–63; Scott Gordon, "Shell No! OCAW and the Labor-Environmental Alliance," *Environmental History* 4 (1998): 460–487; Brian K. Obach, *Labor and the Environmental Movement: The Quest for Common Ground* (Cambridge, MA: MIT Press, 2004); Gunter Peck, "The Nature of Labor: Fault Lines and Common Ground in Environmental and Labor History," *Environmental History* 2 (2006): 212–238.

2. On the topic of "embodying working-class history," see Ava Baron and Eileen Boris, "'The Body' as a Useful Category in Working-Class History," *Labor: Studies in Working-Class History of the Americas* 2 (2007): 23, and the following debate in the same journal issue. In particular, in this chapter I refer to Baron and Boris's remark on "how bodies come to 'matter' and how they can cause 'trouble'" (26), and to John F. Kasson's call to "keep our eyes on the 'marks of capital' on workers' bodies" (46).

3. See Amalia Signorelli, "Movimenti di popolazione e trasformazioni culturali," in *Storia dell'Italia repubblicana*, vol. 4., *La Trasformazione dell'Italia: sviluppo e squilibri* (Torino: Einaudi, 1995), 589–658; Stefano Musso, "Lavoro e occupazione," in *Guida all'Italia contemporanea, 1861–1997*, ed. Massimo Firpo, Nicola Tranfaglia, and Pier Giorgio Zunino (Milano: Garzanti, 1998), 485–544; Nicola Crepas, "Industria," in *Guida all'Italia contemporanea, 1861–1997*, ed. Massimo Firpo, Nicola Tranfaglia, and Pier Giorgio Zunino (Milano: Garzanti, 1998), 287–422.

4. See Kitty Calavita, "Worker Safety, Law and Social Change: The Italian Case," *Law and Society Review* 2 (1986): 189–228; Francesco Carnevale and Alberto Baldasseroni, *Mal da lavoro: Storia della salute dei lavoratori* (Roma-Bari: Laterza, 1999), 147–229; Giovanni Berlinguer, *Storia e politica della salute* (Milano: Franco Angeli, 1991).

5. See Carnevale and Baldasseroni, *Mal da lavoro*, 230–282; Patrizio Tonelli, "Salute e lavoro," in *Il '900: Alcune istruzioni per l'uso*, ed. Luigi Falossi (Firenze: La Giuntina, 2006), 45–65;Tonelli, "La salute non si vende: Ambiente di lavoro e lotte di fabbrica tra anni '60 e '70," in *I due bienni rossi del '900, 1919–1920 e 1968–1969: Studi e interpretazioni a confronto*, ed. Luigi Falossi and Francesco Loreto (Roma: Ediesse, 2007), 341–352.

6. On the 1968 students' movement in Italy, see Giovanni De Luna, *Le ragioni di un decennio. 1969–1979: Militanza, violenza, sconfitta, memoria* (Milano: Feltrinelli, 2008). On the birth of the "new industrial hygiene" in Italy, see Carnevale and Baldasseroni, *Mal da lavoro*, 238–244. See also CGIL-CISL-UIL Federazione Provinciale di Milano, *Salute e ambiente di lavoro: L'esperienza degli SMAL* (Milano: Mazzotta, 1976), 189–199.

7. CGIL-CISL-UIL, *Salute e ambiente di lavoro*, 12–13.

8. On the Seveso disaster, see Laura Centemeri, *Ritorno a Seveso: Il danno ambientale, il suo riconoscimento, la sua riparazione* (Milano: Mondadori, 2006). See also Saverio Luzzi, *Il virus del benessere: Ambiente, salute, sviluppo nell'Italia repubblicana* (Roma-Bari: Laterza, 2009), 140–155. On Medicina Democratica, see http://www.medicinademocratica .org/.

9. For a discussion of the "strong objectivity" approach in the study of industrial hazards, see Barbara Allen, *Uneasy Alchemy: Citizens and Experts in Louisiana's Chemical Corridor Disputes* (Cambridge, MA: MIT Press, 2003), 6–7, 118, 140, 149.

10. CGIL-CISL-UIL, *Salute e ambiente di lavoro*, 110.

11. Ibid., 74–85.

12. Ibid., 143–149.

13. Ibid., 189.

14. On the ANIC (later renamed Enichem) in Manfredonia, see Giulio Di Luzio, *I fantasmi dell'Enichem* (Milano: Baldini Castoldi Dalai, 2003).

15. On the 1976 accident, see Francesco Tomaiuolo, "1976–2006: Trent'anni di arsenico all'Enichem di Manfredonia," *I Frutti di Demetra* 12 (2006): 33–41; and Luzzi, *Il virus del benessere*, 152–155.

16. See Di Luzio, *I fantasmi dell'Enichem*.

17. Ibid.

18. On ecofeminism and women's action for environmental justice, see Carolyn Merchant, *Radical Ecology: The Search for a Livable World* (London: Routledge, 1995), 193–222; on feminist science and action research, see also Allen, *Uneasy Alchemy*, 117–150.

19. Maurizio Portaluri, interview by the author, April 2009.

20. On the encounter between Lovecchio and Portaluri, see Alessandro Langiu and Maurizio Portaluri, *Di fabbrica si muore* (San Cesario di Lecce, Italy: Manni, 2008).

21. See in particular Myrna Santiago's essay in this volume. See also Christopher Sellers, "Thoureau's Body: Towards an Embodied Environmental History," *Environmental History* 4 (1999): 486–514. On labor and workers' bodies in environmental history, see also Arthur McEvoy, "*Working Environments: An Ecological Approach to Industrial Health*

and Safety," Technology and Culture 36 (1995): S145–S173; Linda Nash, "The Fruits of Ill-Health: Pesticides and Workers' Bodies in Post-World War II California," *Osiris* 19 (2004): 203–219; Chad Montrie, *Making a Living: Work and Environment in the United States* (Chapel Hill: University of North Carolina Press, 2008).

22. See McEvoy, "Working environments."

10

A New Environmental Turn?

How the Environment Came to the Rescue of Occupational Health: Asbestos in France, 1970–1995

EMMANUEL HENRY

M any contributors to *Dangerous Trade* note the peculiar relationship between industrial hazards and environmental consciousness. Sellers argues that the "environmental turn" of the mid-twentieth century was precipitated by occupational health problems that brought to the fore a number of issues in environmental health.[1] Castleman and Tweedale discuss problems facing asbestos workers who struggle against barriers to compensation justice.

Asbestos became the most lethal occupational carcinogen used in France by the late twentieth century, killing approximately three thousand people every year, most of them employed in diverse trades (insulation, shipyards, and asbestos factories) and on construction sites utilizing asbestos-cement. The hazards of the substance were well known by specialists of occupational health in the late 1940s but did not attract the interest of the public media or the political actors at the time. Apart from a spurt of intense publicity in the mid-1970s, asbestos was virtually absent from public discourse until 1994, acquiring a public dimension only when its environmental ramifications were recognized, especially with the detection of asbestos in buildings. Like asbestos, some toxins appear to represent both occupational and environmental hazards. It is notable that occupational issues have attracted limited public attention in very recent years, in contrast to the 1970s, while environmental questions have drawn greater public interest.

By tracing the distortions or discontinuities in public presentation of such hazards, we can uncover the modalities of their management. My contribution to *Dangerous Trade* is concerned with the changing awareness of asbestos in France, which marked a distinctively new, but analogous, "environmental turn" in recent history. Redefining the asbestos problem as an environmental issue also allowed changes in the ways that workers' health issues were addressed, revealing a transformation in the rules for the structuring of public debate that affected the terms in which such problems were formulated in the course of public action. My research draws on semi-structured interviews with key actors and documentary analysis of reports, press, and broadcasting media from the peak of French industrial asbestos consumption during the 1970s until total prohibition in 1997.[2]

At its peak, asbestos-related employment reached almost fifteen thousand persons, mainly devoted to asbestos-cement production. The industry was dominated by two industrial groups: Eternit, originally a family business that gained an international profile,[3] and Saint-Gobain, an archetypal representative of French industrial capitalism.[4] The recent asbestos crisis in France can be dated from May 1995 as the problem became an important and frequent news item, prompting administrative action that included several decrees and regulatory texts. In June 1996 legal charges were brought by the asbestos victims' organization, ANDEVA (Association Nationale de Défense des Victimes de l'Amiante). Political responses, which included an asbestos ban, normalized the problem and marked out a longer-term approach by government.

My first task is an examination of the forces behind the publicizing of the problem in the mid-1970s and its subsequent return to the fringes of public debate. There follows a discussion of the reasons for a fresh public engagement with the asbestos issue redefined as an environmental problem. This can be linked to strategies to circumvent particular forms of occupational hazard management, but also reflects changes in the people mobilized, the evolution of the media, and the terms of political actors' involvement. This analysis highlights profound transformations in the sphere of public debate and in modalities of public action in regard to this particular occupational hazard over twenty-five years.

From the Emergence of a Political Problem to Its Containment

Asbestos in 1970: An Occupational Problem with Political Ramifications

During the 1970s, the asbestos issue was drawn to public attention by the harm caused to workers by occupational exposure. Mobilization around this problem occurred in the wake of the May 1968 protest movements and therefore had a marked and openly political orientation. The Collectif Inter-syndical Jussieu led the movement with its far-left-wing orientation, evident in its subsequent account of mobilization.[5] Asbestos was presented essentially as an occupational toxin through reports of the union movements in firms that used or processed it. The presence of asbestos in the subway and in certain food products, as well as the heavy pollution of the Jussieu University campus, was also covered by the news media. But these environmental aspects did not overshadow the debate in the way they were to do later. Numerous articles and books aimed to reclassify occupational accidents and diseases as personal injuries under common law. Since the 1898 compensation law for occupational accidents (extended in 1919 to occupational diseases), these incidents had been dealt with through a specific process of "compensation," managed from 1946 on by social security institutions. This procedure precluded recourse to the civil and penal institutions responsible for other kinds of accident. The long-established conciliation and compromise process, which led to the relative normalization of occupational hazards, was seriously challenged in the 1970s.[6] Several CEOs were arrested by left-wing judges after serious occupational accidents, before a 1976 law on hygiene and safety at work limited the responsibility of industrialists.[7]

The recognition of asbestos-related diseases as occupational hazards proceeded in a highly political atmosphere. The protest campaigns struggled not only against the mineral but also against the socioeconomic structures that legitimized the use of such lethal toxins. The intense politicization of these discussions enabled the persistence of a contradictory, pro-asbestos discourse in the public sphere, as controlled use continued to be advocated by many political and administrative personnel who were involved in its regulation. These included certain trade unions who feared the consequences of restriction or outright banning, and councillors from towns that housed large asbestos plants (see Allen's and Barca's essays in the present collection for comparative Italian cases). The French debate on asbestos in the 1970s revealed a rift between two ways of defining the problem, which also corresponded to different political positions. The news media similarly reflected these positions, clearly visible in certain asbestos-related labor conflicts, which were covered with empathy by left-wing newspapers (*Libération*, *L'Humanité*) but received minimal coverage in the politically "neutral" press (*Le Monde*) or conservative newspapers (*Le Figaro*).

The social and historical configuration of the period facilitated a political presentation of asbestos as a primarily occupational problem. Extensive publicizing of the asbestos issue in the 1970s was also strongly facilitated by its perception by news broadcasters as a means to reassert their position within a politically polarized media sphere. The news media's positions were thus a transposition, within the media sphere, of conflicts between broader social groups.

A (Relatively) Silent Period

Following this initial phase of controversy and mobilization, the asbestos issue lost almost all of its public visibility. In hindsight this may appear surprising when we compare asbestos to other public health problems, though it corresponds to a pattern in the occupational toxin field. Following Bachrach and Baratz on nondecisions, we can see occupational risk as a "nonproblem," one that certain actors seek to render nonproblematic.[8] Factors that contribute to limiting the scope of occupational health problems include, first, the institutional structures in which decisions are made. These structures reflect the low priority granted in France to this field and the limited public resources devoted to administering it. Some twelve hundred labor inspectors are responsible for inspecting 1.5 million firms and 15 million employees.[9] Faced with such inadequate state supervision, French employees and labor unions assume the burden of implementing and controlling safety standards for industrial hazards. The result is weak implementation of policy and serious underestimation of occupational diseases. Only a very small number of the ailments directly attributable to employment are actually recognized as the result of occupational hazards.[10]

In parallel with this limited administration, and partly related to it, is the Labor Ministry's reliance on consultations with representatives of workers and employers. Health and safety regulations depend on compromises reached between employers and employees, who are generally opposed or antagonistic on other issues. The national consultative Conseil Supérieur de Prévention des Risques Professionnels falls under the state labor administration, bringing together representatives of workers and firms. In practice most decisions taken in the field of French occupational health result from agreements reached between representatives on this committee. The main debates concerning occupational health take place before a restricted audience, limited to the circles of specialists participating or directly interested in it (especially occupational hazard prevention professionals and militants recruited in trade unions or mutual benefit societies). Their decisions are rarely publicized since they primarily concern the regulatory field rather than legislation. This precludes debate in arenas with a wider audience, such as parliamentary sessions. Consequently, these players are deeply engaged in compromises resulting from such negotiations, inducing a strong loyalty to the institution.[11] The actors and stakeholders involved in such procedures often try to shield their agreements and compromises from a critical exposure that could undermine them.

The compensation system is an important factor in the absence of adverse criticism of the processes by which occupational health policies are defined and implemented. Because the management of occupational hazards consist of maintaining an "acceptable" risk level for workers, we need to consider the grounds on which occupational diseases are accepted by the people subjected to them, without triggering opposition in other social spheres. The regulation of such problems by France's national health insurance facilitate such acceptance, for occupational hazards are managed by institutions (mainly social security institutions) whose role is seen as precisely one of compensating victims. The weight of occupational accidents and diseases is perceived primarily in terms of a rate of contributions set annually by the social security funds for firms. The suffering generated by work is scaled and fitted into the organization of production like one piece of data among others, dealt with by specific institutions. In this way, generalization of the financial and social security logic end up making it difficult to impute responsibility for faults.

The system becomes more than insurance coverage; it functions as an instrument of normalization that imposes an ineluctable character on occupational hazards. Firms, the generators of the risk, benefit from a situation of de facto impunity. Because of the rules of the Social Security Code, victims who claim compensation for an occupational hazard or accident lost the possibility of obtaining additional compensation in court, unless they persuade the social security court to recognize their employers' "inexcusable misconduct." The situation is also a result of the very weak criminal liability associated with infringement of labor and social security laws, which make recourse to law, as a way of shifting the constellation of power, very difficult.[12]

The lack of employer accountability in labor and social security laws is even more problematic when workers' physical integrity is at stake and legal infringements may have irreversible consequences for health. The absence of occupational health lawsuits differentiates France from countries such as the United States, where the asbestos issue emerged in the 1970s as lawsuits were filed by victims against firms that exposed them to danger.[13] In the United Kingdom legal action was commonly used by victims in this situation.[14] The peculiarity of French conditions helps explain the strong emergence of the issue in the 1990s, following a long period without judicial conflicts between victims and generators of risk. These factors contribute to the framing of asbestos and, more generally, occupational toxins as problems that emerge only very exceptionally in the public sphere, for reasons unrelated to their occupational characteristics.

An Impossible Change?

In common with other occupational hazards, asbestos could have remained invisible to the public. But it did not. Asbestos emerged from the mid-1990s as a major public health scandal in France, at the same time as the contaminated blood affair and BSE ("mad cow disease"), and became an urgent topic in the French news media. The usual interpretation of the French "asbestos crisis" turns on the persistence of a conspiracy of silence. Firms allegedly concealed the toxicity of asbestos from public authorities to ensure that its use was not limited or banned. Such a historical interpretation often assumes, however, an idealized view of the state and its role as public protector. Such a sanitised representation of government administration and of the regulation of occupational hazards is seriously deficient. Labor administration was instrumental in the production of standards regulating the use of asbestos and other toxins in the workplace. The suggestion that the state was deceived by a false representation of asbestos ignores the basic composition of the state as compound arrangement of diverse groups rather than a single entity.

If we focus on labor administration, the period from 1975 to 1995 can be characterized as a time when the management of asbestos-related occupational hazards was "normal." There was nothing particularly unusual about it compared to the management of other, similar toxins regulated for use in the professional context.[15] We can detect here a major contradiction peculiar to occupational toxins. From 1995 on, the asbestos problem has been, without exception, referred to as a "scandal" or, in other words, the result of reprehensible acts that ought to be morally condemned. Research reveals, however, not a pattern of misappropriation or abnormal or exceptional mismanagement of this risk, but rather the normal, routine functioning of French government labor administration. This process contributes to an explanation of the low level of visibility that French occupational health issues have. At the time of the "scandal," such questions were of limited interest or even unknown to actors capable of reaching a broader audience. Journalists were largely absent from the group of relevant actors in the years of silence. It remained very difficult to directly question the modes of managing occupational illness since the actors who shaped policy had little interest in altering the basis of compromise on which it was grounded. Those not directly involved in these processes were unfamiliar with the nature of the problem or not concerned to address it. Actors were locked in a system of checks and balances that compelled those who wanted change to deploy highly particular strategies to circumvent those constraints.

The Reemergence of Absestos in the 1990s as a "Valence Issue": Asbestos as an Environmental Problem

Faced with the impossibility of changing the system from the inside, the actors who mobilized to alter the established balances were forced to do so not by changing the system but by circumventing it, that is, by trying to undermine it from the outside. They achieved this by leaving the sphere of occupational relations and redefining the problem in environmental terms. The recasting of the question as one of general environmental health transformed it into a matter of general interest, including the focus on public buildings and housing. More than two-thirds of the reports on national television news broadcasts, from September 1995 to June 1996, were devoted to asbestos in schools. The main French channel, TF1, used a skull and crossbones to introduce its first reports. The aim was to frame asbestos as "an epidemic concerning us all," as the magazine *Sciences et Avenir* phrased it in a landmark 1995 issue. Two reports in September 1995 and 1996 on *Envoyé Spécial* (a major documentary programme on France 2 television) emphasized the risk for the whole population. Journalists increasingly denounced a new public health scandal, with public authorities and industry standing accused, the former for their failure to act and the latter for having multiplied the uses of asbestos.

It is important to emphasize that the redefinition of asbestos as an environmental problem was *not* an explicit, conscious strategy by frustrated reformers to manipulate public discourse. It was more the outcome of factors that, when combined, gave a similar orientation toward radical change. These are now considered.

The Appearance of New Actors and New Repertoires of Mobilization

An important difference between the 1970s and the 1990s can be seen in the changing actors involved in discussions of asbestos. Workers in asbestos industries were now called "victims of asbestos." A key role was assumed by ANDEVA, the national asbestos victims' organization, and its federation of several local victims groups. This particular body relegated unions to the background, resulting in their virtual absence from public discourse, which reinforced the marginalization, and even exclusion, of occupational aspects of the issue. However, there were also some continuities in support and action; some victims' organizations, especially local ones, continued in different forms activities mounted by workers groups that had members affected by heavy asbestos use. Those who worked with asbestos remained practically involved as key actors in the story.

The appearance of new victims at the forefront of the scene can therefore be interpreted as a modification of the views that the actors had of themselves and of the image that they wanted to project. This change was by no means self-evident for all those concerned. For a long period, those who were to became the most recognisable victims of asbestos were far from seeing themselves in this light. They were, in their own view, first and foremost workers exposed to an occupational toxin. For them this meant accepting the related risks and reaching compromises that might enable them to carry on working in the industry. Exposure to asbestos was, in this sense, simply one aspect of their social identity—and a somewhat peripheral one, as their identity remained centred on their membership in a structured social group. As the 1980s and 1990s witnessed a series of factory closings and staff reductions, leading to retrenchment plans or early retirement, the established facets of identity among exposed workers crumbled, leaving "the victim" as the ultimate point in their identity structure. This recognition of being a victim prevailed not merely by default but also positively, as these actors were encouraged to play this role in court cases, thereby increasing their prospects of winning compensation. They were also requested by local news media to testify to their victim's condition. Such developments prompted the relevant actors to highlight a fresh facet of their identity, rather than it merely being presented as a calculated strategy on their part. This transformation of actors accompanied the investment of new repertoires of collective action by the organizations mobilised.[16]

Even though occupational issues are rarely resolved in courts, victims associations turned to the law—social, civil, and penal—to give exposure to the asbestos issue.[17] This "judicialization" of asbestos provided one of the vectors of its redefinition, since the complaints filed in courts were aimed as much at the legal system itself as at the media. In 1994 a complaint filed by the widows of teachers who had died after teaching in a polluted technical high school triggered the first media discussions. This complaint was the first to take asbestos out of the occupational sphere where it had been confined. The case highlighted the risk of passive contamination through exposure to asbestos without direct contact, and brought forward victims who were not employed in risky manual occupations. The media were also able to present the situation in simplified, moralistic terms.[18] The increasing numbers of legal proceedings in the following months reinforced the image of asbestos as a scandal with future legal ramifications. Public redefinition compelled the actors involved to address the problem within frames of interpretation peculiar to public health rather than occupational hazard. This process necessarily involved the media.

Transformations of the Media Sphere

It is important to note that the French media underwent profound political and economic changes during the 1990s, including an ideological neutralization. In 1970 ideological opposition structured the French press; twenty years later ideology had been largely replaced by the rules of economic competition as the media faced recurrent financial difficulties. Journalists previously approached their work in a militant or politicized mode, but this way of working was transformed into a workplace mentality that embraced values related to skills and professionalization. Journalists' work became legitimized by technical expertise in explaining complex issues rather than by a specific social perspective.[19] It is possible to speculate that if the problem of asbestos had been addressed in the same terms and by the same actors as in 1970, it would have received little attention or none at all from the news media. By contrast, the definition of asbestos as a public health problem prompted the engagement of journalists with it as a key or headline issue. Defining asbestos in this way meant constructing it as a "valence issue," that is, one upon which everybody agrees.[20] As asbestos became recognised as a public health scandal with victims in the general population, implicating recognised culprits (those firms disseminating asbestos into the environment), it became impossible to resist the condemnation of such a situation. The consensual nature of this definition seems to have been one of the factors facilitating the media's commitment to this type of cause—one that in several respects resembled humanitarian causes. Very little coverage emphasized the occupational dimensions of the problem in the first months of its media reemergence during 1995–1996. Those covering it were mostly specialized journalists with prior knowledge of the asbestos issue. The definition of asbestos as a threat to the entire population was first and foremost an effect of limited technical knowledge of the problem.

This broad definition proved very effective in that journalists were able to promote and to construct it from beginning to end. Several televisions reports focused on a para-occupational victim, contaminated by asbestos as a child because he lived close to a family of workers in an asbestos factory. This illustrates vividly how journalists and, in particular, television reporters worked. The portraits of the victim, a 29-year-old father of two little girls who had died in the weeks following the airings of the first reports, emphasized his pain as well as the completely unpredictable and random aspect of the illness, which could affect anyone.[21] Journalists found it easier to work on public health issues affecting the general population than on an occupational disease, for several reasons. As we have seen, the actors involved with occupational health issues did not particularly wish to publicize them. The way such problems were discussed and resolved rendered them highly technical (necessitating knowledge of metrology, toxicology, medicine, or epidemiology), so they appeared beyond the grasp of the nonexpert.[22] Occupational dangers often appeared remote, affecting only limited numbers in society and being far removed from the world and experience of middle- and upper-class journalists, who rarely penetrated the cloak of workplace disease as a "normal" form of occupational risk.

Precedents also helped to frame the asbestos issue. By the time journalists became aware of what appeared as the asbestos scandal, they had already covered a number of "public health crises," including the contaminated blood affair in the early 1990s.[23] The regular coverage of public health concerns influenced their inclination to compare asbestos problems with other toxins affecting the general population. This characterization stemmed essentially from the short circuit between two competing definitions of asbestos: on the one hand an occupational toxin that was a large-scale killer in France (some three thousand annual deaths) but was little known to journalists; on the other hand, a scandal, one emphasizing the omnipresence of asbestos producing risks for the population at large and the failure of regulatory action. This encounter and reformulation of asbestos as a public health problem had an immediate galvanising effect on actors who had no former knowledge of issues relating to occupational risk. These actors were shocked and surprised by the dimension of the problem, unusual for problems affecting the general population, and they responded with indignation. The political consequences were profound.

Politicians "Playing the Game" of Redefinition

Political actors played a crucial part in redefining the asbestos problem. They were not so much "facing" the crisis as they were "in the crisis."[24] In late May 1995, France's Health Minister appeared on the evening news on TF1 (his appearance was covered the next day in the national daily *Le Monde*) to announce a decree requiring all property owners to check for asbestos in their buildings. Thereafter, political actors regularly weighed in on the issue publicly. The 1995 announcement of this future decree (which would be adopted in 1996) provides an excellent example of a formative administrative solution that enabled the state administration to exhibit political resolution in the face of an important public problem.[25] The solution accentuated the environmental elements of the problems posed by asbestos and contributed to setting the agenda of their redefinition. Journalists, faced with what they perceived to be a subject for the Health Minister, turned to him for answers regarding the risk affecting the population as a whole. At the same time, the minister, by presenting a solution to a serious public problem, recognized the media's definition as a means by which to affirm a capacity for action. In agreeing to a definition in terms of a public health scandal, the political actors placed themselves in a risky position, but they also confronted a problem for which they had an immediate response. They demonstrated that they knew how to assume their "responsibilities" at a time when it was precisely the absence of resolution that was the ground for complaint.

The situation reinforced the expected social roles of politicians (taking action) and journalists (denouncing scandal). This strengthening arguably played a key part in redefining the problem. While the political actors played the game of redefinition, they were not followed by all actors in the public administration, some of whom maintained autonomy in responding to the asbestos scandal. Government authorities in France hesitated at the junction of two routes out of "the crisis." The first consisted of presenting asbestos as an exception among other occupational toxins and, a fortiori, among public health policies. In this version of events, the management of the asbestos problem was firmly differentiated from the standard regulation of occupational toxins, and an attempt was made to show a series of mistakes caused by a lack of prior evaluation of asbestos-related mortalities. This definition of the problem as exceptional addressed public concerns by showing that the crisis was well defined and indicating ways of resolving it. The characteristic resolution was a ban. Despite its limited immediate impact, such a course possessed all the attributes of a "final" decision. In practice the ban amounted to a prohibition of asbestos-cement, accounting in 1996 for 95 percent of the 35,000 tonnes of asbestos France imported. Other uses were almost all abandoned, as successive restrictions on commercialization were imposed by European regulations. The prohibition was made more easily since asbestos was of little importance to the French economy, the firms that produced asbestos-cement having delocalized their production.[26]

Before and after the ban announcement, problems posed by asbestos remained much the same. Workers' exposure in the building industry would last for several decades, as long as asbestos remained. The creation of the Fund for the Compensation of Asbestos Victims (FIVA) fell within a similar category of decision making, isolating asbestos among occupational toxic products. FIVA's mission was (and is) to preserve the existing system of insurance for occupational hazards by seeing to it that the state partly finances the compensation of victims whose pathologies have clearly occupational causes, thereby releasing private business from the burden.

The second and alternative route out of the crisis lay in dealing administratively with problems posed by asbestos. By reducing it to narrower dimensions than those identified in public discussions, the intention was to render asbestos a manageable problem. The reshaping of regulations on its use in the working environment, orchestrated by the Labor Ministry in 1995–1996, fell into this category. Although it had a much greater impact in terms of public health, this type of decision received much less attention from the news media because it was less likely to resonate with the more public dimensions of the problem.

Conclusion

The paradoxes that appear to attend the handling of the asbestos problem in France reveal very specific relationships between occupational health issues and the public sphere in the contemporary period. Occupational health issues are managed with relative discretion. The most public facet of occupational health policies are those presented as protection of workers. This facet is the best known because it corresponds most closely to the official objectives of public health policies in Western countries—namely, to protect their populations. Put into perspective in relation to all public health policies, those involving occupational health can also be analyzed as participating in a *differentiated management* of public health. The objectives and modalities of public action are not the same for the entire population. They are, on the contrary, differentiated in relation to the status of the individuals concerned, in relation to the circumstances in which their health is altered, or in relation to the type of actors responsible for the deterioration of their health. By knowingly allowing workers to be exposed to health risks, occupational health policies discriminate against the workers concerned, who are placed in situations of less protection than other groups not targeted by these policies. This aspect of workplace health policy has to remain understated in order to avoid weakening its legitimacy.

We are therefore observing a set of paradoxes between the public dimensions of the problems and the way in which these problems are addressed in a political and administrative mode. The environmental dimensions are almost the only ones that are able to attract public attention. However, many of these problems (like asbestos or glycol ethers) would not have become public had they not been major occupational hazards. On the other hand, the main administrative and political approach to such problems is undertaken in confined arenas of negotiation that specialize in occupational problems. Indirectly, through fear of litigation or fear of the broadcasting of such risks, the intense publicity given to these questions has affected public policy processes, accelerating them or prioritizing these questions on the political agenda. In the longer run, environmental questions may well have more and more effects on the occupational health field. This can be seen through the progressive but regular transformation of expertise in this field, one of the most significant aspects of which, in France, is the creation of new public agencies exclusively dedicated to occupational and environmental health.[27] Such processes may offer a parallel to the discussion of expertise by Melling and Sellers in the present volume.

The contemporary "environmental shift" distinguishes itself quite clearly from the awareness of new environmental risks expressed through studies of workers. Today almost the opposite process is taking place, as the presentation of occupational hazards as a risk for the general population transforms the modalities of their public management. This results from several transformative factors, including transformation of the actors mobilized and of their modes of mobilization, transformation of the arenas of public debate, and transformation of the understanding, treatment, and formulation of public health issues. Constraints on the mobilizations related to occupational problems persist, limiting the possible definitions of problems that now appear as valence issues, and not as problems likely to trigger more resistance. Such restrictions encourage new forms of mobilization, facilitating those that crystallize around actors who present themselves as victims of an injustice, and preempting those that begin with workers affected by workplace hazards. If mobilizations continue to develop in other forms, the recognition of and respect for these constraints remain a guarantee of efficiency for collective action, since they allocate the actors involved to their expected and idealized social roles: the journalist is led to denounce scandals; the politicians are led to act on a situation in order to transform it; and lawyers are led to intervene. In the medium term, the victims are expected to be recognized and compensated and the accused are supposed to be punished. This stylization of problems and actors reveals the constraints imposed by the contemporary spaces of public and media debate, which increasingly limit the possible definitions of actors and problems. Access to spaces of public debate is increasingly linked to this stylization, which raises issues for health-related problems because they do not easily fit within these preconceived frames, or at least not unless they are radically redefined.

NOTES

1. Christopher Sellers, *Hazards of the Job: From Industrial Disease to Environmental Health Science* (Chapel Hill: University of North Carolina Press, 1997).
2. Emmanuel Henry, "Un scandale improbable. Amiante: d'une maladie professionnelle à une 'crise de santé publique'" (Ph.D. diss., Université de technologie de Compiègne, 2000); Emmanuel Henry, *Amiante: Un scandale improbable. Sociologie d'un problème public* (Rennes, France: Presses Universitaires de Rennes, 2007).
3. Odette Hardy-Hémery, *Eternit et l'amiante, 1922–2000: Aux sources du profit, une industrie du risque* (Villeneuve d'Ascq, France: Presses Universitaires du Septentrion, 2005).
4. François Malye, *Amiante: 100,000 morts à venir* (Paris: Le Cherche Midi, 2004).
5. Collectif Intersyndical Sécurité des Universités Jussieu, Confédération Française Démocratique du Travail, Confédération Générale du Travail, and Fédération de l'Education Nationale, *Danger! Amiante* (Paris: François Maspéro, 1977).
6. François Ewald, ed., "Justice, Discipline, Production," *Les temps modernes* 354 (1976): 969–1091.
7. Pierre Cam, "Juges rouges et droit du travail," *Actes de la Recherche en Sciences Sociales* 19 (1978): 2–27; Willem de Haan, Jos Silvis, and Philip A. Thomas, "Radical French Judges: Syndicat de la Magistrature," *Journal of Law and Society* 16, no. 4 (1989): 477–482.
8. Peter Bachrach and Morton S. Baratz, "Two Faces of Power," *American Political Science Review* 56, no. 4 (1962): 947–952. Many studies have shown that no problem is per se a public or political problem, as it needs to be constructed and carried by actors or social groups who work toward framing it as a problem. See, for example, William L. F. Felstiner, Richard L. Abel, and Austin Sarat, "The Emergence and Transformation of Disputes: Naming, Blaming, Claiming," *Law and Society Review* 15, no. 3/4 (1980): 631–654. At the same time, potentially problematical situations have to be consistently reduced to limited dimensions if too much public attention is to be avoided. See, for example, Roger W. Cobb and Marc H. Ross, eds., *Cultural Strategies of Agenda Denial: Avoidance, Attack, and Redefinition* (Lawrence: University Press of Kansas, 1997).
9. Ministère du Travail, des Relations Sociales, de la Famille, de la Solidarité et de la Ville, *L'inspection du travail en France en 2008: Rapport rédigé en application des articles*

20 et 21 de la Convention 81 de l'Organisation Internationale du Travail (OIT) (Paris: Direction Générale du Travail, 2009).

10. Annie Thébaud-Mony, *De la connaissance à la reconnaissance des maladies professionnelles en France: Acteurs et logiques sociales* (Paris: La Documentation Française, 1991); Ellen Imbernon, *Estimation du nombre de cas de certains cancers attribuables à des facteurs professionnels en France* (Paris: Institut de Veille Sanitaire, 2002).

11. Albert O Hirschman, *Exit, Voice, and Loyalty: Responses to Decline in Firms, Organizations, and States* (Cambridge, MA: Harvard University Press, 1970).

12. Evelyne Serverin, "L'application des sanctions pénales en droit social: Un traitement juridictionnel marginal," *Droit Social* 7–8 (1994): 654–662; Emmanuel Henry, "Intéresser les tribunaux à sa cause: Contournement de la difficile judiciarisation du problème de l'amiante" *Sociétés contemporaines* 52 (2003): 39–59.

13. Paul Brodeur, *Outrageous Misconduct: The Asbestos Industry on Trial* (New York: Pantheon Books, 1985); Paul Brodeur, *Expendable Americans* (New York: Viking Press, 1974).

14. Geoffrey Tweedale, *Magic Mineral to Killer Dust: Turner & Newall and the Asbestos Hazard* (Oxford: Oxford University Press, 2000).

15. In other ministries concerned about the asbestos issue (such as Health or Housing), this was always a very secondary question. There appears to have been no immediate need for action since the Ministry of Work was particularly active in a field that primarily concerned it.

16. Charles Tilly, *The Contentious French* (Cambridge, MA: Harvard University Press, 1986).

17. Henry, "Intéresser les tribunaux à sa cause."

18. Emmanuel Henry, "Le droit comme vecteur de publicisation des problèmes sociaux: Effets publics du recours au droit dans le cas de l'amiante," in *Sur la portée sociale du droit: Usages et légitimité du registre juridique*, ed. Liora Israël et al., 187–200 (Paris: Presses Universitaires de France, 2005).

19. Erik Neveu, *Sociologie du journalisme*, 2nd ed. (Paris: La Découverte, 2004); Sandrine Lévêque, *Les journalistes sociaux: Histoire et sociologie d'une spécialité journalistique* (Rennes, France: Presses Universitaires de Rennes, 2000).

20. Barbara J. Nelson, *Making an Issue of Child Abuse: Political Agenda Setting for Social Problems* (Chicago: University of Chicago Press, 1984), 27.

21. See in particular the report broadcasted on *Envoyé Special*, France 2, September 28, 1995.

22. We should not, however, lose sight of the fact that this technical nature of problems was not a given it was constructed. As Cobb and Elder point out, "Perhaps the most effective way to restrict or localize the scope of an issue is to redefine it technically so that most people will not understand it." Roger W. Cobb and Charles D. Elder, *Participation in American Politics: The Dynamics of Agenda-Building* (Baltimore: Johns Hopkins University Press, 1983), 45.

23. Mark A. P. Bovens, Paul 't Hart, and B. Guy Peters, eds., *Success and Failure in Public Governance: A Comparative Analysis. New Horizons in Public Policy* (Cheltenham, UK: Edward Elgar, 2001); Eric A. Feldman and Ronald Bayer, eds. *Blood Feuds: AIDS, Blood, and the Politics of Medical Disaster* (New York: Oxford University Press, 1999).

24. Claude Gilbert, "Risques sanitaires et sciences humaines et sociales: Quelques pistes de recherche," *Revue Française des Affaires Sociales* 1 (1999): 9–20.

25. These solutions seeking a problem were fairly close to the "solutions looking for issues to which they might be the answer" described in the case of organizations. Michael D. Cohen, James G. March, and Johan P. Olsen, "A Garbage Can Model of Organizational Choice," *Administrative Science Quarterly* 17, no. 1 (1972): 2.

26. Barry I. Castleman, "Global Corporate Policies and International 'Double Standards' in Occupational and Environmental Health," *International Journal of Occupational and Environmental Health* 14, no. 5 (1999): 61–64; Jane H. Ives, ed., *The Export of Hazard: Transnational Corporations and Environmental Control Issues* (London: Routledge and Kegan Paul, 1985).

27. Emmanuel Henry, "Nouvelles dynamiques de savoirs et permanence des rapports de pouvoir: L'impact—limité—des transformations—importantes—de l'expertise en santé au travail," *Revue française de science politique* 61, no. 4 (2011): 707–726.

New Arenas of Contest

11

A Tale of Two Lawsuits

Making Policy-Relevant Environmental
Health Knowledge in Italian and U.S. Chemical Regions

BARBARA L. ALLEN

Contributions to this volume frequently note the impact of popular movements on the transformation of environmental health politics during the later twentieth century and the early years of this one. Activist groups have brought pressure to bear on governments to take seriously citizens' complaints about industrial and social hazards. The origins of such disquiet can often be traced to the failure of the powerful and commercial or professional experts to provide effective answers to questions about hazards presented by industrial facilities. For those residing near chemical plants, an important question has been the long-term health effects of exposure to low levels of pollution. For workers employed at such installations, rather different questions arise about the effects of more concentrated chemicals on their bodies.

Knowledge about hazards remains a vital, contested area. Remarkably, little research has been carried out on the effects of low-level, mixed-chemical exposure.[1] While workers' questions are somewhat easier to design studies for, traditional research methods and protocols are expensive and controversial.[2] There seems to be no government incentive to prioritize the types of long-term laboratory and epidemiological studies that are needed to verify causal links between certain chemical exposures and human illnesses. Other problems explaining the lack of research on industrial hazards and illness lie in the tangled intersection of legal institutions, with their adversarial model of proof, and the scientific system, with a set of different problems. The first of these problems is the scientific method's bias against false positive results. This means that scientists studying an effect of a chemical on a human or animal subject are more likely to find a false negative than a false positive impact. The second problem is the misuse of the concept of "scientific uncertainty," meaning that scientific facts are never absolute and always in progress. This concept, unfortunately, is easily manipulated into the maxim "Do nothing until you know for sure."

My earlier research on activism in neighborhoods impacted by industrial pollution found that successful environmental movements share three characteristics: (1) they ally themselves with citizen-oriented scientists, (2) they ally themselves with larger national or international environmental groups, and (3) they are heterogeneous groups of citizens, not from any one class, race, or profession.[3] My aim in this research was to understand the mechanisms that promote better environmental science and regulation in collaboration with better monitoring of public health.

In order to further understand successful environmental case studies, particularly in a comparative perspective, the framework of the new political sociology of science (NPSS) is useful. This framework provides an *analytical structure* in which to connect case studies and other micro or local observations to broader cultural, political, and institutional dynamics.[4] Specifically, NPSS encourages the examination of how rules, legal institutions, organizations, and social/political networks condition the availability and distribution of power in the production of knowledge. It is at this intersection of local action and larger-scale institutions that the fulcrums for productive policy change and reform can be seen. There are many institutions, networks, and practices that shape environmental health knowledge and policy outcomes. However, legal systems and, more specifically, legal actions, such as lawsuits, create apparent social and professional networks as well as cultural practices that pressure knowledge making and outcomes in significant ways. Additionally, legal proceedings provide a more translucent lens through which to view the workings of science and the impacts of institutions in making policy-relevant environmental health knowledge. Looking at case studies comparatively and internationally serves to illuminate processes and procedures and to identify relevant differences toward improving both the environment and public health in the future.

In 2004 two lawsuits—one in Marghera, Italy, and one in Louisiana—regarding environmental health and science were decided. Both cases were heard in a context of considerable suspicion regarding the impacts of petrochemical facilities and their waste products on human health. The outcomes of the two cases differed dramatically and had divergent implications for policy actions, for corporate change, and for the making of publicly available environmental health science. These two cases and the regions in which they were located (namely, the chemical corridor of south Louisiana and Porto Marghera near Venice) form the basis of my present analysis. Both regions were large producers of chlorine-based chemicals for plastics (polyvinyl chloride [PVC] and vinyl chloride monomer [VCM]) and share some of the same large corporations.[5] They both had high unemployment and adjacent residential communities. Both first established themselves as industrial regions in the early twentieth century and experienced large-scale growth in the 1960s with the expansion of plastics demand in the United States and Europe. Geographically, each area was prone to flooding, being located near fragile wetlands and aquatic resources.

Such comparative approaches also provide a *methodological strategy* for moving beyond the local situatedness of each case study and toward building a causal hypothesis and more widely applicable explanations. The present study, in its comparison of two large chemical regions, examines how institutional arrangements, professional networks, and cultural norms can be both productive and repressive in the coproduction of environmental knowledge. As both a lens for viewing the making of environmental knowledge and an ingredient of national differentiation explaining alternate outcomes, the legal system is an important element in comparative research. The following two sections provide a narrative of events in the Italian case; they are followed by a parallel discussion of a case in Louisiana.

The Italian Case

Marghera, a small town on the Venice Lagoon, housed one of the largest chemical complexes in Italy, providing about half of the PVC produced in the country.[6] It originated as an industrial center after the First World War on land purchased from the city of Venice.[7] Workers' housing was built adjacent to industry and was predominantly small apartments and dormitory housing for laborers.[8] The district became a hybrid of various types of industrial production and was destroyed by allied forces in the Second World War. Rebuilt in the late 1950s and early 1960s, it became a center of chlorine-based chemicals in Europe; by 1994 there were about eighty-five chemical plants around Porto Marghera.

In the 1970s chemical workers and, subsequently, residents expressed suspicions about the dangers posed by the petrochemical plants, especially the accidental releases and unexplained illnesses in the community. In 1971 the Institute of Medicine in Padova conducted a pediatric study in Marghera, finding that 90 percent of children between the ages of six and eleven had respiratory ailments and other illnesses.[9] This occurred at a time when both labor activism (see Barca's essay in this volume) and the local environmental movement dedicated to cleaning up the Venice Lagoon, the Fronte per la Difesa di Venezia e della Laguna, were at their height. Citizen protest attributed blame for the pollution to Porto Marghera and chemical industry practices, and labor activists were breaking from union solidarity to ask occupational safety questions.[10]

This period was also a fertile one for Italian environmental health research into the effects of PVC and VCM on human and animal health. In 1966, a private meeting of U.S. and European chemical companies discussed health problems related to the production and use of these substances. Such problems included skin thickening, bone disease, and liver pathologies. European vinyl chloride producers commissioned their own research by Cesare Maltoni of the Bologna Centre for the Prevention and Detection of Tumors and Oncological Research. In 1972 Maltoni found cancer from VCM occurring in rats at very low exposures and in various sites, including the liver. European and American PVC manufacturers, concerned about these findings, made a pact of secrecy during the early 1970s regarding all research about the toxicity and carcinogenicity of PVC/VCM chemical processes.[11] It had become clear by early 1973 that there was a relationship between angiosarcoma of the liver and low-level VCM exposure.

In the spring of 1974, Maltoni's work on the carcinogenicity of PVC and VCM appeared in print. He claimed that epidemiological proof only after deaths have occurred is insufficient to address the issue of safe levels of exposure to toxic substances. Maltoni believed that animal studies, such as his, were a preferable mechanism to predict effect and set safe exposure levels *before* damage is done.[12]

Industry disagreed, claiming that human disease must be the proof of harm, not animal studies. On discovering the deadly effects of their chemicals, the industry *had* made some adjustments to production. They voluntarily discontinued the use of VCM in spray products (hairspray, room deodorants, insecticides, paint), without notifying any public authorities of their concerns. They also stopped using PVC in the packaging of alcohol (wine, beer, etc.) since it leached into the beverage.[13] In food safety, the burden of proof is shouldered by industry, unlike environmental pollution or worker safety where industry can proceed without clear evidence of harm.

At the beginning of 1974 VCM was suspected in the deaths of four workers at a plant in the United States—they died of angiosarcoma of the liver, a rare cancer identical to the cancer reported in Maltoni's rat studies. The National Institute for Occupational Safety and Health (NIOSH) was quickly informed of the potential link between PVC/VCM exposure and cancer, and it sided with Maltoni's conclusions. One consequence was a radical reduction in the industry standard for worker exposure to VCM over an eight-hour period, from 500 ppm to 50 ppm in 1974 and to 1 ppm by 1976.[14] The response of Montedison, the largest PVC/VCM producer in Marghera, to the sharp lowering of exposure limits was creative. According to some scientists, the company changed the monitoring system in 1975 and dramatic drops in VCM concentrations occurred overnight.[15] The new system had a maximum reading of only 25 ppm and averaged concentrations across different workspaces. It did not give point source readings at the locations of maximum exposure; nor did it monitor the exposure of individual workers.

This was a period of workforce decline in Marghera's chemical companies due largely to plant automation. The scarcity of work and the fear of closures reduced the inclination of many workers, unions, and even townspeople to criticize their industry.[16] The chemical workers' union, FULC, investigated claims once it became clear that PVC/VCM was harmful, but they appeared satisfied with industry's assertion that levels had been immediately reduced to meet the new standards. The union's reluctance to contest the issue can be partly explained by the tension between environmental issues and regulation that was perceived as a threat to employment.

One person who remained unsatisfied with Montedison's response to the known hazards of vinyl chloride production was Gabriele Bortolozzo, a worker for the company since 1956. He had worked in the PVC/VCM unit for some years with five other men cleaning the vats where the chemical was mixed at exposures reaching 32,000 ppm or higher: all were dead, four of them from a rare liver cancer. In 1979 Bortolozzo discussed his complaints with others, keeping a log of deaths and illnesses at the plant. Perceived by management as a "problem," he was moved and isolated from other workers. Presenting himself as a "conscientious objector" to carcinogenic industry practices, Bortolozzo continued his campaign of exposure after retirement in 1990, battling to secure information from public health officials as well as from Montedison.[17] Using his own experience in the industry as a basis for a forensic investigation into the suspected causes of human and environmental health degradation in the region, he made the study, collection, and assimilation of information regarding pollution and health problems in Porto Marghera his retirement passion.

In the spring of 1994, Bortolozzo wrote nine short articles for a thematic issue of *Medicina Democratica*, a union-allied professional journal dedicated to topics of health and environmental safety as well as the rights of workers. This particular issue was devoted to cancer and exposure to vinyl chloride in the Porto Marghera area. Wide ranging in their scope and meticulously detailed with charts and statistics, Bortolozzo's contributions explained the vinyl chloride production process and the history of VCM production in Italy, as well as mortality rates for Marghera's VCM workers and the wider environmental impacts of pollution. In the years following his tireless enquiries and the eventual publication of his concerns in *Medicina Democratica*, Bortolozzo had become acknowledged as an expert and authority.[18] In August of 1994, armed with his volume of *Medicina Democratica*, he succeeded in meeting Felice Casson, the attorney general of Venice, who would eventually become the government prosecutor in the Montedison case. Casson quickly assembled a group of experts to investigate Bortolozzo's health and pollution claims. In September 1995, Bortolozzo, an avid naturalist and bicyclist, was struck and killed by a truck while biking near Marghera. It was deemed an accident.

In 1997 the Venice attorney general's office indicted twenty-eight executives and managers of petrochemical companies on charges ranging from manslaughter to environmental pollution. The next year, the case went to trial with about 550 plaintiffs, including state and local governments, several environmental organizations, trade unions, 103 sick workers, and the families of 156 dead workers. Before the court reached a decision, the chemical companies settled with the state, paying €270 million to clean up the Venice Lagoon. They also settled with many of the worker plaintiffs, effectively clearing the courtroom.[19]

When the trial ended in 2001, the chemical plant managers and executives were found not guilty. The court's siding with the defendants in the most heinous allegation, manslaughter, hinged on "who knew what when" with respect to the effect of certain levels of PVC/VCM on human health. It agreed with the chemical companies that 1974 was the year that industry knew, without a doubt, the causal relationship between PVC/VCM exposure and fatal disease. However, neither Casson nor all of the remaining plaintiffs were convinced. The trial revealed much earlier corporate knowledge of health problems and even a secrecy pact among multinational corporations.

In the Italian legal system, a trial has potentially three parts or levels of appeal. If one or both parties do not agree with the verdict of the first part, they can file for an appeal, as in the U.S. court system. Casson filed an appeal and the facts, including those relating to worker protection regulations, were re-presented and reanalyzed. While no fresh historic information could be introduced at this second stage, new information on events that had transpired between the filing of the first case and the second appeal could be entered. A pivotal event had occurred in 1999 when another worker, Tulio Faggan, died of a rare liver cancer. He had been employed at the Montedison plant after 1974, when supposedly new, stringent precautions were in place. In 2004 a verdict in the second trial was reached—five chief executive officers and former managers were convicted of over 150 counts of manslaughter for the deaths of former chemical workers.

In Italy defendants may avoid punishment if too much time has passed, or if they are elderly, as judges have considerable discretion in sentencing. The five convicted executives never served a day in prison. However, the judgment did allow for additional civil suits for damages, both by individuals and by the government for environmental harm. It also verified and legally reinforced claims of the health effects of vinyl chloride production as well as served as a deterrent to future negligent behavior. In 2006, the third and last level of the trial procedure confirmed the guilty verdict of the second trial.

The catalyst for the lawsuit brought by the attorney general of Venice could be attributed to the tenacity of one worker, Gabrielle Bortolozzo. The history of activism and legal action are not that straightforward. Bortolozzo did not act alone, either in the acquisition of information or as sole plaintiff in the lawsuit. Initially, his allies were the medical institutions that offered their research, enabling him to write a series of articles that he published in a union-affiliated medical journal. Additionally he joined in the efforts of national environmental groups that were concerned about pollution in the lagoon. After enlisting the Venice attorney general in Bortolozzo's cause, other international environmental groups, such as Greenpeace, joined the legal actions, as did unions, governmental agencies, and many individuals. The lawsuit gained wide attention and became a public media circus, with all three national newspapers and many smaller local and regional papers regularly reporting its progress. Both scientists and journalists wrote books in the time leading up to the various stages of the lawsuit.

The lawsuit was no longer the cause of Borlolozzo alone, but had grown into a large heterogeneous "movement" with an accompanying media entourage. Many actors, scientists, citizens, workers, residents, environmentalists, and union officials held a stake in finding the chemical companies and their officials guilty. The boundaries had been blurred between local and cosmo-politan knowledge as well as between science and politics. The overall impact of this unwieldy network and its alliances was positive for the advance of environmental knowledge and for the fostering of policy action.

The following section switches attention to a comparable case involving the American chemical industry and one particular region where production is heavily concentrated.

The U.S. Case

The chemical corridor of Louisiana is home to over one hundred thirty chemical plants and petroleum processors that stretch along the Mississippi River between New Orleans and Baton Rouge, on a river bank once lined with large sugar plantations, shipping docks, and pipelines interspersed with small communities. Industry was established in the region in the early part of the twentieth century, first oil refineries and then petrochemicals in the late 1950s and 1960s. Between the various facilities that took the place of planta-tions, there remained small, predominantly African American communities. Many had been formed, in part, on land grants deeded by the U.S govern-ment after the abolition of slavery. Additionally, communities of working-class and poor whites dotted the landscape, near industry but usually not sharing the fenceline with it. Chemical companies hired mostly white work-ers, who commuted to the plants, rather than the poor and minority people living nearby.[20] Hiring workers from outside of the community was one strategy that industry used to protect itself from local scrutiny. Additionally, the people who lived near the plants often lacked the education necessary for employment in this highly technical and automated industry.

Citizens' awareness of the environmental hazards posed by industry in this area can be traced to the late 1970s with the death of a local truck driver, overcome by fumes while dumping toxic waste into an open pit on the banks of the Mississippi River. That event prompted the Louisiana attorney gen-eral to hire an environmental community liaison officer to educate citizens about their rights with regard to polluting facilities and other environmental hazards.[21] In 1980, the group Save Our Selves (SOS), led by two white rural housewives, fought the siting of a large incinerator near their homes. They won their case in 1984, the result being that the state would have to consider not only economic development but also alternative sites and technologies as well as environmental protection in the permitting of new industrial facilities.[22]

BASF, a multinational petrochemical giant, unintentionally contributed to this momentum of environmental and labor resistance by having effec-tively locked out its union employees, the Oil, Chemical and Atomic Workers (OCAW), for five and a half years over disagreements regarding wages and benefits. During this period, disenfranchised labor allied itself with the bur-geoning grassroots environmental movement to fight industry permits and to blow the whistle on dangerous plants. Upon reentering the plant in December of 1989, OCAW members agreed to jointly fund, with the National Toxics Campaign, the Louisiana Labor-Neighbor Project, which would facilitate community/environment awareness of health and safety issues. Over the next twelve years the organization helped support a public water system and an industrial air monitor in Geismar, the town adjacent to BASF, as well as to promote the hiring of African American workers by local industry contractors. The organization also helped to block permission for the location in a nearby community of Shintech Corporation, a facility that would have been the largest PVC plant in the United States. Unfortunately, this activity marked the beginning of the end for the organization, as the BASF workers were divided and accusations of job blackmail were prevalent. The Labor-Neighbor Project halted operation in 2002.[23]

In the mid-1980s Kay Gaudet, a young pharmacist in St. Gabriel (then home to sixteen chemical facilities), noticed that increasing numbers of women were coming into her pharmacy for the breast cancer drug Nolvadex as well as for medication prescribed after they had miscarried. She began keeping a journal of the women who talked to her anecdotally and determined that one-third of the pregnancies in her town had resulted in fetal death, which was over twice the national average of 15 percent.[24] She contacted several state agencies asking them to investigate the problem. The state funded a geographically and demographically large epidemiological study that included residents near the plants as well as many women who lived far away. The report concluded that the miscarriage rates were within national norms.

Patricia Williams, director of the Louisiana State University (LSU) Medical School's Occupational Toxicology Outreach Program, had noted Gaudet's campaign, though she had never actually spoken to her about it. Williams's own research was in reproductive health outcomes, including fetal and early childhood chemical exposure. She shared some suspicions about health problems in the chemical corridor, notably cancer and, more specifically, elevated incidence of pediatric cancer. She was not alone in having such concerns. Many citizens in the region were so convinced that there was an abnormally high incidence of cancer along the chemical corridor that in the 1980s they christened the region "Cancer Alley." Evidence of elevated rates of cancer was lacking, however, since no official data disproving the case was released by the state. Officials purposefully secreted the disease data, only releasing it once it had been manipulated into broad, multiregional data sets.

The fight over data, which had begun in the late 1990s and was decided by the Louisiana State Court of Appeals in 2004, indirectly served to guide health policy and industrial development in Louisiana. The battle against cancer data restrictions had gained pace in the late 1990s, when the River Region Crime Commission (RRCC), a small, fairly homogeneous group of citizens led by Patricia Williams and her son, attorney Eric Williams, filed a lawsuit against the Louisiana Tumor Registry (LTR). The RRCC had been organized as a private, nonprofit corporation whose purpose was to foster honesty and integrity in government, political campaigns, and regulation. The

LTR was the state agency responsible for collecting and compiling data sets on cancer. Formally founded in 1979 under the auspices of Louisiana's Office of Public Health, it represented a systematic and taxpayer-funded venue for collecting and disseminating population-based cancer incidence and survival information across a state that had been collecting partial data since 1947.

The LTR made several decisions at the outset, which would later have great consequences for the residents of the chemical corridor. One was the decision to publish cancer data in five-year increments; another was the decision to break the state down into eight large geographic regions, thus aggregating the data into multiyear blocks and large areas. While scientists will argue that a one-year reporting standard, as set by state statute, is arbitrary, a five-year reporting timetable is equally arbitrary and less sensitive to changing health patterns. More problematic, however, were the eight large geographic regions. Each one consisted of as many as twelve parishes (counties in Louisiana), including both industrial and nonindustrial locales, making the determination of elevated cancer rates near chemical plants impossible to verify.

The Louisiana Chemical Association (LCA) carefully watched the formation and early progress of the LTR. In 1988 it contracted with a private research group to review all past LTR reports to see if there were any indications of a link between cancer and proximity to industry.[25] The report revealed that the LTR's data had not shown such a link. A year later the LCA itself funded a project by the LTR to examine cancer and proximity to industry. The resulting report held few surprises in giving industry a clean bill of health, its findings based on the LTR's epidemiological data. Many citizens in south Louisiana, however, particularly those living in Cancer Alley, remained skeptical of the LTR's reports claiming no evidence of a correlation between living in the industrial region of Louisiana and cancer. The citizens' own empirical evidence from everyday life seemed to contradict those reports. Weakening the citizens' case was the fact that their evidence was anecdotal and thus not equivalent, in the eyes of the regulators, to the official scientific data produced by the LTR.

By the mid-1990s Patricia Williams had seen enough anecdotal evidence of rare pediatric cancers to persuade her of the need for further research. Through the RRCC, she made a public records request to the LTR for raw data by zip code, which would enable her to correlate cancers with their distance from industry. The request was denied, severely weakening any potential application to state and federal agencies for funding further study of pediatric cancer in petrochemical areas. In refusing the RRCC's application for access to such data, the LTR claimed that it did not keep data in the form that the citizens' group wanted and that such data would have to be created at huge public expense. Additionally, it explained that if it created the data tables asked for by the RRCC at the level of specificity requested (i.e., type of cancer for both parish and zip code on a per-year basis), many of the tabulated cancer numbers might be 1, which by definition would be "case-specific and thus exempt from disclosure" due to privacy regulations.[26]

The RRCC responded by stating that it did not want confidential information regarding individual cases and claiming that LTR's interpretation of the privacy rules was intended to avoid releasing public information.[27]

The court that heard the appeal instructed the two parties to attempt a reasonable compromise. In response to the RRCC's concerns about Louisiana's pediatric cancer rates, in 2001 the LTR published *Childhood Cancer in Louisiana, 1988–1996* and furnished researchers and citizens with data on sixteen childhood cancers by parish (though not zip code) for all sixty-four parishes. It continued to delete data categories tabulated as 0 or 1 as case-specific information exempt from reporting. The main recipients (medical researchers and citizens) rejected this approach since as many as sixteen cases of rare childhood cancers might be missed in a parish every year if even one case of each kind of cancer was diagnosed. The RRCC appealed to the court in 2001, arguing that a reasonable compromise had not been reached; however, the judge found for the LTR. In 2002, citizens and medical researchers again filed, this time in Louisiana's First Circuit Court of Appeal.

In addition to their arguments that data retrieval for zip codes was difficult and, where possible, could violate patients' right to privacy, the LTR claimed that data might be used in an unscientific way. It asserted that "The entire scientific community of cancer research professionals regards zip code-specific cancer incidence data as statistically and clinically meaningless."[28] This raised an important question about the interpretation and presentation of information. The LTR had repeatedly stated that there was no evidence of elevated cancer rates in the industrial regions of Louisiana. Its careful formulation of the data collected did not prove a relationship between location and illness, but one can easily slip into an assumption that there is *no* relationship between cancer and proximity to industry. The LTR's refusal to permit citizens and experts access to the original data to establish proximity correlations left open the question of what the evidence does demonstrate.

Interviews with Patricia Williams made it clear that she did not view the epidemiological data as proof of causation. But she and others maintained that state cancer registry data may reveal a *possibility* of elevated pediatric cancers around industrial facilities, justifying funding for further medical surveillance programs to address citizens' questions more fully. The plaintiffs also believed that an accumulation of anecdotal evidence showing a cluster of cancers around plants might pressure state environmental regulatory agencies to caution against expansion of facilities in such areas. Finally, they reasoned that pediatricians in the areas could be alerted to the prevalence of these rare cancers, thus facilitating early detection and treatment.

In the last legal round, the citizen's group won a partial victory. In 2004, the LTR was ordered to give the group all cancer data by parish, including parishes with only one instance. The judge ruled that the LTR's interpretation of patient privacy was extreme and did not align with that of other cancer registries. While he was not convinced that it would be a time-consuming task to compile parish-level data from their computer files, he agreed with LTR that compiling the zip code statistics, necessary for cancer cluster studies, would be costly and thus they did not have to release them. The lawsuit brought by Williams and her son via the RRCC never expanded into the larger, more diverse movement that was characteristic of the Marghera experience. Williams is a traditionally trained scientist who has shown some aversion to media attention and other forms of activism that might make science appear undignified or politically motivated.[29] This isolation of the RRCC from outside groups as well as from other local groups arguably did not facilitate a positive outcome toward expanding environmental health knowledge for the citizens of Louisiana.

Analysis and Conclusion

The decisions in the two lawsuits decided in 2004 have very different implications for environmental regulation and policy and the likelihood of change. In the Marghera case, the court affirmed that anecdotal worker observations and popular epidemiology amplified and confirmed traditional laboratory studies and statistical epidemiology. This legitimized new environmental health knowledge regarding citizen-protective policies and regulations. The outcome of the Louisiana case had very different implications. Contrary to the Italian case, anecdotal and citizen-collected epidemiological data on the relationship between residence near hazardous facilities and illness could not be demonstrated through the official science of the state's epidemiology office. The data could not be released in a useful fashion. The lawsuit filed by Patricia Williams and the RRCC focused narrowly on data and traditional scientific explanations, deliberately steering clear of social or political discourse. This ultimately proved an unproductive strategy for the citizens of Louisiana: They gained no new environmental health knowledge and so are unable to push for research and stronger regulations.

In Italy, the ability to combine civil and criminal cases in one trial was productive for local citizens and workers. The conviction of the five CEOs and managers of Marghera's petrochemical companies sent a strong message that the government expected individual and corporate responsibility with regard to worker safety and environmental stewardship. Additional outcomes of the lawsuit included monetary damages to workers and their families as well as funding to clean up the Venice Lagoon. Among the secondary impacts were funding for Fondazione Bortolozzo (a foundation for the health and safety of workers), the closing of some PVC/VCM plants, and improved legal regulation (and enforcement) regarding exposure and pollution. There has also been an expansion of the Interuniversity National Consortium "Chemistry for the Environment" (INCA), the green chemistry research organization with laboratories in Marghera and six other locations in Italy dedicated to environmental innovation in chemical science. The goal is to develop new and alternative chemical processes and products that have a less negative impact on people and the environment.

The citizens were clearly losers in the Louisiana lawsuit. Without release of the cancer data by zip code, neither cancer clusters nor cancer incidence with a geographic relationship to industry could be ascertained. This information, though not causal, would have prompted more laboratory studies and medical surveillance of the impacted populations. To date no such initiatives are under way and citizens have no idea if they really are living in a "cancer alley." Furthermore, the number of PVC/VCM facilities has actually grown in the chemical corridor, with three new plants either built or in process since 2000.[30] For the citizens of Louisiana, it is business as usual without any further understanding of either the health or the environmental costs of this "economic development" trajectory. In 2003, bowing to the pressure of RRCC's ongoing lawsuit for public health knowledge, the state passed Legislative Act 666, which mandated the establishment of an environmental health surveillance system in Louisiana. Thus far the only completed study is one of "groundwater and drinking water near abandoned or inactive wood preservation and treatment facilities throughout the state."[31] None of them have been undertaken near the petrochemical plants in question.

While both legal cases had beginnings with a vocal private citizen, Bortolozzo the laborer and Williams the scientist, only the former was able or willing to enroll sufficient public and institutional resources to change environmental policy and practices. My earlier research suggested three criteria of a successful environmental outcome—working with scientists, working with national/international groups, and heterogeneous group composition. The Italian case met all three. In the end the unions, Greenpeace, the attorney general of Venice, and dozens of other interested parties joined in the Porto Marghera struggle, effectively changing the region forever. The group in the Louisiana case was a small homogenous organization that was driven by a scientist, Patricia Williams, but had no affiliation with outside environmental or health advocates. The outcome of the two cases is evidence of the strength of one heterogeneous group as contrasted with the weakness of another, homogeneous group. It is also significant that Williams' pursuit of environmental knowledge remained within the strict bounds of the legal system and was argued using traditional medical and scientific justifications. Bortolozzo "mixed it up," so to speak, combining both politics and science to create a powerful hybrid knowledge. In the Italian case, scientists were part of a larger coalition arguing for a cleaner environment and better environmental health knowledge. This "winning" coalition was diverse and included activists, unions, scientists, citizen groups, government agencies, and other participants.[32]

This comparative project has illuminated the ways in which rules, institutions, and networks are successful in creating new environmental health knowledge. The next step is to further unpack the legal system as well as networks of medical science workers to understand where and how power and knowledge coalesce toward legitimizing advances in environmental health science. For example, in the study of chemical exposure, scientists' networks in Italy have done groundbreaking work—"science for the people." There is a noticeable lack of this kind of work in the United States. What are the social and institutional arrangements that facilitate (or deter) science initiated from citizens' questions? What kind of legal structures and rules for the admission of scientific evidence lead to the acceptance of new policy/citizen-relevant science and promote corporate responsibility? Through examining industrial pollution and practices comparatively and internationally, we can better understand the embeddedness of scientific knowledge within sociopolitical systems. It is in the unpacking of this complex dynamic that catalysts for expanding environmental health knowledge can be found.

NOTES

1. See M. Fay, "Exposures to Contaminant Mixtures at US Hazardous Waste Sites," in *Environmental Exposure and Health*, ed. M. M. Aral, C. A. Brebia, M. L. Masalia, and T. Sinks (Billerca, MA: Computational Mechanics/WIT Press, 1995), 227–231.
2. In Italy, the laboratories of the Ramazzini Foundation seek to answer questions about occupational and environmental health. For more see Morando Soffritti, Fiorella Belpoggi, Franco Minardi, and Cesare Maltoni, "Ramazzini Foundation Cancer Program," *Annals of the New York Academy of Sciences* 982 (2002): 26–45.
3. See Barbara L. Allen, *Uneasy Alchemy: Citizens and Experts in Louisiana's Chemical Corridor Disputes* (Cambridge, MA: MIT Press, 2003).
4. See Scott Frickel and Kelly Moore, "Prospects and Challenges for a New Political Sociology of Science," in *The New Political Sociology of Science*, ed. S. Frickel and K. Moore (Madison: University of Wisconsin Press, 2006), 3–31.
5. Polyvinyl chloride (PVC), the base material for plastics, is produced from the inherently unstable chemical chlorine and combined with hydrocarbons to produce vinyl chloride monomer (VCM).
6. In 1994 Italy was the fourth largest producer of PVC in the world after the United States, Japan, and Germany. See Gabriele Bortolozzo, "La produzione di CVM e PVC al Petrolchimico di Porto Marghera," *Medicina Democratica* 92/93 (January-April 1994): 42–45.
7. For a history of the region, including the first court decision in the lawsuit against industry, see Nicoletta Benatelli, Gianni Favarato, and Elisio Trevisan, eds., *Processo a Marghera: L'inchesta sul petrolchimico il CVM e le morti degli operai storia di una tragedia umana e ambientale* (Venice: Nuova Dimensione, 2002).
8. For a history of the residential section of Marghera, see Sergio Barizza, Claudio Cogo, and Gianni Facca, *Marghera: Il quartiere urbano* (Fosso, Italy: Alcione Editore, 2000).
9. See Gianfranco Bettin, *Petrolkimiko: Le voci e le storie di un crimine di pace* (Milan: Baldini and Castoldi, 1998).
10. See Giannadrea Mencini, *Il Fronte per la difesa di Venezia e della Laguna e le denunce di Indro Montanelli* (Venice: Supernova, 2005).
11. See Gerald Markowitz and David Rosner, *Deceit and Denial* (Berkeley: University of California Press, 2002), 183.
12. Ibid., 201
13. Ibid., 185.
14. Gabriele Bortolozzo, " La cancerogenesi da CVM," *Medicina Democratica* 92/93 (January-April, 1994): 46–56.
15. Paolo Rabitti was an engineering expert for the state prosecutor's office and testified at the trial. His book *Cronache dalla chimica: Marghera e le alter* (Naples: Cuen, 1998) is a documentation of the technical issues in the case prior to the trial.
16. Bettin, *Petrolkimiko*.
17. Rabitti, *Cronache dalla chimica*.
18. For an excellent discussion of the "expertification" of laypeople, see Steven Epstein, *Impure Science* (Berkeley: University of California Press, 1996).
19. Felice Casson, interview with the author, November 13, 2006, Venice, Italy.
20. For the development of the chemical corridor, see Barbara L. Allen, "Cradle of a Revolution? The Industrial Transformation of Louisiana's Lower Mississippi River," *Technology and Culture* 47 (January 2006): 112–119.

21. For an in-depth history, see Barbara L. Allen, *Uneasy Alchemy: Citizen's and Experts in Louisiana's Chemical Disputes* (Cambridge, MA: MIT Press, 2003); and J. Timmons Roberts and Melissa M. Toffolon-Weiss, *Chronicles from the Environmental Justice Frontline* (New York: Cambridge University Press, 2001).

22. Allen *Uneasy Alchemy*, 54.

23. Louisiana's Labor-Neighbor project is discussed by Thomas Estabrook, *Labor-Neighbor Coalitions: Lessons from a Louisiana Petrochemical Region* (Amityville, NY: Baywood Publishing Company, 2007).

24. Allen, *Uneasy Alchemy*, 129.

25. Ibid., 134.

26. Taylor, Porter, Brooks & Phillips, L.L.P., *Brief Filed on Behalf of Defendant-Appellee, Board of Supervisors of Louisiana State University and A&M College*, Docket No. 2003-CA-0079, 2003, 3.

27. Williams & Krause, L.L.C. & Williams Law Firm, *Original Brief on Behalf of Williams Law Firm and Carey Brown Plaintiffs-Appellants*, Docket No. 2003-CA-0079, 2003, 6.

28. Taylor et al., *Brief*, 14–15.

29. See Barbara Allen, "Shifting Boundary Work: Issues and Tensions in Environmental Health Science in the Case of Grand Bois, Louisiana," *Science as Culture* 13 (2004): 429–448.

30. From a draft transcript of environmental scientist Wilma Subra's contribution to "Toxic Environments/Toxic Bodies Workshop," presented at a meeting of the American Society for Environmental History, Baton Rouge, Louisiana, March 2, 2007.

31. From *Three Year Progress Report, CDC Program Announcement 03074, Environmental and Health Effects Tracking* (Baton Rouge: State of Louisiana Department of Health and Hospitals, Office of Public Health, April 30, 2007), 14.

32. Allen, in "Shifting Boundary Work," argues that traditional science combined with citizen activism and hybrid forms of science making leads to more successful outcomes than simply relying on laboratory science and the courts to resolve environmental problems.

12

Pesticide Regulation, Citizen Action, and Toxic Trade

The Role of the Nation-State
in the Transnational History of DBCP

Susanna Rankin Bohme

In 1977, the pesticide dibromochloropropane (DBCP) came under public scrutiny in the United States as production workers linked their high rates of sterility to exposure to the toxic chemical. Over the following years, DBCP use in the United States was increasingly restricted and ended altogether in 1985.[1] In Central America, in contrast, transnational fruit grower Dole[2] continued to use the chemical in the absence of even the most basic safety measures.[3]

This scenario evokes the image of globalization as a "race to the bottom," in which hyper-mobile transnational corporations sell, use, or produce dangerous goods in the least regulated markets, or follow radically different regimes of protection in the various nations in which they operate.[4] Dole's continued use of DBCP shows that this analysis has merit. However, the history of DBCP's transnational circulation is complicated by the fact that national regulations worked in tandem with the transnational practices of corporate actors, producing different regimes of protection for U.S. workers compared to non-U.S. workers. U.S. pesticide regulations concerning export and allowable residues explicitly or implicitly underwrote the continued use of DBCP outside of U.S. borders. In this way they authorized and affirmed the transnational corporations' uneven occupational health policies.

The U.S. government's problematic role in allowing heightened health risks for non-U.S. workers was underscored when, in the mid-1980s, some of the estimated tens of thousands of Central American workers sterilized by exposure to DBCP began bringing suit in the United States.[5] The

DBCP cases asserted a certain symmetry to the processes of globalization—if corporations based in the United States could cross national boundaries in their trade and operations, then workers should be able to traverse those same borders in the course of their efforts to hold transnational companies accountable for the harm they caused. However, for more than 30 years, Central American DBCP plaintiffs were largely excluded from courts in the United States, despite establishing jurisdiction, on the basis that these trials would more "conveniently" take place in plaintiffs' home countries. While U.S. regulations had earlier enabled the use of DBCP in Central America, the U.S. legal system effectively prevented most of those who had been exposed from bringing their grievances to trial.

In Nicaragua, DBCP-affected banana workers responded by launching a movement that defined DBCP damage as a national problem and brought political pressure to bear on the Nicaraguan state. By achieving the passage of a national law that facilitated the trial of DBCP cases in Nicaragua, the activists leveraged the state as an ally in the transnational sphere, transforming the legal playing field and turning their own nation into a counterweight to exclusionary U.S. rulings.

The role of the nation-state in the history of DBCP exposure and struggles for accountability is significant to the study of occupational health in context of late-twentieth- and early-twenty-first-century neoliberalism. It is of course impossible to speak of a singular "state." A repressive or failed state is likely to be antagonistic or indifferent to worker health. At the same time, political and economic demands may lead to state-led "management" of labor hazards in a variety of contexts. A key theme in the study of the current era of globalization has been the profound change in the role of the welfare state as post-WWII social policies are increasingly subordinated to the interests of capital, sacrificing welfare and labor protections, rolling back social and environmental regulations, and privatizing public assets. However, the state has not disappeared but instead is reconfiguring its own institutions and authority in a manner consonant with an increasingly global economy.[6]

Globalization and the changing role of the state have provoked debate about the implications for people's movements and, more broadly, for the prospects for democracy.[7] While the history of DBCP shows how the state can enact policies that create uneven exposure to toxins and unequal access to the legal forum, it also suggests not only that the state still has relevance as an object of protest but that citizen demands can transform the state into an agent for change on a transnational level.

Development, Testing, and Regulation of DBCP

DBCP is a soil fumigant that was widely used by agriculturalists—including banana growers—in the 1960s and 1970s to fight nematodes that damage crop roots. Shell and Dow produced the first branded versions of the compound, respectively called Nemagon and Fumazone. Early testing on DBCP found testicular damage in experimental animals.[8] As more research showed

that DBCP seriously affected sperm production and testicle size,[9] researchers became "very upset by the effect noted on the testes."[10] For Dow and
Shell, the research raised questions not only about the safety of the chemical
for humans but about its viability as a marketable product. Bad news from
toxicologists could mean that regulators would refuse permission to market
the chemical, or require a strong warning label that might have "an adverse
effect on [its] sale."[11] As they ushered DBCP through the regulatory process,
scientists at Dow and Shell developed an explanation for the chemical's toxicity that downplayed its dangers. Ultimately, the companies' close relationship
with and influence over regulators led to a lenient government interpretation
of DBCP toxicology.[12] By 1964, DBCP could be sold and used in the United
States with minimal precautions and with a warning label with no mention
of testicular or reproductive risk. Although Dow and Shell jointly published
their findings of testicular damage,[13] most people who came into contact
with the chemical had no way of knowing about this danger.

Indeed, the risks of DBCP would not draw much attention until the summer of 1977, when pesticide production workers at an Occidental Chemical
plant in California linked their epidemic of childlessness to their exposure
to the chemical.[14] The news drew media attention and public concern, and
regulators reacted by increasingly tightening the restrictions on DBCP use in
the United States until it was completely withdrawn in 1985.

DBCP Use in Central America

As early as 1957, Shell was promoting the use of DBCP on bananas.[15] By the
early 1960s, Standard was seeking information on the chemical, and United
Fruit's own researchers reported that it helped eliminate nematode damage
in the early stages of banana planting.[16] Although U.S. policy exempted
exported pesticides from national labeling and application rules, U.S. limits
on the amount of residue that could appear on agricultural products did
apply to imported foods. The widespread use of DBCP on banana plantations, therefore, would not be feasible without U.S. regulators' approval.
Dow and Shell—with the help of United Fruit—asked the Food and Drug
Administration (FDA) to set a rule specifying how much DBCP residue or
breakdown product could appear on produce—including bananas—sold in
the United States.[17] Because the United States was the primary destination
for bananas exported from Central America, such a "tolerance" was fundamental to the adoption of DBCP on banana plantations. In 1963, the FDA
granted the tolerance, clearing the way for use of DBCP in Central America.
By 1977, Dow Chemical estimated, 600,000 gallons of DBCP were being
used on Latin American banana plantations per year. According to Dow,
"at an average cost of about $6 per gallon, this represent[ed] a total material
cost of $3.6 million per year."[18] Despite the growing importance of DBCP to
banana production, workers exposed to the chemical had no knowledge of
and few defenses against the chemical's hazards.

In 1977, when Occidental Chemical workers linked their sterility to DBCP, Dow and Shell announced they would suspend DBCP sales.[19] In response, United Brands instructed all managers in its Central American division to stop using DBCP but soon quietly resumed experimental use of the pesticide.[20] Dole, on the other hand, made it clear to its supplier, Dow, that the banana company would consider any failure to deliver the chemical a "breach of contract."[21] In a Telex to Dow in August 1977, the fruit company maintained that they would

> continue to use DBCP as long as (a) its use is not forbidden by U.S. govt agencies or the provincial or state govts in a specific location in which we operate or (b) there is no evidence the people who apply the chemical have been rendered sterile or have been harmed in any other ways.[22]

This logic justified the continued use of DBCP by arguing that just because men laboring in U.S. factories had been harmed by the chemical, there was no evidence that farm workers would also be sterilized by their exposure. In fact, by 1977 urologists in Costa Rica had noted a number of unexplained sterility cases among banana workers in that country.[23]

The telex's language regarding legal requirements spoke in complicated ways to the impact of national regulations on transnational companies. It seemed to claim that Dole would follow rules set by both U.S. and Central American governments. However, the company's language was ambiguous, leaving it unclear whether it would stop using DBCP only if the U.S. government banned its use *"in a specific location* in which we operate."[24] Such a prohibition was unlikely, as U.S. regulations explicitly exempted chemicals produced for export from the strictures of the Federal Insecticide Rodenticide and Fungicide Act (FIRFA).[25] However, the telex's reference to U.S. laws showed that the company knew that, just as U.S. residue tolerances could shape pesticide use elsewhere, the fate of DBCP in the United States would have ramifications beyond its borders as well.

In fact, the EPA's initial (and inadequate)[26] efforts to codify safe conditions for the use of DBCP in the United States would be used by Dow and Dole to justify ongoing DBCP use in Central America under unsafe conditions. By early September, the EPA proclaimed its intention to suspend the use of DBCP on nineteen crops (not including bananas) and require protections for applicators.[27] Dow agreed to restart sales to Dole subject to "conditions of use" that echoed the new U.S. rules. In return, Standard agreed to indemnify Dow for any claims relating to DBCP damage.[28]

However, writing U.S. regulations into a contract for DBCP sales to Central America could not guarantee safety for banana workers. Transposing the EPA's guidelines into a private contract effectively divorced the regulations from any oversight or enforcement mechanism. The United States would not enforce the rules outside of its own boundaries, and officials in the various nations where Dole operated were unlikely to even know of the agreement. Indeed, Dole quickly dismissed some of the agreement's key elements. Where it called for notification of workers before spraying DBCP, or stipulated that DBCP not be sprayed near workers' housing, Dole leadership declared that these measures were "not operationally feasible and [did] not need to be implemented."[29] Ironically, then, the fruit and chemical companies' use of U.S. regulations in their transnational dealings opened the door to continued use of DBCP abroad, but without the protections intended by the rules as they were enacted.

U.S. regulations would also affirm continued DBCP use in Central America more directly. In the wake of the Occidental Chemical workers' disclosures, the EPA used a risk-benefit analysis to determine the policies for DBCP use on particular crops.[30] Dow and Dole lobbied the Agency, arguing that DBCP was essential to the banana trade, which in turn was essential to maintaining Americans' health and developing the economies of banana-producing countries.[31] In a position document released in 1978, the EPA adopted much of this reasoning, ultimately placing non-U.S. workers' health explicitly outside the framework of risk consideration.[32] On DBCP's "benefit" side was the cost savings DBCP afforded U.S. consumers: a savings in the price of bananas of 3.5 cents a pound. EPA did not consider any health risks for DBCP application to banana crops because "little or no DBCP is known to be applied to bananas" in the United States (because, ultimately, very few bananas were grown in the mostly temperate country). The health of Central Americans or other non-U.S. workers, then, only figured in the analysis through its omission; the risk-benefit analysis was made in exclusively national terms.

Eventually, however, it was U.S. regulation that would bring DBCP use on bananas to an end. In early 1985, the EPA published its "Intent to Cancel" use of the pesticide.[33] Registrations for all crops would be canceled, although pineapple growers would get an extra year for their DBCP use. The EPA also recommended that residue limits—including for bananas—be revoked. Dole personnel quickly realized that the loss of residue limits "wipe[d] out our last legal avenue for use of the product," calling it "the death rattle insofar as use of DBCP on bananas is concerned."[34] By 1986, DBCP had been included on the World Health Organization's "Obsolete Pesticide" list.[35]

Directly and indirectly, then, U.S. governmental decisions helped to produce unequal regimes of exposure in Central America and the United States, prolonging the dangerous use of DBCP by a number of years. Some of the U.S. laws and regulations explicitly defined non-U.S. bodies as outside the realm of their protection. Others, such as the EPA regulations written into Dow and Dole's 1978 agreement, affected DBCP use as they were taken out of the national context by transnational corporations that ultimately used them to justify the chemical's ongoing sale and use. The actions of the U.S. state, then, had important repercussions not only for the health of those within the United States but also for those Central American banana workers who were exposed to the chemical both before and after it was restricted in the United States.

DBCP-Affected Workers' Quest for Accountability in the United States

The mid-1980s marked a watershed in the history of DBCP, when the central question turned from one of exposure to one of accountability. Just as the nation-state had played a key role in shaping the trade in this dangerous chemical, it was central to injured workers' attempts to obtain compensation from the fruit and chemical companies. In legal struggles over DBCP, important questions emerged regarding the role of the state in defining both its own legal boundaries and the extent of its engagement with a transnational field of contestation.

Since 1983, over 400 DBCP cases with sterility claims have been filed in the United States against corporate defendants, including the Dow, Shell, and Occidental chemical companies and Dole and Chiquita (United Fruit).[36] The cases have mostly been filed in states where the presence of defendants' headquarters or substantial business dealings has established jurisdiction. They mirror the export of DBCP—whereas the chemical has flowed from the United States to Central America, the legal cases have crossed borders in the opposite direction.

That seeming symmetry, however, was interrupted when the first DBCP lawsuit, brought by fifty-eight Costa Rican plaintiffs in 1983, was dismissed. The sitting District Court judge ruled that, while the case did have jurisdiction in Florida, it would not be tried there.[37] Instead, the court invoked the legal doctrine of *forum non conveniens* (FNC), ruling that Costa Rican plaintiffs should return to their own country and seek justice in courts there. Latin for "inconvenient forum," the FNC doctrine is ostensibly meant to prevent plaintiffs from harassing defendants by choosing a purposefully inconvenient forum.[38] In the DBCP cases, however, the defendants' use of the doctrine meant that most cases became mired in procedural hearings, sometimes for years, only to eventually be dismissed. Theoretically intended by U.S. judges to be heard in the plaintiffs' nation of origin, a case dismissed in the United States is usually left unpursued.[39] In these cases, an FNC dismissal is best understood as a victory for the defendant.

Following this first decision, all other non-U.S. plaintiffs with DBCP cases in U.S. courts faced the FNC specter. Filed in 1984, *Castro Alfaro v. Dow* spent almost a decade in the courts as an FNC dismissal was debated and considered by lawyers and judges. Ultimately, the Texas Supreme Court ruled that FNC was not legally allowable in Texas.[40] While the *Alfaro* plaintiffs won a settlement from the fruit and chemical company defendants, a similar outcome was foreclosed to others when the Texas legislature passed a law specifically authorizing FNC dismissals.[41] Over the next decades, cases involving tens of thousands of DBCP-affected individuals would be dismissed from state and federal courts under the doctrine.

What is notable about the FNC doctrine is how, while the regulatory machinery of the state worked to authorize the transborder flow of DBCP, the power of the legal realm worked to *close* the nation's borders to those who had been harmed by it. This double standard helps us understand how, even in an era of globalization in which the power and significance of the nation-state is waning, the state does continue, in sociologist Saskia Sassen's words, to "[assert] its sovereign right to control its borders."[42] This control is exerted not only over the entry of physical bodies (i.e., immigrants) but also over the entry of legal claims that—paradoxically—have their origin in the transgressions of U.S.-based transnational corporations and the inequities of U.S. regulations.

A National Movement in Nicaragua

The Nicaraguan response to the history of DBCP exposure and exclusion from U.S. courts exemplifies another potential role of the state in the context of late-twentieth- and early-twenty-first-century globalization. In Nicaragua, as in Costa Rica and other Central American nations, DBCP-affected workers unsatisfied by the outcome of the U.S. court cases turned to domestic political processes to pursue some level of compensation and to hold fruit and chemical companies accountable. The movement they created was based in domestic traditions of democracy and resistance, and ultimately engaged the Nicaraguan state in a transnational field of contestation over DBCP.

The discovery of sterility and other health effects came at what was already a tumultuous time for Nicaragua. After years of war with the U.S.-backed Contras, the revolutionary Sandinista government had been voted out of power in 1990. Underemployment and unemployment were over 70 percent, social services such as health and education were severely limited, and the legacy of the Sandinista era remained uncertain.[43] In the early 1990s, DBCP-affected Nicaraguans organized as the Asociación de Trabajadores y Ex-Trabajadores Damnificados de Nemagón (ASOTRAEXDAN, Association of Workers and Ex-Workers Victimized by Nemagon; later the name was changed to Association of Worker and Ex-Worker Nemagon Plaintiffs [Demandantes]). Emerging out of the Asociación de Trabajadores del Campo (ATC, Association of Rural Workers), one of the mass organizations formed as part of the Sandinista strategy for participatory democracy in the 1980s, ASOTRAEXDAN drew on a history of citizen engagement to work for changes in state policy.[44] Activists focused on achieving the passage of a law that would both facilitate the trial of fruit and chemical companies in Nicaragua and frustrate the defendants' FNC strategy in the United States. In doing so, they converted the Nicaraguan state into their ally in the transnational struggle for DBCP accountability.

Activists mounted large-scale protests, including walks from the banana-growing region to the capital of Managua, extended campouts in front of the National Assembly, and dramatic public protests. In 2000, they won the passage of Law 364, the "Special Law for the Processing of Claims Filed by People Affected by Pesticides Containing DBCP,"[45] which set forth a number of rules for DBCP litigation in Nicaragua. Among its key provisions was the assumption that the fruit and chemical companies had prior knowledge of DBCP's harm, meaning that the defendants could not argue that they had not known that DBCP would cause sterility or other health problems in farm workers. The law also established that, in cases where a plaintiff could prove both exposure and sterility, there was an "irrefutable presumption" of causation. In other words, any plaintiff who had medical test results showing low or no sperm production and could prove that he had been exposed to DBCP would be entitled to the minimum compensation (set at U.S. $100,000 in the case of total sterility). DBCP-affected workers and their lawyers hoped that these rules would make litigation quicker and easier and that the cases would not involve lengthy discussions of individual causation or company knowledge of DBCP's dangers, as any cases litigated in the United States were likely to do.

The passage of Law 364 quickly drew fire from both the U.S. government and the fruit and chemical companies. Soon after passage, news emerged that the U.S. ambassador's opposition to the law had led the Nicaraguan attorney general to pen an opinion that it was unconstitutional.[46] It was reported that Dow and Shell had not only hired lobbyists in Washington but planned to send either then-vice president Dick Cheney or a State Department official to Nicaragua to pressure the government. Indeed, a high-ranking representative of the State Department reportedly visited Nicaragua and met with the "highest functionaries" of Nicaraguan President Bolaños' administration.[47] DBCP- affected Nicaraguans responded by renewing their public protests and calling on the government to retain Law 364. Drawing on populist anger about (and a long history of resistance to) U.S. interference in Nicaraguan affairs, they once again used a mass march and extended protest to call attention to their issue and pressure elected officials.[48] Their effort won government affirmation of Law 364 and promises of other support, while the Supreme Court and a majority of the National Assembly also assured the protestors that Law 364 was safe.[49] Efforts by the State Department, the U.S. Trade Representative, multinational firms, and the U.S. Chamber of Commerce to erode or remove Law 364 were also unsuccessful.[50] The threat of *afectado* protest, later magnified by efforts on the part of labor and solidarity activists from around the world, outweighed the pressures on the Nicaraguan state by powerful outsiders.

Within weeks of the defeat of the first challenges to Law 364, a Nicaraguan court issued the first decision under the new rules, awarding a total of over U.S.$489 million to almost six hundred plaintiffs.[51] Subsequent cases added to the number of judgments against the fruit and chemical companies, pushing total verdicts closer to the billion-dollar point, with many times that claimed in cases yet to be decided.[52]

Despite the *afectados*' victories, the Nicaraguan court has been unable to enforce judicial rulings against transnational corporations, revealing the limits of state power. The defendants hold few assets in Nicaragua and cannot be compelled to pay the substantial verdicts. In 2006, one judge's effort to enforce her own verdict starkly revealed the limits of Nicaraguan state power. The judge ordered the seizure of Shell's trademark to pay its share of a total verdict of over $500 million.[53] If the chemical company did not compensate workers as ordered, rights to the trademark in Nicaragua would be sold to the highest bidder. Shell responded by filing a request for arbitration at the International Center for Settlement of Investment Disputes (ICSID), an organization associated with and funded by the World Bank that serves as a forum for dispute resolution between investors and national states.[54] Nicaragua had already consented to ICSID arbitration by signing an investment treaty with the Netherlands, leaving it in the ironic position of being brought to a private tribunal by a company that would not respect the verdicts of its national judicial system. Nicaragua's situation was made desperate by the projected costs of ICSID arbitration, about U.S.$3,000 per day, a significant figure for a nation with a GDP of U.S.$5.3 billion in 2006.[55] (In comparison, Royal Dutch Shell had revenues of $318.8 billion in 2006.)[56] Unsurprisingly, the Nicaraguan court eventually reversed the embargo.[57]

While advocates for the *afectado*s are still searching for ways to enforce the Nicaraguan courts' decisions, Law 364 had perhaps its most profound impacts transnationally by countering the fruit and chemical companies' FNC strategy in the United States. With cases filed in Nicaragua returning verdicts totaling up to hundreds of millions of dollars, defendants no longer had the incentive to argue that Nicaragua constituted a more "convenient" forum than the United States. By passing Law 364, Nicaraguan *afectado*s leveraged their power as citizens into the transnational realm. Facing what they saw as unfair legal conditions in Nicaragua, most defendants would choose a U.S. trial rather than seek FNC dismissal. Indeed, the first-ever U.S. DBCP trial in a case with non-U.S. plaintiffs, *Tellez et al. v. Dole Food Co. et al.*, took place in 2007; the plaintiffs were twelve Nicaraguans whose cases would almost surely have been dismissed under FNC a few years before. Despite this achievement, the litigation has been marked by setbacks for the plaintiffs—of the original twelve, half were awarded a jury verdict of U.S.$5.7 million, which was later reduced by the judge.[58] By 2010, defendants had raised charges of corruption against a number of lawyers involved in the *Tellez* and other Nicaraguan DBCP cases (a strategy echoed in other recent U.S. litigation with developing-world plaintiffs).[59] While this book was in production, those charges resulted in judicial overturn of the *Tellez* verdict, a significant victory for the defendants that continues to be disputed by plaintiffs and their lawyers in U.S. courts.[60]

Conclusion

The history of DBCP shows that the nation-state can foster global inequalities, but it also offers the potential that state-level changes can work in the interest of grassroots movements in a transnational context. Both U.S. pesticide regulations and Nicaraguan *afectado*s' political victories show that the impact of actions taken at the nation-state level do not necessarily stop at the border. This history helps us understand some of the dynamics underlying both hazardous trade and citizen action and offers a more nuanced understanding of the dynamics of globalization, reminding us to look not only at the movement across space of goods, people, and so forth, but also at the national regulations, traditions, and laws that shape and authorize or limit transnational exchanges. The DBCP experience can be helpful for activists interested in halting dangerous trade or seeking accountability for past harms. Taking U.S. pesticide regulation as an example of what *not* to do, it is clear that national regulation (or regional regulation in the case of the EU) can be a powerful measure against the exportation of hazard. Moreover, it is clear that, if political pressure can be built, states can represent national citizen movements in transnational struggles. At the same time, corporate defendants' legal strategies have been successful at forestalling verdicts against them, and the potential of the state to intervene in transnational processes is threatened by trade agreements that grant investors authority to engage states in costly "dispute resolution." Even in the changing global landscape, the state remains one of a very few institutions with enough power to represent grassroots efforts for change transnationally. Certainly it is the only such institution with at least a formal commitment to structures of accountability and representation. The erosion of state power vis-à-vis investors threatens citizens' ability to work for political change at the level of the state and, by extension, their ability to project nation-level change into the transnational sphere as the Nicaraguan DBCP movement has been able to do.

NOTES

1. "Status of Chemicals in Special Review" (Washington, DC: Environmental Protection Agency, 2000).

2. The name of the corporate entity has changed several times over the course of history discussed here. Vaccaro Brothers & Company was one of the early leaders in the transnational banana market; in 1924 the company changed its name to Dole Company, and in 1926 became Dole and Steamship. In 1968, Dole was taken over by Castle & Cooke, a Hawaii-based company with roots in the shipping and agricultural industries. Castle & Cooke had already merged with the company founded by James Dole in Hawaii; building on that association and the success of Dole Pineapples, the company began placing "Dole" labels on its bananas in 1972. In 1991, Castle & Cooke (which already had divisions named "Dole Fresh Fruit Company" and "Dole Fresh Vegetable") changed its name to Dole Food Company, Inc. Sacrificing specificity for continuity, I refer to all of these entities simply as "Dole."

3. Memo from Jack DeMent, Director of Agricultural Research, Castle & Cooke, to Distribution, "DBCP Safe Handling Procedures," March 3, 1978, in private holdings of the author. Other cited primary letters, memos, and reports are in the private holdings of the author unless otherwise specified. These documents are available at http://www.dbcpdocuments.com.

4. Tim Costello and Jeremy Brecher, *Global Village or Global Pillage: Economic Reconstruction from the Bottom Up* (Boston: South End Press, 1994).

5. Saul Munoz Sibaja et al. v. Dow Chemical Company et al., 757 F.2d 1215 (1985); M. Slutsky, J. L. Levin, and B. S. Levy, "Azoospermia and Oligospermia among a Large Cohort of DBCP Applicators in Twelve Countries," *International Journal of Occupational and Environmental Health* 5 (1999): 116–122.

6. Saskia Sassen, *Losing Control? Sovereignty in an Age of Globalization* (New York: Columbia University Press, 1996).

7. John A. Guidry, Michael D. Kennedy, and Mayer N. Zald, "Globalizations and Social Movements," in *Globalizations and Social Movements: Culture, Power and the Transnational Public Sphere,* ed. John A. Guidry, Michael D. Kennedy, and Mayer N. Zald, 1–34 (Ann Arbor: University of Michigan Press, 2000).

8. T. R. Torkelson, "Summary of a Chronic Vapor Toxicity Experiment 1,2 Dibromo-3 Chloropropane (1956)" (technical report, Dow Chemical Company, 1957), 2.

9. H. H. Anderson, C. H. Hine, and R. J. Guzman, "U.C. Report No. 278: Dibromochloropropane: 50 Vapor Exposures and Ancillary Blood Studies" (San Francisco Department of Pharmacology and Experimental Therapeutics, University of California School of Medicine, 1958); "Results of Repeated Exposure of Laboratory Animals to Various Concentration Sof 1,2-Dibromo-3-Chloropropane" (Biochemical Research Laboratory, Dow Chemical Company, 1958).

10. Letter from Louis Lykken, Shell Technical Service Department, New York, to Mitchell Zavon, Kettering Laboratory, Cincinnati, June 4, 1958.

11. Memo from M. R. Sprinkle, manager of manufacturing for Shell Agricultural Chemicals Division, New York, to Shell Agricultural Chemicals Division manager, Denver, "Use Experience with Nemagon Soil Fumigant to Support Precautionary Labelling," November 9, 1961.

12. Douglas L. Murray, "The Politics of Pesticides: Corporate Power and Popular Struggle over the Regulatory Process" (Ph.D. diss., University of California, Santa Cruz, 1983).

13. T. R. Torkelson et al., "Toxicological Investigations of 1,2-Dibromo-3-Chloropropane," *Toxicology and Applied Pharmacology* 3 (1961): 545–559.

14. "Chemical Plant Workers Found Sterile," *Los Angeles Times*, August 4, 1977.

15. John Soluri, *Banana Cultures: Agriculture, Consumption, and Environmental Change in Honduras and the United States* (Austin: University of Texas Press, 2005), 195.

16. Letter from H. C. Thornton, United Fruit, Boston, to Dr. M. J. Sloan, Shell Oil, April 21, 1961.

17. Shell Chemical Company and Dow Chemical Company, "Petition Proposing Tolerances for the Pesticide Chemical 1,2-Dibromo-3-Chloropropane in or on Certain Raw Agricultural Commodities," submitted to the FDA in 1961, D-28.

18. Letter from A. E. Schober, Dow Chemical, Midland, MI, to Jeff Kempter, EPA, "Subject: DBCP—Additional Information," December 6, 1977.

19. Murray, "The Politics of Pesticides," 144.

20. Paige Lee Taylor, "Nematode Experiments with DBCP" (Changuinola, Nicaragua: United Fruit, Division of Tropical Research, 1977); Memo from F. C. Butler to F. S. Mentz, United Brands Company, "DBCP," August 25, 1977.

21. Telex from Henry Cassity, Castle & Cooke, San Francisco, to Budd Daley, Dow Chemical, August 18, 1977.

22. Cassity to Daley.

23. Lori Ann Thrupp, "Sterilization of Workers from Pesticide Exposure: The Causes and Consequences of DBCP-Induced Damage in Costa Rica and Beyond," *International Journal of Health Services* 21, no. 4 (1991): 731–757.

24. Cassity to Daley.

25. Federal Insecticide Rodenticide and Fungicide Act, United States Statutes, 61 P.L. 104 (1947).

26. Murray, "The Politics of Pesticides."

27. "Notice of Rebuttable Presumptions against Registration and Continued Registration of Pesticide Products Containing Dibromochloropropane (DBCP)," in *OPP 30000/19* (Washington, DC: Office of Pesticide Programs, Environmental Protection Agency, 1977).

28. Letter from Dow Chemical to Standard Fruit, "Agreement," February 6, 1978.

29. DeMent to Distribution.

30. J. Kempter and M. Bernstein, "Dibromochloropropane: Final Position Document" (Washington, DC: Office of Pesticide Programs, U.S. Environmental Protection Agency, September 1978), 156.

31. Castle & Cooke, "Benefits of DBCP Use on Bananas" (unpublished report, November 29, 1977); Schober to Kempter, "DBCP—Additional Information."

32. Kempter and Bernstein, "Dibromochloropropane: Final Position Document."

33. *Intent to Cancel Registration of Pesticide Products Containing Dibromochloropropane (DBCP)*, 50 Federal Register 1122-23 (1985).

34. Letter from Jack DeMent to Dave Green, Dole/Standard Fruit and Steamship Company, Boca Raton, FL, "DBCP," January 22, 1985.

35. Pesticide Action Network North America, "DBCP: Identification, Toxicity, Use, Water Pollution Potential, Ecological Toxicity and Regulatory Information," available at http://www.pesticideinfo.org/Detail_Chemical.jsp?Rec_Id=PC33459.
36. Don Mayer and Kyle Sable, "Yes! We Have No Bananas: Forum Non Conveniens and Corporate Evasion," *International Business Law Review* 4 (2004): 131–164.
37. Saul Munoz Sibaja et al. v. Dow Chemical Company, et al., 757 F.2d 1215 (1985).
38. Mayer and Sable, "Yes! We Have No Bananas"; Gulf Oil v. Gilbert, 330 U.S. 501 (1947).
39. David W. Robertson, "Forum Non Conveniens in America and England: A Rather Fantastic Fiction," *Law Quarterly Review* 103 (1987): 398–427.
40. Dow Chemical, et al. v. Domingo Castro Alfaro, et al., 786 S.W.2d 674 (1990).
41. *Forum Non Conveniens*, Texas Civil Practice and Remedies Code, 71.051 (1993).
42. Sassen, *Losing Control?* 59.
43. Phillip J. Williams, "Dual Transitions from Authoritarian Rule: Popular and Electoral Democracy in Nicaragua," *Comparative Politics* 26, no. 2 (1994):169–185.
44. Victoríno Espinales Reyes, interview by author, November 18 2006, Chinandega, Nicaragua.
45. *Ley 364; Ley especial para la tramitación de juicios promovidos para las personas afectadas por el uso de pesticidas fabricados a base de DBCP*, La Gaceta, Diario Oficial, 12 (2001).
46. Octavio Enríquez and Juan Carlos Bow, "EmbUSA intervino en caso Nemagon," *El Nuevo Diario*, October 9, 2002, available at http://archivo.elnuevodiario.com.ni/2002/octubre/09-octubre-2002/nacional/nacional2.html.
47. Luis Galeano and Roberto Collado Octavio Enriquez, "El dictamen vino de EEUU," *El Nuevo Diario*, November 6, 2002, available at http://archivo.elnuevodiario.com.ni/2002/noviembre/06-noviembre-2002/nacional/nacional5.html.
48. Ramón Cruz Dolmus, "Avanza a Managua marcha de víctimas del Nemagón," *El Nuevo Diario*, November 16, 2002, available at http://archivo.elnuevodiario.com.ni/2002/noviembre/16-noviembre-2002/nacional/nacional18.html.
49. María Haydee Brenes Flores, "Logran apoyo marchistas del Nemagón," *El Nuevo Diario*, November 21, 2002, available at http://archivo.elnuevodiario.com.ni/2002/noviembre/21-noviembre-2002/nacional/nacional10.html.
50. "National Trade Estimate Report on Foreign Trade Barriers" (United States Trade Representative, 2003); David Gonzalez and Samuel Loewenberg, "Banana Workers Get Day in Court," *New York Times*, January 18, 2003, available at http://www.nytimes.com/2003/01/18/business/worldbusiness/18BANA.html.
51. Roberto Collado Narvaez, "Víctimas de Nemagón ganan gran demanda," *El Nuevo Diario*, December 13, 2002, available at http://archivo.elnuevodiario.com.ni/2002/diciembre/14-diciembre-2002/nacional/nacional18.html.
52. "Dole Food Company Inc. 10k: Fiscal Year Ended December 28, 2002" (Washington, DC: Securities and Exchange Commission, 2003).
53. Valeria Imhof and Carlos Salinas, "Histórica decisión judicial," *El Nuevo Diario*, January 13, 2006, available at http://impreso.elnuevodiario.com.ni/2006/01/13/nacionales/10199.
54. International Centre for Settlement of Investment Disputes, available at http://icsid.worldbank.org/ICSID/Index.jsp.
55. Luis Galeano, "Shell nos clava en un arbitraje," *El Nuevo Diario*, August 29, 2006, available at http://impreso.elnuevodiario.com.ni/2006/08/29/nacionales/27650; U.S. Department of State, "Background Note: Nicaragua," available at http://www.state.gov/r/pa/ei/bgn/1850.htm.
56. Royal Dutch Shell, *Delivery and Growth: Annual Review and Summary Financial Statements, 2006* (Washington, DC: Royal Dutch Shell, 2006). Available at http://www-static.shell.com/static/investor/downloads/financial_information/reports/2006/2006_annual_review.pdf.
57. Luis Galeano, "Juez suplente levanta el embargo a la Shell," *El Nuevo Diario*, July 8, 2006, available at http://archivo.elnuevodiario.com.ni/2006/07/08/nacionales/23642.

58. John Spano, "Dole Must Pay $2.5 Million to Farmhands," *Los Angeles Times*, November 16, 2007, available at http://articles.latimes.com/2007/nov/16/local/me-dole16; John Spano, "Dole Must Pay Farmworkers $3.2 Million," *Los Angeles Times*, November 6, 2007, available at http://articles.latimes.com/2007/nov/06/local/me-dole6.

59. Victoria Kim, "Judge Hears Evidence as Dole Food Co. Seeks to Overturn Pesticide Verdict," *Los Angeles Times*, May 12, 2010, available at http://articles.latimes.com/2010/may/12/local/la-me-dole-20100512; Chevron Corporation, "Illegitimate Judgment against Chevron in Ecuador Lawsuit: Chevron to Appeal in Ecuador, Enforcement Blocked by U.S. And International Tribunals" (press release), available at http://www.chevron.com/chevron/pressreleases/article/02142011_illegitimatejudgmentagainstchevroninecuadorlawsuit.news.

60. Amanda Bronstad, "California Bar Drops Complaint against Dole's Lawyers," *National Law Journal*, February 28, 2011, available at http://www.law.com/jsp/nlj/PubArticleNLJ.jsp?id=1202483509606.

13

Turning the Tide

The Struggle for Compensation for Asbestos-Related Diseases and the Banning of Asbestos

BARRY CASTLEMAN AND GEOFFREY TWEEDALE

sbestos—a mineral once used for fireproofing and insulation, and still used in some parts of the world for building products— can cause potentially fatal diseases: asbestosis (lung scarring), asbestos-related lung cancer, and mesothelioma (a virulent malignancy of the lining of the lung or gut). By the 1960s, substantial numbers of workers in asbestos factories were suffering from these asbestos-related diseases (ARDs); so, too, were people who worked outside the asbestos industry (see the essay in this volume by Melling and Sellers). This did not prevent the growth of world production of asbestos from 3.5 million tonnes to 4.7 million tonnes between 1960 and about 1980.[1] The asbestos multinationals—Johns-Manville (United States), Turner & Newall (United Kingdom, Canada, and South Africa), Cape Asbestos (United Kingdom and South Africa), Eternit (Switzerland, France, Belgium, and Latin America), and James Hardie (Australia)—were powerful enough to distort the media and the scientific debate. Because the industry was for so long immune to litigation, victims had few claims to compensation and they had no voice.

Today that has changed. The asbestos industry has disappeared in most countries of the industrialised world and the mineral has been replaced by safer products, including man-made mineral fibres. Many countries have banned asbestos. In place of the industry's propaganda, victims' action groups have sprouted alongside a well-organised movement to ban asbestos *worldwide*. How this sea change occurred— through events beyond those scientific and professional innovations depicted in Melling and Seller's essay on Irving Selikoff—is the subject of this chapter. It is jointly written by a business historian who has spent nearly fifteen years researching the history of the asbestos industry and by an environmental consultant with over thirty years' experience in asbestos public health work.

The Origins of the Compensation Scandal

The World Health Organisation (WHO) has cited estimates that asbestos—a product that was known to be potentially lethal in the early twentieth century—kills at least 107,000 workers worldwide each year at present.[2] According to another report, the asbestos cancer epidemic could take at least 5 million (and possibly as many as 10 million) lives before asbestos is globally banned.[3] Even if these estimates are regarded as the upper limit, it is certain that the global trend for ARDs is still upward and in several countries (such as the United Kingdom, France, Japan, and Australia) mesothelioma incidence may not crest for at least another decade or so. The profile of victims is changing: They are presenting with mesothelioma at a younger age and include increasing numbers of women.[4] This trend appears to be reflected in Australia and the United Kingdom, where victims in their thirties and forties are not unknown. Mesothelioma is not simply a disease of old age.[5]

Mesothelioma is the worst ARD (and is synonymous with the term "terminal illness"), but all ARDs—including asbestosis (lung scarring) and asbestos-related lung cancer—are incurable. Against this bleak backdrop, monetary compensation remains an individual's only form of restitution. It is especially important in the United States, which was once the world's greatest consumer of asbestos but has no universal health care scheme. Compensation for ARDs can involve looking for someone to blame (and bringing someone to account for an individual's illness is an understandable motivation), but more often it revolves around the critical issue of financial survival for families when the main wage earner dies or a working life is ruined. Even in the early twentieth century, governments in the leading asbestos-consuming countries in North America and Europe accepted that workmen's compensation would be needed.

Although medical recognition of asbestosis came in the 1920s, compensation was much slower to develop. Compensation for some work-related diseases had been introduced in Switzerland, Germany, and Austria by about 1900, with the United Kingdom following in 1906. But the emphasis remained on compensating injuries. Only slowly were occupational dust illnesses added to many countries' lists (or "schedules") of compensable diseases. Before the Second World War, it appears that only Britain, Germany, Finland, and certain states in America compensated asbestosis, even though most industrialised countries either used or mined the mineral (see Table 13.1).

Until recently, historians knew very little about these schemes, but parts of the picture are now clearer. In Britain and the United States, asbestos compensation laws eventually provided more economic protection for the

TABLE 13.1   COMPENSATION FOR ASBESTOSIS

YEAR ESTABLISHED	COUNTRY
1931	Britain
1936	Germany
1943	Italy
1945	France
1946	Czechoslovakia
1947	Japan
1949	The Netherlands
1953	Belgium and Switzerland
1955	Austria
1956	Norway

Limited state compensation schemes operated in the United States and Canada. The introduction of such schemes in the United States proceeded slowly during the interwar period. In some states, such as Massachusetts and California, there was no list, and any illness that could be shown to be caused by work was compensable. In Canada, state asbestosis compensation was introduced in Ontario and Quebec in 1943.

industry than for workers. Compensation was hedged with so many limitations that the compensation schemes were cheap to operate. In the United States, asbestosis claims rarely troubled the leading companies. In the 1930s, only a trickle of asbestosis claims were lodged and were settled for average payments of between $2,000 and $3,000. Even in successful claims, the top benefit was usually well under a worker's average weekly income and was cut off when a statutory limit was reached—this for workers who were typically low-income earners. Often benefits were so paltry that they were hardly worth pursuing, and most workers were not even within the ambit of compensation. Industrialists may have feared workmen's compensation, especially in America in the 1930s when a wave of silicosis cases appeared,[6] but by 1964 it had long been apparent that the exorbitant costs had not materialised. In the United States and most of Europe (including the United Kingdom), the growing knowledge throughout the 1940s and 1950s of asbestos-related lung cancer had little impact on the compensation system.[7] A few lung cancer cases were compensated in the United States and Canada in the 1950s. But even as late as the early 1960s, the only countries that had formally introduced compensation for asbestos-related lung cancer were Germany in 1943 and Czechoslovakia in 1948.

The lack of compensation for ARDs hid their extent and perpetrated "a swindle . . . in which men and women . . . were cheated out of just recompense."[8] The social "bargain," by which workers in both North America and Europe had relinquished the right to sue employers for negligence under common law, had failed to deliver. And not only workers had been duped. Leading American occupational health physician Dr. Irving Selikoff once remarked:

> One of my great disappointments has been my naiveté in accepting, as a younger physician, the assertions concerning workers'

compensation, that the expense would lead to employers attempting to prevent disease, rather than to pay for it, and that suffering would be lessened thereby. It certainly has not worked out that way. [I] reflect on the basic decision (*White v. New York Central Railroad*), that it was just and fair to take basic rights from a large number of people, because there was a quid pro quo and that instead of their basic day in court they would get certainty, adequacy and speed in the no-fault system the state legislators propose. Well, the quid has disappeared and the quo has remained.[9]

Compensation Problems after the 1960s

After the 1960s, some attempt was made to restore the quid in both Europe and the United States by ending the virtual immunity of manufacturers from litigation. This was partly because of the widely perceived failure of workmen's compensation. The solution in America in 1965 was the introduction of a new law of strict product liability, which made the *sellers* of products liable for a failure to warn ordinary consumers and users of an "unreasonably dangerous" product.[10] No longer would plaintiffs need to prove cases against their employers to receive the derisory sums available under workmen's compensation law. They could sue companies that sold the products they had used for failure to warn against a hidden lethal danger. They could sue companies that had contracted their services and failed to warn or protect them against asbestos hazards on their industrial premises. These legal actions fell outside the workmen's compensation regime with its limitations on payments for medical costs and disability and with its lack of payment for pain and suffering. For the defendants whose failure to warn could be proven to be wilful and to demonstrate a reckless disregard for the effects on the victims, it was even possible to sue for additional punitive damages.

Product liability launched the modern era of American asbestos litigation, which has received so much publicity. Before 1980, under a thousand asbestos cases were filed in U.S. federal courts (no corresponding figures exist for state courts), but by 2005 that total was about 750,000 in all courts, state and federal. By 2002, the compensation net had ensnared over eight thousand defendants in litigation, including major companies such as Ford, Dow Chemical, General Electric, Shell, Texaco, Metropolitan Life, and leading railroads. Cases now settled for millions of dollars instead of a few thousand (or nothing), and some personal injury attorneys became multimillionaires (even billionaires).[11] Cases were sometimes much delayed for trial, but many people did get their day in court; very often the immediate prospect of a trial led to settlements.

But although the highest American asbestos awards were well publicised, not everyone was able to sue and not everyone with asbestos disease was compensated. Moreover, U.S. asbestos companies were able to seek shelter in a bankruptcy procedure known as Chapter 11, by which a firm does not even need to be insolvent to file for bankruptcy and while restructuring takes place it enjoys protection from creditors (in other words, asbestos claimants). The mechanism was first used to great effect by Johns-Manville, which in 1982 sought refuge from thousands of lawsuits. After 1994, when the federal government allowed companies to seek bankruptcy protection from *future* liability, Chapter 11 bankruptcies escalated. By 2006, over eighty companies had sought Chapter 11 relief, attributing their bankruptcies to asbestos claims.

Outside the United States, most corporations were able to either avoid the worst effects of asbestos litigation or avoid the courts entirely. In the United Kingdom, for example, claims had to be directed against the employer because there was no product liability route for damages. Cases were decided by judges, with no juries and no punitive damages. Legal aid from the government was sometimes available and necessary, but in the United Kingdom the loser of a lawsuit paid the winner's costs and legal discovery was a tepid affair compared with its U.S. counterpart (with no court documents made available to the public). The awards typical in American cases, where the average mesothelioma payment was well over $1 million by 2001, were not seen in Britain, where typical awards ranged between £50,000 and £100,000 (about $75,000 to $150,000) during the 1990s and early 2000s.

By the 1980s, apart from America and the United Kingdom, the only other countries in which litigation registered were Australia and Japan. In Australia, the first mesothelioma case was not won by a plaintiff until 1985; not until the 1990s, with the relaxation of the statutes of limitations and the impact of entrepreneurial legal firms, did the pace of litigation begin to quicken.[12] In Japan, civil actions for damages were rare: only twenty such cases had been launched by 2006. The first asbestosis legal action was not until 1980; the first asbestos-related lung cancer case was settled in 1997; and Japan's Supreme Court ruling for the first mesothelioma case was not until 2006.[13] Most Japanese cases involved the shipyards, particularly in Yokosuka City near Tokyo, which was renowned for its shipbuilding industry and American naval base. In 1988, eight former workers in Yokosuka sued Sumitomo Heavy Industries Ltd., thus beginning a long legal action that was only settled, in the workers' favour, in 1997. By the 1990s, litigation was appearing in the Netherlands and Belgium, but this involved only a handful of cases that had to battle their way through the usual thicket of statutory limitations.[14] In Switzerland and Italy few legal cases have reached the courts.[15] In France, civil courts recently found in favour of a group of shipyard workers, and in 2004 thirteen former miners at Eternit's Corsican asbestos mine were awarded €1.5 million ($1.92 million) after action by the French national health services and the victims. In 2006, a court in northern France fined Alstom Power Boiler for exposing employees to asbestos; however, no charge against Alstom has yet been filed in a French criminal court.[16]

Most countries still relied heavily on some form of state social security. The present European situation is summarised in Table 13.2. The schemes are characterised by low payment levels (both in terms of numbers covered and size of awards) and the blocking of legal action. Not surprisingly, these

TABLE 13.2   EUROPEAN ASBESTOS COMPENSATION SCHEMES

COUNTRY	SCHEME	COMMENTS
United Kingdom	Pneumoconiosis (Workers' Compensation) Act of 1979	Modest compensation if employers are defunct.
Germany	Berufsgenossenschafts (BG)	Effectively blocks civil actions.
Switzerland	Swiss Accident Insurance Organisation (SUVA)	Restrictive with small awards.
Italy	National Institute of Insurance for Professional Illness & Injury (INAIL)	Rejects most claims.
France	Fond D'Indemnisation des Victimes de L'Amiante (FIVA)	Claimants surrender their right to sue negligent employers; awards are lower than those paid by courts.
Belgium	Asbestos Fund (AFA)	Beneficiaries relinquish any legal rights to sue employers.
The Netherlands	Institute for Asbestos Victims (IAS)	Confined to mesothelioma cases, many of which are deemed ineligible for compensation. Decisions are not legally binding.

schemes have been criticised for destroying the "polluter pays" principle and for having a negative impact on court awards. In the Netherlands, for example, it has been said that, because of the emergence of the Institute for Asbestos Victims (IAS), asbestos litigation has "almost disappeared. . . . All the public anger about the injustice of the fate that asbestos victims suffer has evaporated. There is no media involved in their cases any more, they are now neither seen nor heard."[17] In the minority of mesothelioma cases that are eligible, the IAS mandates an advance lump sum of €16,500 ($21,100)—a very modest amount but enough to make victims think twice about suing a company. Even in Germany, payments are only two-thirds of salary and there are no awards for pain and suffering. It is rare for any victim in Europe to get more than €100,000 ($128,000), and without a civil action (impossible in many countries), many payments do not even reach €20,000 ($25,600)— even for mesothelioma.

As with asbestosis, the introduction of compensation for cancers has been a drawn out affair. Asbestos-related lung cancer has only minimally been accepted for compensation. Many countries did not make it officially compensable until the 1980s—more than thirty years after its medical recognition. In Belgium, asbestos-related lung cancer was listed for compensation only in 1999. Often it was a requirement that asbestosis be present alongside the lung cancer as evidence of asbestos exposure—despite medical evidence that asbestos could trigger lung cancer without it.[18] A comparison of the ratio of asbestos-related lung cancers to mesotheliomas from epidemiology shows that there are at least one to two lung cancers for every mesothelioma; however, the compensation of lung cancer from asbestos falls far short of that ratio.

Mesothelioma follows a similar pattern. The disease was compensated in the United Kingdom after 1966 and in the Netherlands after 1968. But national laws in France, Germany, Spain, and Japan did not make it compensable until the late 1970s. In Canada, Belgium, Poland, Switzerland, and in some states in Australia, it was not compensable until the 1980s. In Italy, mesothelioma (without asbestosis) was not listed for compensation until 1994. In some Central and Eastern European countries, such as Czechoslovakia and Hungary, mesothelioma had not been officially listed as a specific occupational disease by the mid-1990s.[19] In some countries in the developing world, such as India, it is still not statutorily recognised as an occupational disease.

Moreover, statutory recognition does not guarantee compensation. Generally, mesotheliomas are largely uncompensated even in industrialized nations, despite the relative ease of establishing asbestos as their cause. For example, in the United Kingdom during the 1990s well over half of those with mesothelioma were not compensated by the government (the self-employed and many household and environmental cases being unable to claim benefits at all). In France by the year 2000, annual mesothelioma deaths had surpassed a thousand a year, yet not many more than a quarter of the victims were compensated and there were wide regional differences.[20] In Canada, 832 mesotheliomas were diagnosed in Quebec between 1982 and 1996, but the Workers' Compensation Board registered only 261 between 1967 and 1997.[21] In Japan, 7,013 mesothelioma deaths had been recorded between 1995 and 2004, but only 419 had been compensated by the government.[22] These statistics demonstrate that most asbestos victims go uncompensated.

The Fight Back: Victims' Action Groups

The inequalities and injustices of the compensation system fuelled a sustained attempt by workers to fight back. By the late 1970s, the first victims' action groups (see Table 13.3) had appeared, as had a recognisable anti-asbestos lobby. The first groups appeared in Britain and the United States, where much of the world's asbestos had been used. The asbestos industry claimed that such groups were filled with left-wing subversives or linked with trade unions. However, the invariable driving force behind the foundation of these groups was the physical and emotional damage caused by asbestos, either to an individual or to his or her close family and relatives. The experience of Nancy Tait (1920–2009) in Britain provides a classic example. She was married to a telephone engineer, Bill Tait, who died of mesothelioma in 1968. Mrs Tait launched a battle to establish a connection between his death and the asbestos to which he had been exposed. Not until 1972 did the authorities admit that Bill Tait's mesothelioma was a result of occupational exposure, at which point the employers offered her a paltry £4,000 (which she refused). The experience of fighting the systematic obstructionism of employers, the government, and the medical community transformed Tait into an asbestos activist, who attempted to highlight the dangers of asbestos and also fight for better compensation. In the early 1970s, she researched, lobbied, and helped victims from her house in north London. In 1978, angered by the asbestos

TABLE 13.3   ASBESTOS ACTION GROUPS WORLDWIDE

YEAR ESTABLISHED	GROUP	COUNTRY
1978	Society for Prevention of Asbestosis & Industrial Diseases (SPAID) (Occupational & Environmental Diseases Association after 1996)	United Kingdom
1979	White Lung Association	United States
1979	Asbestos Diseases Society of Australia	Australia
1983	Hull Asbestos Action Group	United Kingdom
1986	Clydeside Action on Asbestos	United Kingdom
1987	Ban Asbestos Network Japan (BANJAN)	Japan
1989	Associazione Eposti Amianto (AEA)	Italy
1990	Asbestos Diseases Foundation of Australia	Australia
1990	Asbestos Diseases Association	New Zealand
1991	Ban Asbestos Network (BAN)	International
1992	Clydebank Asbestos Group	United Kingdom
1993	Merseyside Asbestos Victims Support Group	United Kingdom
1993	Gippsland Asbestos-Related Diseases Support (GARDS)	Australia
1994	Greater Manchester Asbestos Victims Support Group	United Kingdom
1994	Association Nationale de Défense des Victimes de L'Amiante (ANDEVA)	France
1995	Dutch Committee of Asbestos Victims	The Netherlands
1995	Brazilian Association of Asbestos Exposed (ABREA)	Brazil
1996	Concerned People against Asbestos (CPA)	South Africa
1998	Asosiacon de ex Trabajadores de Nicalit (AEXNIC)	Nicaragua
1999	International Ban Asbestos Secretariat (IBAS)	International
2000	Association Belge des Victims de l'Amiante (ABEVA)	Belgium
2001	Association of Asbestos Victims (ACHVA)	Chile
2002	Ban Asbestos Network India (BANI)	India
2002	Association Against Asbestos—Program for Study of the Occupational Risks of Asbestos (AFA-PEART)	Peru
2002	Justice for Asbestos Victims	United Kingdom
2002	Comité d'Aide et d'Orientation des Victimes de l'Amiante (CAOVA)	Switzerland
2003	Ban Asbestos Canada	Canada
2004	Asbestos Diseases Awareness Organization (ADAO)	United States
2004	Japan Association of Mesothelioma and Asbestos-Related Disease Victims and their Families	Japan
2005	Philippines Ban Asbestos Network	Philippines
2005	Asbestos Victims Support Group Forum	United Kingdom
2008	Ban Asbestos Network Korea	Korea
2009	Asian Ban Asbestos Network	Asia
2009	Korean National Network of Asbestos Victims	Korea
2010	Northern Asbestos Support and Campaign Group	United Kingdom

industry's well-financed lobbying efforts, she formally launched the world's first victims' action group—the Society for the Prevention of Asbestosis and Industrial Diseases (SPAID).

Others groups were established in industrial regions of the United Kingdom where asbestos had been most used (such as those associated with shipbuilding). In Scotland, asbestos damaged the lungs of Glasgow lagger (insulator) John Todd (c. 1921–2004) and killed his father as well several members of his family. He began raising health and safety concerns as early as 1959, when he was spraying asbestos, and by the 1960s he was actively campaigning for better working conditions. His unremitting efforts led to the foundation of Clydeside Action on Asbestos in 1986. Similarly, shipyard workers were influential in the foundation in 1979 of the White Lung Association (WLA) in San Pedro, California. These workers included individuals from the labour movement in Long Beach, San Diego, and San Pedro—alongside Jim Fite who had worked at shipyards and at General Motors in California. After the group expanded, in 1984 it transferred its activities to a national office in Baltimore—another major shipping and industrial area. In Japan, victims of ARDs were concentrated in the naval yards at Yokosuka. The relief funds and support groups that developed to deal with the fallout over ARDs in Yokosuka paved the way for the launch in 1987 of the Ban Asbestos Network of Japan.

Other groups flourished in asbestos disaster areas. The catalyst for the founding of the Asbestos Diseases Society in Perth, Western Australia, was the large number of ARD cases from the blue asbestos mine at Wittenoom. A key individual in the development of the society was Robert Vojakovic, a Croat who had worked at Wittenoom for only three months. Vojakovic is still living, but many of his colleagues are dead from the effects of Wittenoom asbestos. Other Australians who were hit by ARDs lived in the Latrobe Valley in Victoria, where coal-fired power stations were a source of asbestos exposure and a trigger for the Gippsland support group.[23] In South Africa, the group Concerned People Against Asbestos was a direct reaction to the disastrous impact of mining and milling in the small towns of the Northern Cape. In France, a powerful spur to the creation of the Association Nationale de Défense des Victimes de L'Amiante (ANDEVA) was provided by former workers, mostly women, at the Amisol asbestos textile factory in Clermont-Ferrand. ANDEVA welcomed teachers and students who were protesting against the contamination caused by sprayed asbestos inside university buildings, such as Jussieu in Paris. An Italian group was mostly composed of former workers at an Eternit asbestos-cement factory in Casale Monferrato.[24] In Brazil, workers at a Eternit factory were the driving force behind the country's first asbestos action group.

As outsiders to medical circles and government bureaucracies, these groups had first to educate themselves and then write their own literature. Nancy Tait taught herself about asbestos, and in 1976 won a Churchill fellowship, which allowed her to travel abroad to meet international experts. She then wrote a paperback booklet *Asbestos Kills*, which she published in 1976 and then updated. Tait emphasised the dangers of white asbestos and the problems with environmental exposure, and she attacked injustices in the compensation system. Also in the United Kingdom, Alan Dalton (1946–2003) published an activists' handbook, *Asbestos Killer Dust* (1979), which he dedicated to "the many working-class people who have been murdered by the asbestos industry and to those beginning to fight back." In France, by the mid-1970s, a group of researchers led by Henri Pézerat (1929–2009), a toxicologist, and trades unionists had formed a syndicate to demand measures to deal with asbestos. The syndicate published *Danger! Amiante* (1977), which became an important text for the "social movement" that succeeded in pushing the French government toward a ban on asbestos and recognition of mesothelioma as an occupational disease.[25]

By the 1980s, when industry doctors and experts attended asbestos-related inquests and trials, they were finding that victims' action groups had become highly expert organisations. In Australia, the Asbestos Diseases Society had grown into a professional operation with more than 8,500 members and eight full-time staff in its Perth offices. Moreover, during the 1980s and 1990s, victims' action groups had moved beyond compensation to tackle other issues. They became educators themselves. For example, the White Lung Association in 1982 decided to direct its attention to educational efforts that might help prevent exposure of children to asbestos through building products.[26] Other groups ran seminars and issued publications. One example is the Clydebank Asbestos Group, part of a local partnership composed of health and council groups, which published a book on asbestos.[27] In Australia, the Asbestos Diseases Foundation lent its support to the New South Wales government's Asbestos Diseases Research Institute, which was founded in 2002.

Inevitably, such campaigns and groups were attacked. The asbestos industry published a critical *Commentary* on *Asbestos Kills* that took Tait to task for her "extreme view." Alan Dalton was sued for libel and bankrupted by Dr Robert Murray, the medical adviser to the Trades Union Congress and a secret collaborator with asbestos giant Turner & Newall (Murray would later testify as a witness in defence of T&N in U.S. court cases). In 2008, ANDEVA was sued for defamation by the asbestos industry's main public relations body—the Chrysotile Institute (CI; formerly the Asbestos Institute) in Canada—for statements that had appeared on ANDEVA's Web site about CI's role in the global pro-asbestos lobby. CI dropped the case in the following year. Fernanda Giannasi, a Brazilian labour inspector and a founding member of Brazil's asbestos victims' group, faced pressures from the Canadian industry as well as repeated (failed) criminal defamation charges from the Brazil industry.

Victims' action groups initially led a precarious existence. They were usually staffed by volunteers and often had difficulty coping. Eventually, as the asbestos crisis deepened, city and local authorities offered small amounts of money or office space, which was supplemented by appeals, raffles, bequests, and donations. Tait's organisation was funded for about twenty years by local authorities; so too were Scottish organisations, such as the Clydebank Asbestos Group. Some support came from the trade union movement. For example, the Asbestos Diseases Foundation of Australia (ADFA) in New South Wales was supported by the Australian Manufacturing Workers Union, which provided an office for its first meetings. However, victims' groups and activists have not always felt that their interests have been well represented by trade unions—indeed, that was one reason that the victims' groups were established. Similarly, although many groups have developed links with personal injury lawyers, the relationship has not always been easy. The White Lung Association, for example, has been a fierce critic of some asbestos attorneys.

Victims' action groups are not easily characterised. Put simply, they have cultivated and accepted whatever support they have been able to find while offering support to others. In the 1960s and 1970s, the asbestos industry in the United Kingdom could count on the expert testimony of leading scientists and physicians, such as Sir Richard Doll and Christopher Wagner. Gradually, campaigning groups and plaintiffs found their own supporters. Besides Irving Selikoff, help and advice came from Henri Pézerat in France, Morris Greenberg in Britain, and Thomas Mancuso, David Ozonoff, and David Egilman in the United States. Ozonoff, for example, a professor of environmental health in Boston, reviewed the history of the asbestos medical literature—knowledge that he put to good effect as an expert witness in numerous trials. One of us (Castleman) also testified as an expert on the public health and corporate history of asbestos, usually at the request of plaintiffs. The media proved another influential ally of victims' action groups. In 1982, Yorkshire TV in Britain broadcast *Alice—A Fight for Life*, a two-hour documentary that was so hard-hitting that it led directly to changes in U.K. health and safety laws. Journalists such as Laurie Flynn—who produced "World in Action" documentaries for Granada television and in 1974 wrote a series of articles in the *Socialist Worker* about the horrors experienced by Glasgow shipyard laggers—effectively publicised ARDs.[28] In America, Paul Brodeur's equally devastating portrayals of the American asbestos industry, in *Expendable Americans* (1974) and *Outrageous Misconduct* (1985), were particularly influential. As one reviewer put it, "Even the confirmed skeptic will find astonishing Brodeur's account of the asbestos industry's avaricious inhumanity."[29] Such publicity helped pave the way for the movement to rid the world of asbestos as an industrial material.

The End Game: Banning Asbestos

A universal priority among victims' action groups was the banning of asbestos worldwide. To achieve this, by about 1990 they were becoming more overtly political and more global. Two developments occurred. One was the global proliferation of groups in countries such as Brazil, South Africa, Nicaragua, Chile, India, Peru, and even Canada. The other was an international organisation that specifically aimed for a worldwide asbestos ban. This began in 1991, when campaigning groups gathered in Strasbourg at the European Parliament, where a decision was taken to form a federation of international groups. Thus was born the Ban Asbestos Network (BAN). During the 1990s, as the movement gathered force, a global peregrination of meetings took in cities as far afield as Milan and São Paulo. During the

World Trade Organisation (WTO) case brought by Canada over the French ban on asbestos, BAN became part of a coalition of interests that succeeded in having the Canadian challenge rebuffed. This proved a landmark case. Asbestos activists have not been without scientific support, particularly from the Collegium Ramazzini—a global group of occupational health physicians that has supported calls for the banning of asbestos since 1999.

In 1999, the International Ban Asbestos Secretariat (IBAS) was established to campaign for a global ban and for justice for victims. A key individual in its operation is Laurie Kazan-Allen, based in London, who publishes the *British Asbestos Newsletter*. In 2010, this publication celebrated its twentieth anniversary.[30] IBAS, working with BAN and the groups discussed previously, has organised and coordinated conferences on asbestos around the world, including São Paulo (2000), Tokyo (2004), and Hong Kong (2009). International events, workshops, and rallies have been organised across six of the seven continents. A range of publications has been issued, with some translated into Japanese, Chinese, Bengali, Farsi, Portuguese, Italian, Flemish, and French.[31]

BAN and the various victims' action groups (listed in Table 13.3) have made an important contribution to the global retreat of asbestos, which is currently banned in 52 countries.[32] Nevertheless, world production stands at about 2 million tonnes. Many workers—in countries led by Russia, India, and China—are still exposed to raw asbestos fibre and asbestos-containing materials. The mining of chrysotile (white) asbestos continues in Canada, the fibre (some 180,000 tonnes in 2009) is hardly used there; almost all of it is shipped to countries such as India and Indonesia, where the Quebec mining industry recommends that it be used under conditions of "controlled use" (in other words, with appropriate dust control). Since such conditions are rarely if at all experienced in the poorest countries, Canada's continued promotion and mining of asbestos has provoked considerable opposition. In 2010, the Quebec government announced plans for a "loan" of Can$58 million (U.S.$54.7 million) to revive a large Quebec asbestos mine. The announcement provoked global protests—and not only from the various anti-asbestos groups. In response the Collegium Ramazzini restated its opposition to asbestos.[33] Even the Quebec Medical Association registered its disapproval. So far Canada has remained immoveable, and in 2011 it once more opposed the listing of chysotile as a hazardous chemical under the Rotterdam Convention. Whatever the final outcome, it is clear that the victims' action groups and IBAS—once branded by industrial interests as extremists who had little understanding of science or of the developing world—now occupy a position not too distant from the government consensus in the industrialised world (and the consensus of key international bodies, such as the World Health Organisation and the World Bank) that asbestos is too hazardous to use. It is now the pro-asbestos lobby that is in the minority and its long-standing defence of asbestos—that the risks of chrysotile are negligible and that workers have more to gain than to lose by working with the mineral—has been discredited by the weight of scientific evidence and over three decades of fighting back.

NOTES

1. J. McCulloch and G. Tweedale, *Defending the Indefensible: The Global Asbestos Industry and Its Fight for Survival* (Oxford: Oxford University Press, 2008).

2. World Health Organisation, *Asbestos: Elimination of Asbestos-Related Diseases* (Geneva: World Health Organisation, 2010). Available at http://www.who.int/mediacentre/factsheets/fs343/en/index.html.

3. Joseph LaDou, "The Asbestos Cancer Epidemic," *Environmental Health Perspectives* 112 (March 2003): 285–290. Available at http://www.ehponline.org/docs/2004/112-3/toc.html.

4. *British Asbestos Newsletter*, no. 68 (Autumn 2007): 2. Available at http://www.britishasbestosnewsletter.org/ban68.htm.

5. Forum of Asbestos Victims Support Groups, *Mesothelioma: The Human Face of an Asbestos Epidemic* (2007), DVD. British victims profiled in this DVD include men and women in their forties and fifties, including a former electrician, Andrew Burns, who was born in 1969. Available at http://www.youtube.com/watch?v=gLTDknLVm4A.

6. D. Rosner and G. Markowitz, *Deadly Dust: Silicosis and the Politics of Occupational Disease in Twentieth-Century America*, 2nd. ed. (Ann Arbor: University of Michigan Press, 2006); D. Ozonoff, "Failed Warnings: Asbestos-Related Disease and Industrial Medicine," in *The Health and Safety of Workers*, ed. R. Bayer (New York: Oxford University Press, 1988), 139–218.

7. B. I. Castleman, *Asbestos: Medical and Legal Aspects*, 5th ed. (New York: Aspen Publishers, 2005), 195. Castleman highlights that during the 1960s and 1970s employers in New York State compensated only about five cases of occupational cancer per year.

8. P. Brodeur, *Outrageous Misconduct* (New York: Pantheon Books, 1985), 23.

9. Letter from Irving Selikoff to Jack B. Weinstein, Chief Judge, United States District Court, April 21, 1986, Mount Sinai Hospital, Selikoff papers, New York.

10. Brodeur, *Outrageous Misconduct*, 27–28.

11. S. J. Carroll et al., *Asbestos Litigation* (Santa Monica, CA: RAND Institute for Civil Justice, 2005). Available at http://www.rand.org/pubs/monographs/2005/RAND_MG162.pdf.

12. Ben Hills, *Blue Murder* (Melbourne: Sun Books, 1989), 76–87.

13. Sugio Furuya, "Compensation for Asbestos-Related Diseases in Japan," paper presented at the Third Annual Mealey's International Asbestos Conference, London, October 17–18, 2007.

14. P. Swuste, A. Burdoff, and B. Ruers, "Asbestos, Asbestos-Related Diseases, and Compensation Claims in the Netherlands," *International Journal of Occupational and Environmental Health* 10 (April/June 2004): 159–165; S. Y. Nay, "Asbestos in Belgium: Use and Abuse," *International Journal of Occupational and Environmental Health* 9 (July/September 2003): 287–293.

15. P. Comba, E. Merler, and R. Pasetto, "Asbestos-Related Diseases in Italy: Epidemiological Evidences and Public Health Issues," *International Journal of Occupational and Environmental Health* 11 (2005): 36–44.

16. Annie Thébaud-Mony, *Travailler peut nuire gravement à votre santé* (Paris: La Découverte, 2007).

17. Yvonne Waterman, quoted in Laurie Kazan-Allen, "Commentary: International Asbestos Conference for Fair and Equal Compensation for All Asbestos Victims and Their Families," *Mealey's International Asbestos Liability Report* 6 (April 2008): 6.

18. K. Martischnig et al., "Unsuspected Exposure to Asbestos and Bronchogenic Carcinoma," *British Medical Journal* 1 (1977): 746–749; V. Roggli et al., "Does Asbestos or Asbestosis Cause Carcinoma of the Lung?" *American Journal of Industrial Medicine* 26 (1994): 835–838. Not until 2005 did the U.K. government compensate lung cancer where no asbestosis was present but where there was evidence of substantial asbestos exposure.

19. P. Brhel, "Occupational Respiratory Diseases in the Czech Republic," *Industrial Health* 41 (2003): 121–123; E. Fabianova, N. Szeszenia-Dabrowska, K. Kjaerheim, and P. Boffetta, "Occupational Cancer in Central European Countries," *Environmental Health Perspectives* 107, no. S2 (May 1999): 279–282.

20. M. Goldberg, S. Goldberg, and D. Luce, "Regional Differences in the Compensation of Pleural Mesothelioma as an Occupational Disease in France, 1986–1993," *Revue Épidémiologie Santé Publique* 47 (1999): 421–431.

21. L. Kazan-Allen, "Canadian Asbestos: A Global Concern," *International Journal of Occupational and Environmental Health* 10 (April/June 2004): 121–143.

22. Furuya, "Compensation for Asbestos-Related Diseases."

23. George Wragg, *The Asbestos Time Bomb* (Sydney: Catalyst Press, 1995).

24. D. Degiovanni, B. Pesce, and N. Pondrano, "Asbestos in Italy," *International Journal of Occupational and Environmental Health* 10 (April/June 2004):193–197.

25. Francois Malye, *Amiante: 100,000 morts à venir* (Paris: Le Cherche Midi, 2004).

26. Jim Fite, personal communication to author (Tweedale), April 30, 2005.

27. T. Gorman, ed., *Clydebank: Asbestos the Unwanted Legacy* (Glasgow: Clydeside Press, 2000).

28. Letter from Laurie Flynn to J. P. McKenna, Transport and General Workers Union representative, n.d. See also L. Flynn, *Asbestos: The Dust That Kills in the Name of Profit* (pamphlet, London: Socialist Worker, 1973).

29. D. Rosenberg, "The Dusting of America: A Story of Asbestos—Carnage, Cover-Up, and Litigation," *Harvard Law Review* 99 (1986): 1695.

30. *British Asbestos Newsletter: Twentieth Anniversary Edition*, no. 78 (Spring 2010).

31. For example, see David Allen and Laurie Kazan-Allen, eds., *India's Asbestos Time Bomb* (London: IBAS, 2008). Available at http://ibasecretariat.org/india_asb_time_bomb.pdf.

32. R. C. Haynes, "A Worn-Out Welcome: Renewed Call for a Global Ban on Asbestos," *Environmental Health Perspectives* 118 (July 2010): a298–a303. Available at http://ehp03.niehs.nih.gov/article/info:doi/10.1289/ehp.118-a298.

33. Joseph La Dou et al., "The Case for a Global Ban on Asbestos," *Environmental Health Perspectives* 118 (July 2010): 897–901. Available at http://ehsehplp03.niehs.nih.gov/article/fetchArticle.action?articleURI=info%3Adoi%2F10.1289%2Fehp.1002285.

Conclusion

JOSEPH MELLING AND CHRISTOPHER SELLERS
(WITH BARRY CASTLEMAN)

Contributors to this collection share a common aim. We seek to
puncture the complacency that prevails in much of the world
today concerning industrial dangers. Those of us living in affluent,
developed nations find it only too easy to congratulate ourselves on the
accomplishments of the past century in both occupational and environmental health. Even more commonly, citizens in wealthier societies take
these historic achievements entirely for granted. Such complacency is
misplaced. To paraphrase the novelist William Faulkner, many of history's worst hazards are not dead; they are not even past. Impressive as
many of our protective schemes have become, the essays in this volume
demonstrate just how short-sighted even tales of past accomplishment
can be. Repeatedly, discovery and rigorous regulation of a hazard in one
part of the world dovetail with an eruption of the very same hazard in
another, less shielded, corner. In this and other ways, profound inequalities have long existed in where and for whom the risk and damage of the
dangerous trades are the worst. These inequities may even be a defining
feature of modern global production. If we are to stand a better chance of
ameliorating them, we need a longer, deeper, and broader understanding
of their genesis and staying power. We must appreciate the limits of both
our past and our present weapons against industrial hazards.

Toward this end, these essays represent a modest step forward. What
intellectual foundation they provide has come from a range of disci-
plines. Our essayists, drawing from a rich legacy of writing on hazards,
include practitioners and activists who bring to the table a firm grasp of

contemporary knowledge and an appreciation of today's most pressing issues and conflicts. This concluding essay itself finishes with thoughts developed in collaboration with Barry Castleman, who continues to contribute to campaigns to improve awareness of exploitation in dangerous industries around the world.

Yet the social forces, contexts, and legacies at work are illuminated by other types of professional culture as well. Much of the terrain sketched here draws on the repertoires of those trained and working in history and other social sciences and the humanities—that is to say, academics. In few fields of public health or environment do such scholarly methods and answers have as great a relevance for those working on the front lines. To the interdisciplinary beachhead sketched by this volume, we invite others to add. As a whole, these essays do hint at some initial conclusions about the historical allocation and transfer of workplace-related hazards since the nineteenth century, even while suggesting a great many avenues for further inquiry.

First, and most obviously, the volume points to how the current unequal distribution of industrial hazards across the world is nothing new. Already in the early twentieth century, the colonial plantations in Malayan jungles, British trade in hides from the Middle East, and the search by American companies for Mexican oil had inflicted an inordinate burden of danger on developing-world workers. Beyond this generalization, however, the trajectories sketched by our contributors pose at least as many questions as answers. Whereas infectious hazards predominate in our earlier developing-world episodes, later hazards appear more likely to emanate from manufactured products, whether chemical pesticides in Nicaragua or lead batteries in Uruguay. But is this trend a result of changes in hazards themselves or of changes in the lenses through which past actors viewed them? Might other histories, for instance, of the long-standing and distinctive dangers associated with mining, defy this tentative chronology? Our studies join others in suggesting that by the later twentieth century, the newest processes and products of hazardous manufacture more readily afflicted developing nations.[1] But this pattern also deserves much further scrutiny.

Indeed, crude and sweeping distinctions between a "developing" and a "developed" world may well have only modest explanatory power regarding the cross-national differences sketched in these essays, not just in the evolution of hazards themselves but in the responses they stirred. What are we to make, for instance, of the case studies here demonstrating the recent emergence in developing countries of those same sorts of movements that led to the containment of dangerous production in more developed states? Contrasting levels of economic development alone would seem to offer little leverage for understanding such a pattern. It remains to be seen what concepts or categories may serve us better.

Alternative terms of analysis will more likely come to light through a widening base of evidence. A single volume of essays can only gesture at the multitude of places where, and times at which, industrial hazards have arisen throughout the modern era. We need a far better understanding of the histories of industrial hazard in those many nations outside of the United States, Britain, and Europe, especially those that have lately taken on the balance of the world's manufacturing. Over the past half-century, India, Brazil, and, most dramatically, China, have carved out their own pathways toward industrial modernity. Might their histories of industrial hazards together characterize an intermediate, semi-industrialized trajectory of development? Or does China, catapulting from government-controlled economy to a free-market manufacturing powerhouse in less than a generation, have an industrial hazard history that is more entirely its own, sui generis? Given the continuing importance of nation-states to hazard regulation, such national studies will no doubt remain vital to our evolving understanding.

Still, many essays in this volume indicate the value of alternative combinations of scale. Global or cross-national institutions and influences on industrial hazards need more attention, in and of themselves, as well as via their impacts on national, regional, and local arenas of historical change. At all of these levels, we also have much to learn about the passages between periods—both the two eras emphasized in this collection and those before and after. Perhaps, as the studies accumulate, altogether different periodizations will crystallize.

For all of the conundrums it poses, this volume signals a solidifying basis for cross-national comparison and analysis of work heretofore undertaken mostly by isolated, individual scholars. This foundation may be nourished through embellishment of the shared framework that has evolved, out of this volume's making, of the "industrial hazard regime." As more scholars frame projects around this heuristic notion—that of a constellation of production systems and regulatory controls active in a particular moment in a particular place—it may bear further fruit. Easing our ability to situate studies of differing historical perceptions and realities alongside one another, it may aid the collective revelation of patterns that are larger and less expected, cultivating an understanding that is at once firmer and deeper. The broadened knowledge and control of industrial hazards in many contemporary nations may serve as a reference point, yet the idea is not to rush headlong toward judgment of past regimes by this present standard. The goal is more evenhanded: to assess just how and why industrial hazard regimes have varied and evolved across time and place.

We especially hope that the concept of an industrial hazard regime may serve as a corrective lens for viewing scholarship and practice in North America and Europe. On these two continents, dwindling factories and mines have made it all too easy to imagine "postindustrial" societies. However, the very act of looking for an industrial hazard regime in such places returns attention not just to legacies of past hazards but to surviving, often remote, sites of production and extraction within them. Equally important, it beckons further comparable study of those other parts of the world on whose industries "postindustrialism" continues to rely.

In their examination of industrial hazard regimes, our essayists offer a variety of models for investigations to come. Many of these models nevertheless converge on two common lines of inquiry: the boundaries and social scope of a given regime in a given time, and the ways in which these have been compelled to transform.

The Neglected Edges of Industrial Hazard Regimes

Several of the essays here concentrate especially on actors, actions, and consequences that have been ignored or underestimated by the authorities on a particular time and place. It is along these neglected edges of a given regime, many of our contributors argue, that the worst hazards accumulate, and around which the forces of historical change coalesce. In seeking to understand the patterns of hazard that have actually emerged, as well as the movements that have combined and developed to address them, our essayists uncover stories of many challenges to industrial hazard regimes past. They also undermine assumptions prevailing today not only among many practitioners and activists in this field but across much of the related scholarly literature about a global "race to the bottom."

First, while some essays emphasize industrial hazards imposed by the largest, most organized, and most multinational of firms, others do not. Business historians such as Alfred Chandler and Neo-Marxist geographers such as David Harvey portray large-scale corporations and also overwhelmingly older, less-organized styles of production.[2] Multinational corporations figure in many scandalous episodes detailed in our case studies, from the suppression of knowledge regarding carbon disulphide poisoning in Blanc's essay to the pandemic of asbestos-related diseases explored in the essay by Henry as well as that of Castleman and Tweedale. We need to know more about internal monitoring of, debate over, and handling of hazards within this kind of organization, especially as operations were extended from one country to another. But throughout the years covered here, this reputedly "modern" scale and scope of business does not turn out to be so reliable a predictor of a regime's approach to hazards. In common with more revisionist business historians such as Philip Scranton, other essayists stress the persisting significance of subnational, regional, and highly localized industries and enterprises in the making of industrial hazards.[3] From the early-twentieth-century anthrax problem in Britain detailed by Carter and Melling to the lead battery issue in Uruguay described by Renfrew, some of the most lethal dangers to health have been found not in large-scale modern factory production but in "primitive" arenas of capitalist accumulation. As with asbestos in today's India, a dense undergrowth of individual or small-scale subcontractors—not large or organized firms—may prove especially heedless and lethal. As disposal and even recycling of lethal materials bring their own dangers to industrial garbage workers, the developing world continues to provide a toxic cradle for such fledgling and underregulated activities.[4]

Nor are we safe in simply assuming that the risks faced by workers invariably originated with capitalists' drive to make profits at the lowest possible cost. These essays confirm the culpability of private enterprise in creating some of the worst conditions faced by workers over the past century. Yet in many developed and developing countries, governments and local authorities have colluded with, even actively encouraged, industrial undertakings that present a serious threat to public and worker health. This is true whether the regime was at one time a colonial state, like early-twentieth-century Malaya, or a national government seeking to stimulate industrial development, like mid-twentieth-century India and Uruguay. Our studies vividly illustrate the wider social and health costs of such commitments—whether to farmers, importers, or employers, whose livestock and employees were harmed by anthrax, or to residents of the Mexican coast who bore the risks of a new liquefied natural gas plant.

To our list of suspects in the making of these hazards, we must add scientific professionals, not just those who design or build dangerous technologies but those whose job it is to defend the public's health. Historically, from those who looked askance at Selikoff's studies of the asbestos-cancer link to those who questioned the objectivity of any citizen-driven science, that very skepticism that often nourishes scientific careers can impede a more serious contention with newly discovered or underregulated dangers.[5] Examples of this dynamic here come only from the developed world; how it may or may not operate in developing nations remains an open question.

In the patterns of regulation depicted across these essays, we may recognize some larger cross-national drifts, more or less shared by those in developed and developing nations. Throughout the early twentieth century, from European towns to colonial Malaya, labor departments, if they existed, might oversee hazards inside factories, while public health departments often did the investigating of other industry-related outbreaks, mostly of infectious disease. Later in the century, many developed countries passed product liability and antipollution laws, giving consumers as well as communities additional rights against toxic exposures. New controls thereby coalesced over poisons afflicting environments outside the workplace, which might affect children as well as working family members. Our developing-world cases, while offering less scrutiny of any comparable regulation, do establish that contaminants in spaces beyond the workplace became matters of wide concern, whether among those living near the oil fields of Nigeria or among those living near the battery fires of Montevideo.

Altogether, these studies offer an array of precedents for what historical as well as contemporary investigation of an industrial hazard regime must entail. Whatever their place coverage, most investigations seek out the variety of boundaries that private as well as public actors have drawn—culturally, legally, and politically—across many different social spaces. The costs of injurious production may be borne not just by those working in factories but by those who reside and work in the neighborhood and region or who mine or till its land, as well as those who shop in the markets these activities supply. Beyond the coverage of this volume, more consideration of consumer exposures to industrial hazards, and of the health care institutions that serve working and other affected families, would deepen and strengthen our terms for comparing regimes.

One overarching conclusion follows from these essays about historical means for defining or detecting harms, be they those of acute or chronic disease or of the workplace or other environments, be they wielded by courts or an agency or a professional group. Their agendas are defined not only by hazards they actually cover but also by those they do not. Most strikingly, industrial hazards rarely stayed within the narrow confines of production, where early-twentieth-century regulatory schemes most often looked for them. Instead, sites of production created additional damage beyond: via air and water pollution, poor housing, and agricultural or still wider ecological depredation. Historical and other scholarly study of industrial hazard regimes needs to be attentive to those effects whose industrial antecedents were temporally or spatially more remote and more difficult to pinpoint. Existing regimes often found these hazards the easiest to ignore. That so many who historically sought to delimit the reach of industrial dangers later appeared shortsighted raises questions about how contingent and contestable today's boundaries of the "industrial" may prove. Policy makers of the twenty-first century, when industrial hazards arguably will extend from heavy metals and synthetic organics to the far more copious greenhouse gases, would do well to take note.

Just how, then, have existing industrial hazard regimes been overturned? From the mesothelioma that turned up in American asbestos workers to the unanticipated sterility that pesticides caused in Nicaraguan farm workers, change may well require that significant damage, even disaster, occur. But it is a myth that such episodes automatically cause regulatory change. The consequences of an industry's actions must become visible, beyond what a given hazard regime has been able to anticipate or recognize. Potential or actual damage also has to register on someone's radar screen, and more. Countervailing social and political forces need to arise to anchor and spread this awareness, and to ensure that it is translated into political pressure. Our essays offer important insights into how these processes unfold.

Regime Change: Between Knowing and Mobilizing

Workers and nearby residents bore the early brunt of so many of the hazards explored in these pages: workers shipped from India to Malaya or those living in the vicinity of Nigerian oil fields. Communities of the exposed thereby forged their own acute awareness and local knowledge of the hazards involved, but not necessarily in the service of any social movement.[6] In the case of Indian migrants to Malaya, it might have as well propelled local residents to change jobs or living quarters or, at least for a while, propelled early-twentieth-century Mexican oil workers to push for higher wages. That this inexpert knowledge did not always lead to collective action suggests that we need to know much about its content and the subjective and collective contexts that helped to mold it. Many of our essays also suggest an additional theme that could prove historically important in generating change: the ways in which this lay awareness and know-how of hazards did or did not evolve through interaction with existing experts.

Santiago's study of a 1930s rebellion in the Mexican oil fields offers one instance of how workers' own knowledge of hazards could be channeled into popular mobilization. In the context of a revolution-minded worker culture, this knowledge helped motivate a takeover of oil companies by the Mexican state. Yet Santiago also questions the effectiveness of the resulting regime in actually correcting that industry's dangers. On the other hand, two studies of the later developed world—Barca's of 1970s labor environmentalism in Italy and Allen's of 1980s and 1990s citizen suits in the Louisiana Delta and in Italy—stress the making of lay-expert coalitions. In these cases, lay community activists acquired voice and agency, not just by organizing among themselves but by striking up with, and learning from, more elite knowers. Barca's and Allen's essays, as well as others', pose an additional question as well: Just how might such sympathetic experts themselves have learned, or otherwise gained, from collaborating with the locals? Even significant shifts in scientific methodology, as exemplified by Selikoff's new approach to the science of asbestos, can owe much to lay mobilizations and advocacy, and to the new laws and oversight they may achieve. Overall, to tell from these essays, a certain reinforcing synergy between lay and expert knowledge, between the subjective, voiced experiences of victims and more objective and codified claims of supportive professionals, may yield farther-reaching and more effective change than either can alone. However, these are empirical questions, invitations to further study and debate.

For all these reasons, one further conclusion seems sure: knowledge about hazards that existed in one corner of the world at a given time was often slow to keep up with the travel of dangerous technologies or toxins themselves. Many further investigations are in order here: of how and why knowledge was or might have been transmitted and of the networks, avenues, and institutions that actually did so. But this very slowness suggests a rejoinder to the many arguments justifying the current imposition of so many industrial hazards on the developing world. Somehow, it is too often supposed, those not born in a better-off corner of the Earth need or deserve to suffer from industrial dangers long since abolished elsewhere. After all, to those who are poor and desperate for any income, the jobs provided *must* seem worth the bodily and ecological costs. But the more we learn, the more this argument itself seems born of complacency and indifference, especially toward those workers and communities who bear the brunt of the damage. In case after case, not they but others made the choices that brought industrial hazards their way. And their own decisions, accepting risky jobs or other exposures, often came with little or no awareness of how much danger was involved.[7]

Double Standards and Beyond: A Third Era?

For all the additional thinking about the history of industrial hazards we wish to encourage, our work on this volume has also yielded some useful clarity about where the struggle against them now seems headed. To the two earlier eras in the globalizing of industrial hazards we describe, we suggest the addition of a third, still in the making, that has wrought further sea change in the industrial hazard landscape.

Ever since our first era, corporations in hazardous industries have complained that regulation within their originating nations creates unfair trade advantages. Some of them have nevertheless gone on to capitalize, through subsidiaries, on whatever cross-national regulatory differences have emerged. Early on, the prevailing strategy was to locate plants in poor rural regions of the corporations' own countries. Especially in the wake of post-1945 environmentalism, however, during our second era, the global balance of lethal manufacturing and extraction began a more definitive shift toward nations of the developing world. During the 1970s there was much talk of wholesale industrial flight, but by the 1980s it had become clear that the main problem was, instead, international "double standards." We believe that out of the initial efforts to contend with these "double standards," a third era of industrial hazard history was born.

Within the few industries engaging in wholesale flight across national borders were the asbestos-based multinationals from Europe and the United States. Dependent on old, discredited, hazardous processes, and on sales of products that also proved deadly, from World War II onward these companies opened factories in the developing world. Conditions there were suffused with dangers that, beginning in the 1970s, were prohibited in their home countries. More typically, Western multinationals helped organize Third-World subsidiaries, whose disregard for the health and ecological impacts of their operations stood in stark contrast to the same corporation's developed-world counterparts. For instance, in Mexico during the 1970s, as well as in South Africa in the 1970s and into the 1980s, Bayer set up subsidiaries for manufacturing chromates that caused horrific pollution and worker illness.[8] Our essays include another striking instance of the double standards of the 1970s and 1980s: the Nicaraguan use of the pesticide DBCO after it was banned in the United States. What most dramatized the double standards of the late-twentieth-century multinationals, however, was the horrific turn of events at a Union Carbide pesticide plant in Bhopal, India—the worst industrial accident in world history.

One winter day in 1984, the Bhopal plant spun out control, releasing tons of lethal methyl isocyanate vapors that killed thousands of people and left a hundred thousand more with permanent disability. Comparisons made with the Union Carbide's plant making the same pesticide in West Virginia revealed numerous shortcomings in the Indian operation. The Bhopal factory was run by poorly trained workers and designed with poor instrumentation and emergency equipment—maintained just enough to keep the plant running. Moreover, vital safety systems had been shut down at the time of the disaster, and a corporate safety audit over two years before had produced no discernible improvements. The government response evinced a further unevenness. Had such a thing occurred in the United States, it would probably have bankrupted the company. But in 1989 the Indian government settled all claims for the air pollution release for $470 million, the announcement of which caused Carbide stock to go up in value.[9]

Change then stirred among major multinationals based in the United States and Europe, starting with their public relations departments. They began to insist, at least through issuance of global corporate policy statements, that they had renounced double standards. Dow Chemical's chairman said that the company would observe the same standards of worker and environmental protection from "Midland [corporate headquarters in Michigan] to Malaysia." Major German chemical companies and the British giant ICI released similar renunciations.[10] But what was the impact of the lofty declared ideals on actual corporate practice? As Zalik notes in this volume, one such company, Royal Dutch Shell, became increasingly responsive to environmental protests over its proposed LNG plants, not just in California but in Nigeria. At the same time, it did not shirk from erecting just such a plant on Mexico's Gulf Coast, where resistance was less vocal or powerful. To what extent do Shell's or others' public commitments to a single cross-national standard mask a continuing exploitation of local differences in industrial hazard regimes? In our third era, corporate rhetoric itself can pose pressing questions about operational realities.

The ground shifted further over the 1990s, especially through the rise of new international regimes connected, as Renfrew notes, with "neoliberalism." With the creation of a free trade agreement in North America and the establishment of the World Trade Organization in 1995, the largest corporate enterprises found it convenient to operate in a new way. Instead of doing their own managing of far-flung subsidiaries that manufactured their needs, they found it attractive to contract work out to outside suppliers and contractors. This strategy held a special attraction for hazardous work. Subcontracting of the more dangerous tasks was not new: oil companies and others in the United States had realized its advantages long before. Subcontracting largely relieved companies of having to confront labor unrest—such as strikes demanding hazard pay or correction of dangerous conditions, calls for government inspection and regulation, and workers' compensation claims. It thus also allowed companies to sidestep adverse media coverage, of this as well as other ecological unpleasantness, which might make consumers wary. During refinery maintenance shutdowns, for instance, oil producers found it easier to bring in contractors to handle jobs like insulation repair, which involves contact with asbestos. During the first round of capitalist "liberalization" from the restraints of union bargaining and the tight enforcement of safety regulation within more developed countries such as the United States starting in the 1970s, more corporations began to resort to subcontracting with small local outfits. More recently, even as the liability of premises ownership has finally been recognized, at least in the United States, and former contractor employees can more easily sue, this strategy has continued to pay off. The cost of worker suits is often long delayed. In many cases, it is then covered by corporate insurance policies, with implicated firms themselves winding up paying only their premiums.[11]

The ploy of having the most dangerous work done not just outside the firm but outside the country has proven even more foolproof. The modern-day version is to have hazardous jobs performed almost entirely by suppliers and contractors outside the country where a product is to be sold, in places where expenditures for prevention or compensation are minimal. If the impacts somehow become a problem—if workers die, if a nearby neighborhood sickens—usually only the firm to which the operation has been outsourced deals with it. On this front, the authoritarian capitalism of China has proven an outsourcer's dream. Given government control of Chinese media, word rarely ever filters out about a supplier's offenses. Still less likely to make headlines is how the offending firm may produce for a well-known global brand. Should the news actually leak out and get back to the United States or Europe, the big corporation can pin the blame on the repressive or simply neglectful country where the deed was done. Denial comes easily: How could it have known that people or environments were being sacrificed for the sake of its own profits? Another announcement then follows: another supplier has been found, and the chastened corporation now plans regular inspections of it. But once the publicity dies down, who will look over this corporation's shoulder?

The trade in dangers at work in today's world is the product of a multinational past; of a history of divergent trajectories; and of intertwined flows of processes and products, knowledge and people, all of which this volume seeks to highlight. Inescapably, unless counter-measures can be devised to deter it, the outsourcing of hazardous tasks and processes from the developed to the developing world seems likely to accelerate, with or without an upturn in the global economy. Corporations gain profit from it, after all, and the wealthy thereby exploit the anonymity and unaccountability that it allows, even as many in the most vulnerable and needy parts of the world grasp after the economic boon it promises. Compounding the dilemmas, in these very places where outsourcing's detrimental consequences to health and environment are most felt, locals owing their power or livelihoods to the offending operation are often among the least eager to make an issue of its damages.

Dire as these prospects seem, the essays in this volume suggest considerable grounds for optimism. New avenues of opposition have begun to address those very vulnerabilities that seem so engrained in the late-twentieth and early-twenty-first-century global economy. New local or national mobilizations have indeed arisen; so, too, have cross-national networks of activists. In an historic irony, while more and better state regulation may still help, many of these groups seek further conscientiousness from multinational corporations themselves, as a vehicle for cross-national change. Because of their activism, leading clothing and footwear corporations disclose their suppliers worldwide, even if chemical corporations do not. Extending this solution across more industries may seem a tall order; any stronger fix, even more remote. But here the past century of hazard regime change has one further lesson to teach. A politics of industrial hazard control that, in an earlier era, may have looked unimaginable, can later on seem well-nigh inevitable.

NOTES

1. Gavin Bridge, "Contested Terrain: Mining and the Environment," *Annual Review of Environment and Resources*, 29 (2004): 205–259; Francisco Ramirez Cuellar and Aviva Chomsky, *The Profits of Extermination: Big Mining in Colombia* (Monroe, ME: Common Courage Press, 2005); Angela Vergara, "The Recognition of Silicosis: Labor Unions and Physicians in the Chilean Copper Industry, 1930s–1960s," *Bulletin of the History of Medicine* 79 (2005): 723–748; David Pellow, *Resisting Global Toxics: Transnational Movements for Environmental Justice* (Cambridge, MA: MIT Press, 2007).

2. Alfred D. Chandler, Jr., *Scale and Scope: The Dynamics of Industrial Capitalism* (Cambridge, MA: Belknap Press, 1994); Alfred D. Chandler, Jr., *The Visible Hand: The Managerial Revolution in American Business* (Cambridge, MA: Belknap Press, 1993); David Harvey, *The Condition of Postmodernity: An Enquiry into the Origins of Cultural Change* (Oxford: Wiley-Blackwell, 1991); David Harvey, *A Brief History of Neoliberalism* (New York: Oxford University Press, 2007).

3. Philip Scranton, *Endless Novelty* (Princeton, NJ: Princeton University Press, 2000).

4. V. Subramanian and N. Madhavan, "Asbestos Problem in India," *Lung Cancer (Amsterdam, Netherlands)* 49, no. S1 (2005): S9–S12; Guadalupe Aguilar-Madrid et al., "Globalization and the Transfer of Hazardous Industry: Asbestos in Mexico, 1979–2000," *International Journal of Occupational and Environmental Health* 9 (2003): 272–279; Jennifer Clapp, *Toxic Exports: The Transfer of Hazardous Wastes from Rich to Poor Countries* (Ithaca, NY: Cornell University Press, 2001); Pellow, *Resisting Global Toxics*; Daniel Faber, *Capitalizing on Environmental Injustice: The Polluter-Industrial Complex in the Age of Globalization* (Lanham, MD: Rowman and Littlefield, 2008).

5. Phil Brown, *Toxic Exposures: Contested Illnesses and the Environmental Health Movement* (New York: Columbia University Press, 2007); Sylvia Noble Tesh, *Uncertain Hazards* (Ithaca, NY: Cornell University Press, 2000).

6. A fine example of how such "environmental suffering" may be studied, without presuming mobilization as an outcome, is offered by Javier Auyero and Débora Alejandra Swistun, *Flammable: Environmental Suffering in an Argentine Shantytown* (New York: Oxford University Press, 2009).

7. For instance, Jay Johnson, Gary Pecquet, and Leon Taylor, "Potential Gains from Trade in Dirty Industries: Revisiting Lawrence Summers' Memo," *Cato Journal* 27 (2007): 397–410.

8. Jock McCulloch and Geoffrey Tweedale, *Defending the Indefensible* (New York: Oxford University Press, 2008); Barry Castleman, "The Double Standard in Industrial Hazards," *Multinational Monitor* 5, no. 9 (1984), available at http://multinationalmonitor.org/hyper/issues/1984/09/castleman.html; Jose Castro, "Una mirada desde la antropologia sobre espacios contaminados con residuos peligrosos en una comunidad: Estudio de caso en la planta de Cromatos en Tulititlan, Estado de Mexico" (Ph.D. diss., Escuela Nacional de Antropologia y Historia, Mexico City, 2006).

9. For a good summary of what has become a huge literature, see Edward Broughton, "The Bhopal Disaster and Its Aftermath: A Review," *Environmental Health* 4 (2005), available at http://www.ehjournal.net/content/4/1/6.

10. B. Castleman, "Global Corporate Policies and International Double Standards in Occupational and Environmental Health," *International Journal of Occupational and Environmental Health* 5 (1999): 61–64.

11. M. Quinlan, C. Mayhew, and P. Bohle, "The Global Expansion of Precarious Employment, Work Disorganization, and Consequences for Occupational Health: A Review of Recent Research," *International Journal of Health Services: Planning, Administration,*

Evaluation 31 (2001): 335–414; Richard Johnstone, Claire Mayhew, and Michael Quinlan, "Outsourcing Risk? The Regulation of Occupational Health and Safety Where Subcontractors Are Employed," *Comparative Labor Law and Policy Journal* 22 (2005): 351–394; Annie Thebaud-Mony, "Non-Standard Employment, Subcontracting, Flexibility, Health," paper presented at the TUTB-SALTSA Conference, Brussels, September 25–27, 2000, 25–33, available at http://hesa.etui-rehs.org/uk/newsevents/files/thebaud.pdf.

Contributors

Barbara L. Allen is the director of the graduate program in Science, Technology and Society (STS) at Virginia Tech's Washington, D.C., campus. She is the author of *Uneasy Alchemy: Citizens and Experts in Louisiana's Chemical Corridor Disputes* (2003) and coeditor of several books, including *Dynamics of Disaster: Lessons on Risk, Response and Recovery* (2011).

Stefania Barca is a senior researcher at the Centre for Social Studies of the University of Coimbra, Portugal. Her education and research span Italy, the United States, and Portugal, and she has written three books, including *Enclosing Water: Nature and Political Economy in a Mediterranean Valley, 1796–1916* (2010).

Paul D. Blanc is a professor of medicine and holds the Endowed Chair in Occupational and Environmental Medicine at the University of California, San Francisco. Among his many publications is the general-interest book *How Everyday Products Make People Sick* (2009).

Susanna Rankin Bohme is a deputy editor of the *International Journal of Occupational and Environmental Health*. Her book on the history of the pesticide DBCP is forthcoming from the University of California Press.

Tim Carter, a specialist in occupational and transport medicine, served as Britain's Medical Director of the Health and Safety Executive, and he is currently a visiting professor at the Norwegian Centre for Maritime Medicine in

Bergen. His Ph.D. studies at the University of Birmingham developed his interest in anthrax and the regulation of its occupational, public, and veterinary health risks.

Barry Castleman has been deeply involved in the struggle over asbestos in the United States and worldwide for over thirty years as a scientist working with environmental nongovernmental organizations. His *Asbestos: Medical and Legal Aspects* (2005) is now in its fifth edition, and others of his publications have pioneered in the study of the "export of hazards" and the "double standards" of multinational corporations.

Emmanuel Henry is an associate professor of political science at the Institute of Political Studies of Strasbourg, France, and a researcher at the Center for European Political Sociology (GSPE), also in Strasbourg. He is the author of, among other works, *Amiante: Un scandale improbable. Sociologie d'un problème public*, or *Asbestos: An Improbable Scandal. Sociology of a Public Problem* (2007).

Amarjit Kaur is a professor in the School of Business Economics and Public Policy at New England University, Armidale, Australia. She has authored many books and articles, among them: *Wage Labour in Southeast Asia since 1840: Globalisation, the International Division of Labour and Labour Transformations* (2004).

Joseph Melling is the director of the Centre for Medical History at the University of Exeter. He is the author (with Bill Forsythe) of *The Politics of Madness* (2006) and (with Alan Booth) of *Making the Modern Workplace* (2008).

Alfredo Menéndez-Navarro is an associate professor in the History of Science Department at the University of Granada, Spain. He has published *A Sunless World: The Health of the Workers of Almaden Mercury Mines, 1750–1900* (1996, in Spanish), a book-length edition of an eighteenth-century manuscript, *Morbid Catastrophe* (1998, in Spanish), and many related articles.

Daniel E. Renfrew is an assistant professor of anthropology in the Division of Sociology and Anthropology at West Virginia University. In addition to his many articles, he is drawing from his doctoral dissertation and ongoing ethnographic research to complete a book on the broad-based societal responses to the discovery of a lead poisoning epidemic in Montevideo, Uruguay.

Myrna Santiago is a professor of history at Saint Mary's College in Moraga, California, where she teaches Latin American and world history. Her first book was *The Ecology of Oil: Environment, Labor, and the Mexican Revolution, 1900–1930* (2007).

Christopher Sellers is an associate professor of history at Stony Brook University and author of *Hazards of the Job: From Industrial Disease to Environmental Health Science* (1997). He is also coeditor or author of various other books and articles.

Geoffrey Tweedale is a professor of business history at Manchester Metropolitan University Business School in Manchester, United Kingdom. He is the author of *Magic Mineral to Killer Dust: Turner & Newall and the Asbestos Hazard* (2000) and (with Jock McCulloch) *Defending the Indefensible* (2008) on the global asbestos disaster.

Anna Zalik is an assistant professor on the faculty of Environmental Studies at York University, in Toronto, Canada. Trained as a sociologist, she is the author of many articles and a forthcoming book on how corporate aid reconstitutes local subject identities and shapes socio-environmental regulation in extractive sites in the Mexican Gulf and the Nigerian Delta.

Index